Motorcycle Journeys Through the
Rocky Mountains

by Toby Ballentine

Whitehorse Press
Center Conway, New Hampshire

Whitehorse Press books are also available at discounts in bulk quantity for sales and promotional use. For details about special sales or for a catalog of motorcycling books, videos, and gear write to the publisher:
Whitehorse Press
107 East Conway Road
Center Conway, New Hampshire 03813
Phone: 603-356-6556 or 800-531-1133
E-mail: CustomerService@WhitehorsePress.com
Internet: www.WhitehorsePress.com

ISBN 1-884313-58-2

5 4 3 2 1

Printed in China

Acknowledgments

During the course of the past year and a half, I have spent countless hours compiling information, doing research and, best of all, re-riding several of these routes. Writing these journeys through the Rocky Mountains has once again reaffirmed my love of motorcycling and of this great country. Many thanks to Whitehorse Press for working with me and giving me the chance to write this book. You have helped each step of the way. Thanks to my wife and riding buddies for their suggestions and for stopping just one more time for that picture perfect photo op! And Mom, thanks for taking the time to edit each chapter and offer up ideas on how to make the words flow a little more smoothly.

Finally, I would like to dedicate this book to my three-year-old grandson, Bryton. I often think of him while I'm riding through the majestic Rocky Mountains . . . and know he is right by my side!

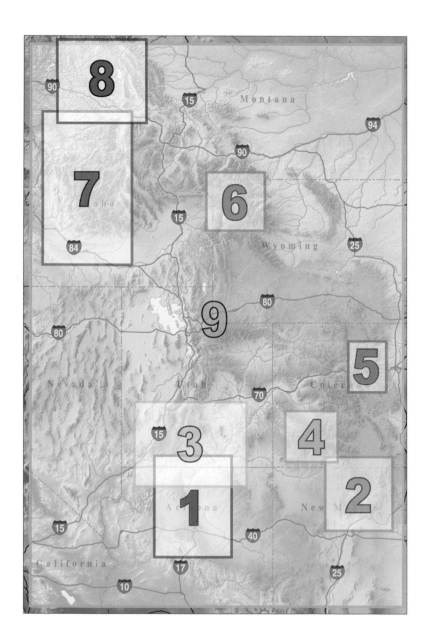

Contents

Introduction

Just about every Memorial Day weekend, I pack up my gear and head north to Monument Valley with a few of my motorcycling buddies. We spend the first night at Goulding's Lodge, either in the campsite or at the hotel. Views of the monolithic buttes cover the horizon. The next morning we tackle the Moki Dugway and climb 1,200 feet via a dirt road to an even higher perch above the valley floor. The panorama below is—well, one of those "you gotta see it to believe it" moments. The road quickly becomes asphalt and bends around the eastern end of Lake Powell. I can count the number of cars on one hand driving toward Hanksville. Over the next couple of days, we head west into Capital Reef, do a little trapeze dance over the Escalante

A high summit crossing in the Colorado Rockies begins a new journey.

Staircase, descend to Bryce, climb back up to Cedar Breaks, hop over to Zion, blast up to Jacob Lake, and spend our final night at the Grand Canyon's north rim. Oh, I forget to mention, we'll usually throw in a few short GS-type dirt tracks and do a little exploring in the backcountry as well. Let's see, last time we did Hell's Backbone Road and the Smithsonian Butte Backway. Are you interested?

After returning from such a trip about two years ago, I decided to write some ideas down and send them to Whitehorse Press. Basically I suggested they hire one of their professional writers and write a book on the Rocky Mountains. Well, one thing led to another and the publisher asked if I would be interested in writing the book myself and suggested I include some backroad adventures as well. I told him my writing skills were a little dusty and that my mom was my only admirer. He felt they could coach me through it and, as a matter of fact, many motorcycle journalists start off doing this in their spare time. So with the encouragement and help of Whitehorse Press, I was hooked and this book is now official (and my mother is very proud!).

The view toward Sedona from Schnebly Hill Road shows the marks of time.

HOW THIS BOOK IS ORGANIZED

When I first approached the subject of writing a book on journeys through the Rocky Mountains, I was overwhelmed with the enormity of the task. There are literally hundreds of rides in the Rockies. Where do I start and how do I get there? To put some reasonable bounds on the project, we agreed to limit the scope from twenty to thirty rides that span the entire mountain range. But, you say, there are that many trips in Colorado alone! So, I put together an outline of journeys and then refined it, based on the following criteria:

- Stick to the Rockies. The mountain states cover a lot of territory and not all of it lies in the Rocky Mountains. I know several treks in Southern Arizona and New Mexico that are great rides, but they're not what I consider "Rocky Mountain" journeys.

- Focus on trips using a common hub. As you read the text you will see that the various chapters are tied to a home base and each section starts with an introduction about this town or city. All trips for a particular area will start and finish at this hub.

- Link these journeys into one Grand Rocky Mountain Loop for those interested in taking a three- to four-week summer extravaganza. I wanted to be sure to cover the entire mountain range from northern Idaho and Montana to Arizona and New Mexico. My final chapter ties all these trips together into one master journey.

- Include some outstanding yet optional backroad adventures that are offshoots to the main trip and accessible on dual sport or GS type bikes. Riding on the backways in the Rocky Mountains is like taking a step back in time. You truly can see the mountains for what they are and share the same feelings the early pioneers and prospectors must have had. I know not everyone rides a dual sport, but due to their increasing popularity, I figured some of these side trips should be included. The average length is around ten to twenty miles round trip. These trips are highlighted in yellow on each map.

So, I ended up with a total of twenty paved trips and fifteen backroad detours in three geographic areas, the Southern, Central, and Northern Rocky Mountains. That may not sound like many, but please be forewarned—

these are not short sixty-mile runs to the Rancher Bar in Wickenburg. These are 200- to 800-mile treks through some of the most magnificent scenery on earth! Because the distances are so expansive, several loops require two to three days to complete in very isolated areas of the Rockies. Other trips are shorter, requiring one day in very well-known and well-traveled areas. Many of the dirt sidetrips pass through old ghost towns built in the 1800s when gold was king and prospectors flooded the west.

As I have written these chapters, I have also tried to include an historical perspective to many of the places on the way. My feeling is if you understand the past, you gain a better appreciation for the present. Hopefully, the historical aspects are fairly accurate and interwoven into the chapter to give you some additional insights into the Rocky Mountains. I have also taken the liberty of suggesting various hikes, boat trips, or local events that might make the trip more fulfilling. Please remember—these are strictly my opinion and mine alone. I'm sure some of you may wonder why a certain trip wasn't included or why such and such backroad not mentioned . . . what can I say? This is not meant to be a comprehensive travel book, but as the title suggests, it takes a more personal outlook on my journeys and discoveries through the Rockies.

ACCOMMODATIONS

Places to stay and restaurants are provided on a limited basis. These are places that I am familiar with and by no means cover all possibilities. For a more definitive list, check out the websites given as references in each of the chapters. Note also that I may mention people's names, restaurants, or owners that were present on my last visit. They may still be there . . . but things have a way of changing.

A couple of comments about the last two chapters. Chapter 9 consolidates the prior twenty trips into one grand loop through the Rocky Mountains. You can start anywhere along the way (Phoenix, Denver, Salt Lake, Missoula, etc.) and journey along a 5,000-mile made-to-order route through some of the world's most majestic scenery. Bring your own bike or rent one when you get here. Take a three to four week vacation and have the time of your life!

The last chapter summarizes some of my favorites. It is a short chapter and includes my top ten list of locations, places to stay and, of course, road trips. My number one choice for favorite journey through the Rocky Mountains will definitely surprise you!

Hmmm . . . made you look, didn't I?

A lonesome sweeper on Lake Mary Road just outside Flagstaff gets the bike to speed.

RENTALS

- **Blue Sky Motorcycle Rentals, Inc.**
(www.blueskymotorcyclerentals.com). They have locations in Phoenix, Scottsdale, Denver, Salt Lake City, and Las Vegas. The website has links and phone numbers for all of these cities.

- **Tourbikes** (www.tourbikes.com, 866-377-7810) in Denver, Colorado, rents BMW, Yamaha, Honda, and Kawasaki Motorcycles.

- **High Desert Harley-Davidson** (www.highdeserthd.com, 800-666-4644) in Boise, Idaho, rents Harleys only. I remember running late one trip and they took me straight to the airport. Great service!

PLANNING YOUR TRIP

A couple of pointers before you get started. First of all, I would suggest taking some emergency camping gear. A small tent and a warm sleeping bag may be just what you need when you get that flat in the middle of nowhere . . . at least you will get a good night's rest. I'm not necessarily suggesting cooking gear, propane, chair, etc., but that pup tent and mummy bag really don't take up much room and may come in handy. Also, some of my best experiences happened when I pulled off the main drag onto that dirt track to

that accidental campsite found overlooking the lake with mountains towering overhead (check out such a spot in the Teton Rendezvous chapter). That
was the cheapest five-star overnighter I ever had!

MAPS

Maps included in this book are only intended to supplement good road
maps. I would suggest you orient your road map to the details in this book
and use a highlighter to plan your trip.

NATIONAL PARK PASS

Also, don't forget to buy the National Park Pass when you enter your very
first park. The Rockies abound with some of the world's greatest parks.
Rather then pay a fee each time you enter, break down and buy the Park
Pass. Some of these trips take you through National Monuments as well, so
get the pass that includes both parks and monuments. You won't regret it
and the savings are significant.

GEAR

Be sure to take well tested rain gear. As I'm sure you know, some rain gear is
better than others. Thunderstorms are commonplace in the mountains and
a warm seventy-five degree afternoon can quickly turn into a forty-five degree storm with rain and sleet. Be prepared for a quick change!

This may sound a little weird, but don't forget your swimsuit! I can't tell
you how many times I've stopped to enjoy a good soak in a roadside hot
spring. Colorado, New Mexico, and Idaho all have natural springs just waiting to soothe that iron-butted motorcyclist. Don't forget your towel, either!

ROAD CONDITIONS

And finally, remember that a lot of these roads are in excess of 10,000 feet in
elevation. If the weather looks questionable, take five and call the State
Highway Department in advance for an update on road conditions. A good
resource for road conditions is usroadconditions.com. Snow flurries are not
uncommon in June or September. For the most part there should be no
problem, but I do recall it was the middle of May a few years back and . . . I
should have called!

SOME MORE THOUGHTS

To me the most exciting aspect of motorcycling is being spontaneous along the way. Sure, the anticipation and planning raise your excitement level while preparing for that cross country trip. But the real fun starts when you kick your leg over the seat, see that side road that says Clearwater Loop or Lake San Cristobal, do a quick downshift, turn around if you have to, and then veer off on that single-laner or dirt track to destinations unknown. That is the real joy of motorcycling! I've done my fair share of downshifting and exploring and made many unforgettable discoveries. Now it's your turn. Start planning that trip, go find that side road, and begin writing your own book of memories. Start creating your own journeys through the majesty and wonder found only in the Rocky Mountains!

Happy Trails!
Toby

Explore the occasional dirt track. Maybe there's a nice campground just around the bend . . .

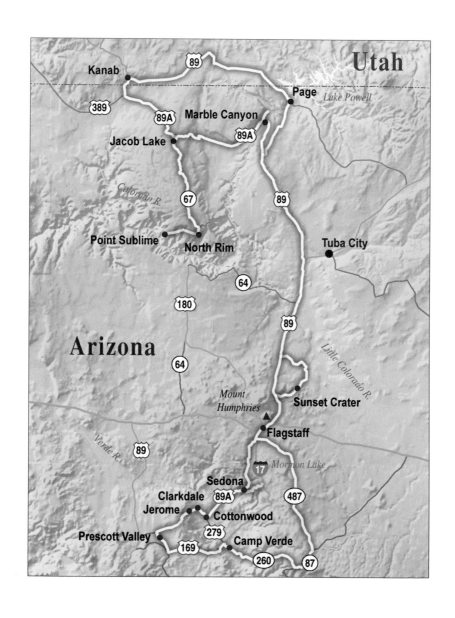

Flagstaff

Route 66. The Main Street of America passes right through this old frontier town of Flagstaff, Arizona, founded in 1881. As a result, the old and the new are intertwined in an eclectic, yet comfortable manner.

The older part of town around Beaver Street offers a rustic, almost cowboy atmosphere. Many of the buildings are historic landmarks with plaques retelling stories from their colorful past. Other parts of Flagstaff capture the more recent past of neon-lit motels, bars, and restaurants lining one of the few remaining active stretches of **Route 66** (www.historic66.com). The two disjointed pasts coexist in distinct harmony, giving Flagstaff a sense of history and modern appeal.

Old Town in Flagstaff has numerous shops and restaurants that make it an ideal spot for an evening stroll.

Flagstaff (pop. 63,000) is located in North Central Arizona at the crossroads of Interstate 40 heading east and west, and Interstate 17 heading north from the Phoenix metropolis. Just two and a half hours from Phoenix, Flagstaff sits at 7,000 feet surrounded by pine forest and Arizona's highest mountains, the San Francisco Peaks. The summer temperatures are ideal, ranging from the mid-seventies during the day to the mid-forties at night.

As a result, you couldn't ask for a better staging point to begin your motorcycle adventure through the Southern Rockies. From Flagstaff you can explore the wonders of ancient Indian Civilizations at Wupatki and Walnut Canyon, drive down the road through Oak Creek Canyon to the majestic red rock monuments of Sedona, or head north to the fabled Grand Canyon via desert view ridge or through lush alpine meadows to the North Rim.

Originally, Flagstaff and the surrounding area were inhabited by nomadic Native Americans as early as 500 BC. From 200 to 500 AD, they built more domestic pithouses and pueblos, eventually reaching a population peak around 1100 AD. For various reasons (mostly unknown), these inhabitants migrated elsewhere, abandoning their villages and homes. Some have been preserved as state and national monuments, while hundreds remain isolated and empty in the backcountry of North Central Arizona.

Starting in the 1820s, trappers became familiar with this area and sent word back east of this "Marvelous Country." Eventually, ranchers and lumber mills created an impetus for settlers to remain. The coming of the railroad in the 1880s further opened the area to more permanent settlements.

While driving around Flagstaff can be a little confusing, just keep your eye out for Mt. Humphreys, the tallest mountain in Arizona, in the background and then point your bike in what you think is the right direction. Eventually, you should get there. Most of the side streets feed off the old Route 66 which is now US Hwy 89 (Beaver Street marks the beginning of the old town) and more recent venues lie off of I-40 heading east.

Flagstaff also offers much in the way of self-contained entertainment and attractions (www.flagguide.com). Being the home of Northern Arizona

The planet Pluto was discovered at the Lowell Observatory in 1930 by Clyde Tombaugh.

Route 66 was once the only piece of continuous asphalt across the continental U.S. Sure was a lot simpler back in those days.

University, a variety of sights exist for both the old and the young. You could easily spend several days meandering around the various locales and sights within the city.

I will suggest two of my favorites. Perched on Mars Hill is the **Lowell Observatory**. It is located only one mile from downtown and it was at this facility that Pluto was discovered in 1930 by Clyde Tombaugh. The visitor center is open daily (April to October) from nine to five. Take the tour and view the heavens from the telescope used to unveil Pluto. At night, the center opens for "Sky Tonight" programs and viewings. Call to check days and times at 928-774-2096 (www.lowell.edu). Well worth a visit.

Over Labor Day Weekend, I would also suggest the Coconino County Fair which has been around for fifty-five years and epitomizes a true slice of "out West" culture and entertainment. If you want to enjoy the sights, tastes, and smells of cattle, hogs, Navajo fry bread, lumberjacks and cotton candy all rolled together, this is the spot for you. The hypnotist has my daughter dancing like Michael Jackson and singing like Elvis Presley every year.

As far as places to stay, Flagstaff has a wealth of basic motel-type lodgings and a host of B&Bs. One of the most delightful is the **Inn at 410** (www.inn410.com, 800-774-2008). Each room is unique and decorated based on its own theme. **Little America** is also right off I-40 near Butler Street on exit 198 (www.littleamerica.com/flagstaff, 800-865-1401). Camping is plentiful in and around Flagstaff as well. There is a KOA campground in the north end of Flagstaff on US Hwy 89 (www.koa.com) and **Fort Tuthill** by the Coconino County fairgrounds also has nice facilities (exit 337 on I-17). There are many state, local, and national park campgrounds as well.

If you want something good to eat after a long drive, **Black Bart's Steakhouse Saloon** (928-779-3142) offers up some cowboy-style portions of steak, ribs, and chicken. A musical revue will entertain as you chow down the porterhouse or prime rib. Another local eatery frequented by the university crowd is **Buster's Restaurant and Bar** located at 1800 South Milton Road (928-774-5155). I guarantee after a long day of motorcycling, a steak cooked medium-rare with cowboy-style beans and Texas Toast tastes mighty fine!

A dust storm is brewing. Not a good idea to unload just yet!

Trip 1   The Grand Canyon's North Rim

Distance   *527 miles (two days, overnight at North Rim or Jacobs Lake)*

Terrain   *Start in Flagstaff, Arizona amidst ponderosa pine and the San Francisco Peaks, drop to 3,500 feet to the Colorado River, and then head up to Douglas Fir at 8,800 feet at the North Rim. Swing back to Kanab, Utah, drive over the Glen Canyon Dam, see some Indian Ruins, and then back home to Flagstaff.*

Highlights   *Diverse scenery. Straightaways, S-curves, river crossings, and twisties. Roads are well marked and in good condition. Backroad side trip to Point Sublime at North Rim (GS or dual sport only).*

The Grand Canyon is without a doubt one of the most awe-inspiring natural phenomenons in the world. The grandeur and majesty will take your breath away. Every time I go back, I am amazed at how this puny river (relatively speaking) carved a hole ten-miles wide and one-mile deep. I keep asking myself "how could this have happened?" The question you need to ask yourself is, "how do I get there and not spend half my time looking for a

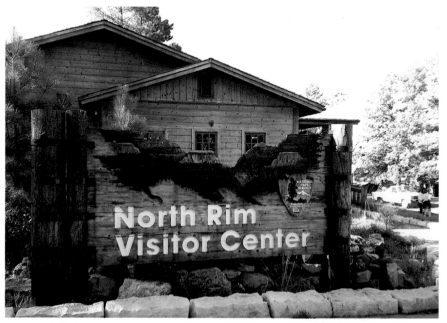

The North Rim visitors' center is a welcoming place to begin this journey.

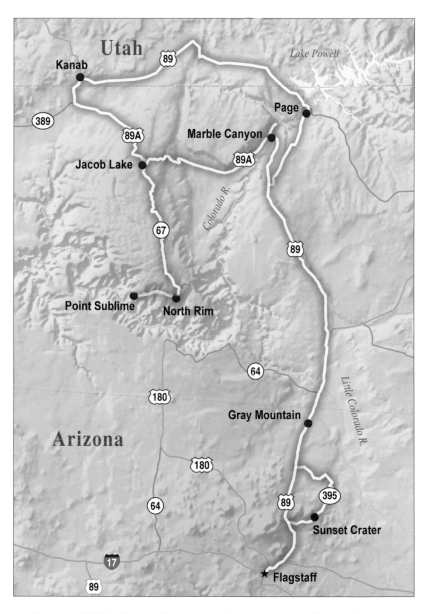

parking spot?" The Grand Canyon receives over five million visitors a year, but guess what? Over ninety percent go to . . . the South Rim. I am taking you to the North Rim on roads that were built just for motorcycles. So settle in and let's take a motorcycle journey of a lifetime on a road less traveled.

First off, pack your bags for an overnighter. I am not a drive-by picture

THE ROUTE FROM FLAGSTAFF

Day One

0   Starting point I-40 and I-17 in Flagstaff
110   Route 66 and US Hwy 89 North to 89A Junction, veer left
123   Take US Hwy 89A to Navajo Bridge Visitors Center
124   Turn right on Lees Ferry Road
129   Follow road to Lonely Dell National Historic District
134   Back to 89A junction, turn right
175   Follow 89A to State Route 67, turn left
214   Turnoff for Point Sublime (unpaved- optional)
217   Follow State Route 67 to the Grand Canyon North Rim

Day Two

217   Starting point Lodge at North Rim
259   State Route 67 to 89A Junction, turn left
296   Take 89A to Kanab, Utah and turn right onto US Hwy 89
368   Stay on US Hwy 89 to Glen Canyon Dam/Lake Powell
472   Follow US 89 across dam and south to Wupatki exit
509   Turn left into Wupatki and Sunset Crater and follow U loop back to US Hwy 89
527   Home to Flagstaff on US 89

taker. It took millions of years for the Grand Canyon to evolve; I figure we can spend a day or two exploring a fraction of that splendor. Even though the North Rim is visited by only ten percent of all Grand Canyon visitors, call in advance to make reservations at the **Grand Canyon Lodge** (www.grandcanyonnorthrim.com, 800-297-2757) which is well worth a visit. The original lodge was destroyed by fire and was then rebuilt in 1937. Designated a National Historic Landmark, the structure with its limestone walls and timbered ceilings blends in beautifully with the rustic landscape and is priced reasonably at $90 to $120 per night. Two other facilities are **Jacob Lake Inn** (www.jacoblake.com, 928-643-7232) and **Kaibab Lodge** (www.kaibab.org, 928-638-2389). Camping facilities are also plentiful (www.nps.gov/grca, 928-638-7888). One final note: the pastries at the Jacob Lake Inn are definitely worth the stop.

This path leads to Bright Angel Overlook and breathtaking photographs.

Our trip begins in Flagstaff and heads North on US Hwy 89, on to 89A and Lees Ferry and then to Jacob Lake and the Grand Canyon on State Route 67. Spend the night in North Rim Country, then swing back around through Kanab, drive across Glen Canyon dam, and then head back into Flagstaff. On the way back, enjoy a detour through the Wupatki Indian ruins and the lava formations at Sunset Crater. Elevation changes from 6,900 to 3,500 to 8,800 feet over the course of this ride. So pack a t-shirt and a warm jacket!

DAY ONE

I-17 north stops at Flagstaff and connects with I-40 going east and west. This is our starting point. It is about two and a half hours from Phoenix if you plan on flying into the area and renting a motorcycle. You can also rent motorcycles in Flagstaff (see my intro for a little more background on Flagstaff). I would suggest driving through Flagstaff even though traffic is heavy just to get a feeling for this town. The downtown area pretty much follows the old Route 66 and is lined with motels and restaurants. Stop by and grab breakfast on the way or just peer up at Mt. Humphreys, the tallest mountain in Arizona, as you drive through this old western town. Flagstaff is a great little city nestled in the San Francisco Peaks and offers many amenities (www.flagguide.com).

Now, please remember that I am taking you to the *North Rim* of the Grand Canyon, not the tourist congested South Rim. When driving up US Hwy 89, pass right on by the Grand Canyon exit. Do *not* turn left. Follow 89 around the backside of Mt. Humphreys (great views looking back) and enjoy the scenery as it unfolds from Ponderosa Pine to Plateau brush to Painted Desert formations. US Hwy 89 is relatively straight with some sweeping curves thrown in. The road is well maintained, but remember this is one of the main thoroughfares from Arizona to Utah. So just sit back and relax. Enjoy the remarkable scenery and pass that slower vehicle when the passing lane opens up every two to five miles. The wind blows out here in the West, so be prepared for a wake up call every now and then. Stop at the historic **Cameron Trading Post** (www.camerontradingpost.com, 800-338-7385) established in 1911 and about fifty-four miles north of Flagstaff to refuel and take a break. The grocery store is tucked way in the back corner. There is also a counter toward the front that caters just to fudge lovers. If your coffee didn't wake you up, a slice of fudge certainly will. Beautiful Native American artifacts and Navajo rugs adorn the trading post, most of which are available for purchase. I would recommend doing your souvenir shopping on your return trip or have them ship your purchases directly to your home.

After a nice break, cross over the Little Colorado River alongside the **Swayback Suspension Bridge** and drive another fifty-seven miles to the 89A turnoff. The **Navajo Cliffs** appear on your right and make for some spectacular scenery. Veer left off 89 to 89A at the posted sign. US Hwy 89A is a nice windy road heading to **Lees Ferry** and **Marble Canyon** across the Colorado River. The **Vermilion Cliffs** rise up like a stone tidal wave in front of you. The color and majesty of these cliffs are best seen at dawn or dusk when the shadows play tricks on the outcroppings and your eyes. I remember traveling through this area at dusk and stopping on the bridge to savor the shadows on the cliffs and sounds of the Colorado River meandering beneath me. The sounds of nature and colors tinged with orange, red, blue, brown, and gray hues make you feel a part of the canyon and that time itself does not exist here. It was like listening to Enya except without Enya.

Cross the bridge and hang an immediate right into the **Navajo Bridge Interpretive Visitors' Center**. The facility is clean and well run. Read the plaques on the edge of the Colorado and you will be impressed with the history and engineering feats explained to you. The original Navajo Bridge is now open only to foot traffic as it has been replaced by a larger suspension

After riding the dirt track to Point Sublime, this was a well-deserved (and well-named) treat.

bridge. Take a walk across it, peer down at the Colorado 470 feet below you and get a feel for the strength of this river. Until 1928, there were no available crossings for over 700 miles. Lees Ferry just up the river from this point provided the only transport across the river for over fifty years (www.nps.gov/glca.com).

Get back on 89A and take an immediate right just before Marble Canyon Lodge into the Lees Ferry park entrance. This is a neat little five-mile road that takes you right past the base of the mammoth stone embodiments, past a campground, and all the way around to the back side of the Vermilion Cliffs. You will end up at the Lonely Dell Ranch Historic District where you can park your bike and walk to an old abandoned log cabin, blacksmith shop, cemetery, and orchard used by the early pioneers. John D. Lee set up housekeeping here with his several wives and started the ferry crossing in 1871. The early Mormon Pioneers used the crossing when they trekked to Utah to be married in the Temple. Hence, the route was named Honeymoon Trail. Some buildings are used by the Park Service, while others you can crawl inside and get an idea how comfortless the lives of the early pioneers must have been.

Hop back on your bike and go down to the staging area for rafters going down the mighty Colorado. Captain John Wesley Powell started his historic venture down the Grand Canyon here. In my opinion, Lees Ferry is a detour that tourists miss on their way to the North Rim. For those of you who are totally enthralled with the breadth and history of this little known oasis, settle in at the campground or spend a night at the Marble Canyon Lodge. Do some fishing on the river, or just sit and listen to the muted roar of the Colorado as you bask in the solitude of a place where time seems to be standing still.

The next stage of the trip takes us up 89A to Jacob Lake, a change in elevation from 3,500 to 8,500 feet. As you drive down the road, the Vermilion Cliffs stick out like King Kong's jagged teeth on your right, and on your left, the Kaibab plateau is level and flat until dropping like a precipice into the Grand Canyon. On your way, stop at the historical marker midway between Marble Canyon and Jacob Lake. You will see the historical marker on your right. Take the time to pull over and indulge yourself in history going back to 1776 when Father Escalante set out on an expedition to find a northern route to California from Santa Fe in the name of the Holy Catholic Church. He was one of the first foreigners to set foot in this territory.

The ride up to Jacob Lake is one of my favorites. The landscape changes from high desert to midrange ponderosa pine to high altitude Douglas fir. The transition is remarkable. But one word of caution: keep your eyes on the road as this one is twisty. The road starts with some hairpins and then proceeds up the side of the mountain. Even though there are several blind curves, you can really get into this piece of pavement. Drag your peg every now and then, gently roll up on your throttle and enjoy this ride upward as the elevation changes from 4,000 to 8,000 feet. This road is an absolute delight, but you may need to stop at an overlook and put on that jacket you packed.

If you want to enjoy the scenery, pull over at one of the scenic overlooks. And if you are going to pull over the first one is the best. It is a large turnout that you can't miss and is about one mile up the road. Stop and take a look back at the plateau and cliffs! I remember stopping here after a desert rainstorm and the colors are still etched in my mind. The blue sky and white billowing clouds contrast with the reds and grays of the cliffs and plateau. Nothing like good ol' Western grandeur!

Take this road up to Jacob Lake and take a break at Jacob Lake lodge if you like. There is a restaurant and gas station here as well. By the way, my mobile phone worked great up here—there must be a transmitter at the top of this mountain—so call home and tell them what a wonderful time you are having. A nice state campground is also at this intersection. If you want

Every time I see the Grand Canyon, I am awestruck by its enormity.

to spend the night, I would recommend the lodge at Jacob Lake. It has a cozy atmosphere, fireplace, and homemade pastries. You can also stay in the park, just be sure you make reservations in advance.

State Route 67 to the North Rim is well worth the wait. Recently paved asphalt flows alongside alpine meadows and Douglas fir (watch out for wildlife in the morning and dusk). The pavement weaves through the alpine meadows like a slow moving snake. Gentle curves, soft pavement, and lush greenery make this an all time Rocky Mountain Scenic Byway. Take your time on State Route 67. Open up your visor. Feel the wind as its crispness massages your face. Smell the pine and Douglas fir. The road is about forty-two miles long and I wish it could go on forever.

Now that I've got you to the Grand Canyon, you can decide what to do. More books than I care to count have been written about it. But for starters, stop at the visitors' center; get some information on hikes and at the very least trek on down to the Bright Angel overlook. A paved half-mile trail leads from the lodge to this point. Dramatic views of Roaring Springs and Bright Angel Canyon can be seen from this overlook. The North Rim is not as crowded as the South and the views are just as magnificent. Go to the lodge, grab a drink, and sit on the outside veranda for more spectacular views. If you are hungry, eat at the restaurant (reservations highly recommended, 928-638-2611) in the lodge that overlooks the canyon, or just grab a snack at the deli and go back out to the veranda. Last time I went was

A daring soul gets ready to bungee jump off Navajo Bridge over the Colorado River.

over Memorial Day weekend and . . . let's see, I think it took me two minutes to find a parking spot. You will not be disappointed!

A couple of other neat motorcycle rides are to Point Imperial, which is about eleven miles from the lodge, and Cape Royal, which is about twenty-three miles from the lodge. Point Imperial is the highest point on the rim at 8,800 feet and overlooks the eastern end of the Grand Canyon all the way from the narrow Marble Canyon at Lees Ferry to its dramatic opening right below you. Cape Royal provides a panoramic view across the Canyon in just about every direction imaginable. On a clear day you better bring two or three disposable cameras. This view is especially breathtaking at sunrise or dusk.

It's best to spend an extra night at the North Rim if you really want to explore some of the backroads or hike down a portion of the Kaibab Trail. For those of you on a GS or dual sport there is a 4 × 4 trail road that heads west to Point Sublime. If you are interested head up State Route 67 about three miles to the Point Sublime Road just before the Point Imperial and Cape Royal turnoff. Turn left and drive slowly. Rocks, boulders, and fallen trees frequently visit this road as well. Plan on around two to four hours round trip depending on your speed, road condition, and number of stops along the way. Geologist Clarence Dutton and Photographer William Holmes came to this same spot over a hundred years ago. Bet they would still recognize it today!

DAY TWO

After a good night's rest at the Lodge and exploring the North Rim to your satisfaction, continue on our loop by heading back up State Route 67 to the 89A turnoff at Jacob Lake. Mornings are a must on State Route 67. You have the road all to yourself. The weather is a bit chilly, but zip in your liners, turn on your heated handgrips, and flow with the road. At the State Route 67 and 89A junction, hang a left (after stopping for a pastry at Jacob Lake Inn) and trek on down the backside of the mountain to Kanab, Utah. Flying down the mountain is a great way to start your morning. Your mind is alert, there is rarely any other traffic, and the twisties force you to focus. The motorcycle, you, and the road are one as you roll and release your grip around the throttle. The pavement is just as enjoyable heading down the mountain as climbing up. There is a scenic turnout about ten miles down the road. The view looks toward the other Vermilion Cliffs in Southern Utah. Great pictures.

At the bottom of the mountain, 89A straightens out and after about thirty miles takes you into Kanab, Utah. Coming into Fredonia (just before Kanab) watch out for the police car with the mannequin in it. Fools me every time (one of these days he will be the real McCoy)!

Kanab is famous for being the crossroads to Zion and Bryce National Parks. Several Westerns have been filmed in the vicinity and at the **Parry Lodge** (www.infowest.com/parry) you can stay in some of these rooms formerly used by movie stars. If you didn't grab a pastry at Jacob Lake Inn, I would recommend you get a bite to eat and tank up. **Houston's Trail End** at 32 E. Center (435-644-2488) is a good place to start.

US Hwy 89 intersects 89A at the light. So, turn right as you enter Kanab and drive past McDonalds. You are now on US Hwy 89 heading southeast to Glen Canyon Dam and Lake Powell. The road is relatively straight for

Heading back from the North Rim on State Route 67 to Jacob Lake, this recently-paved piece of tarmac makes for one great ride!

seventy miles and hugs more of the Vermilion Cliffs until you begin the descent to Lake Powell. As you approach the dam, the road rapidly drops into a gorge and the visitors' center appears on your left. Stop in and get educated. **Glen Canyon Dam** (www.nps.gov/glca, 928-608-6404) is an engineering marvel and not nearly as crowded as the more well known Hoover Dam on the way to Las Vegas. Take in the panoramic view from the glass paneled veranda. Sit and watch some of the videos which take you back to the actual construction of the dam. If you have the time, go on the tour into the dam itself and to the lower levels where the turbines are generating massive amounts of electric current. You can also walk out to some of the viewpoints on the dam and get a feel for the Colorado River and the battle between taming the river and allowing nature to run its course. The views are stupendous.

After getting your fill of the visitors' center, drive across the dam and head toward Page on Hwy 89. There are some fast food restaurants and gas stations along this corridor if you need to stop for fuel (either your own or the bike's). US Hwy 89 then takes you up through the red rock Navajo cliffs where you can enjoy some clean pavement as the road winds around various rock formations and then meanders down the side of the cliffs to the junction of 89 and 89A. These tight curves will give you a nice adrenalin rush. There are some scenic viewpoints if you wish to stop. Drive right by the 89A exit (about twenty-five miles from Glen Canyon Dam) and you are back into familiar territory.

The drive from the 89 and 89A junction to Flagstaff is about 100 miles. To break this up, I suggest another detour which is about seventy-nine miles south of the 89 and 89A junction and just twenty-two miles south of the Cameron Trading Post. You will see a sign on your right that says "**Wupatki Indian Ruins and Sunset Crater National Monument**" (www.nps.gov/sucr, 928-526-1157). If you blink you'll drive right by it, so stay alert! Turn left onto the thirty-seven-mile U Loop Road that weaves through some ancient Indian Ruins, the Painted Desert overlook, and then back around some jagged lava formations at Sunset Crater. You end up about twenty miles from Flagstaff at the end of the U loop when you reconnect with US Hwy 89. I would suggest stopping at the ruins and walking among these ancient dwellings. Around 1250 AD the Indians inexplicably left these masonry pueblos and they have been uninhabited for close to 800 years. You can actually walk inside them as opposed to seeing them from a distance. Wupatki Pueblo Trail located at the visitors' center is a self-guided tour to one of the largest pueblos in the park and is less then half a mile. After getting an idea how basic living conditions were back in those days, hop back

The Colorado River as seen from Navajo Bridge looks a long way down to me!

on your comfy bike, take a picture at the Painted Desert overlook about twenty miles down the road and then drive up to Sunset Crater another seven miles up the road. It's time to work off that Mexican food you ate in Kanab and go on a little hike through the lava and moonscape at the Lava Flow Trail (one-mile walk). This self-guided trail is well marked and worth the effort. If you want to be real aggressive, hike up to the cinder cone on the Lenox Crater Trail (steep one-mile trail). Sunset crater erupted around 1100 AD and is the youngest volcanic explosion on the Colorado Plateau. The landscape is harsh, yet aspen trees and vegetation flourish. After you've worked off a few calories, continue to follow the loop out of the Sunset Crater exit and back on to 89. This U loop is well maintained, fun to ride, and the best part is that you will have it all to yourself.

Follow 89 back into Flagstaff and enjoy the views one last time as you look up at the snow capped San Francisco Peaks. Clean up at your B&B and then head over to Black Bart's Steakhouse Saloon at 2760 E. Butler (928-779-3142) for some fine western dining. Meet up with your riding buddies, rest your weary behind, and reminisce about the trip you just made on the road less traveled to the Grand Canyon.

Trip 2 Sedona and Mormon Lake Loop

Distance *236 miles (full day, including stops)*

Terrain *This trip is a roller coaster of elevation changes. Start in Flagstaff at 7,000 feet, drop 2,600 feet to the red rocks of Sedona through Oak Creek Canyon, and then climb back up Mingus Mountain through Jerome to 7,100 feet. The trip back drops to 3,500 feet at Camp Verde and nudges to 8,000 feet by Mormon Lake and then swings back into Flagstaff.*

Highlights *Numerous hairpins coming down canyons and climbing mountains. Sweeping S-curves on the return trip from Camp Verde to Flagstaff. Beautiful backroad detour on Schnebly Hill Road for some unforgettable vistas.*

You'll enjoy these sweeping curves as you climb Mingus Mountain toward Jerome.

The vortex may swallow your motorcycle on this trip through Sedona and Jerome, but don't let that bother you. The only worry you should have is keeping your eyes on the road as you scrub your tires on hairpins through scenery that continues to amaze with each passing mile.

This loop begins in Flagstaff on Hwy 89A and heads south through Oak Creek Canyon to Sedona and then over Mingus Mountain to Jerome and the Upper Prescott Valley. The trip back returns via sweeping turns up Route 260 from Camp Verde to Clints Well and then back past Happy Jack and Mormon Lake to Flagstaff on Route 487.

Over the course of this drive, elevation changes are dramatic, so be prepared for temperature changes, and more importantly, roads that are as varied as the landscape.

A word of advice before this journey begins: be patient as you drive the hair-pinned spine of Oak Creek Canyon. The run from Flagstaff to Jerome is popular and can be busy. Early mornings and mid-week are best, but nonetheless, you will probably be taking it nice and slow as you gaze down at the sandstone monoliths searching for UFOs landing on top of Bell Rock. The trip back from Camp Verde is another story. This backdoor of sweeping curves into Flagstaff is wide open as you climb back up to 8,000

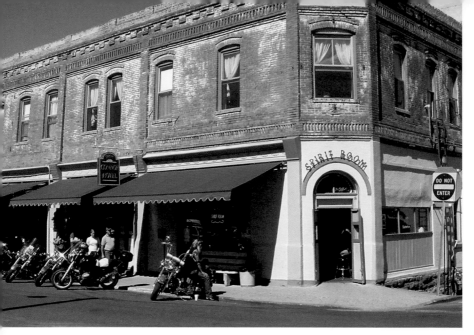

Hotel Conner in Jerome is a well-known watering hole for bikers.

feet and may get the best of you, so be sure to keep a sharp lookout for that State Trooper.

To begin this trip, follow 89A south from Flagstaff past the Coconino County Fairgrounds and begin your twenty-seven-mile, 2,600-foot descent toward Oak Creek Canyon and Sedona. The road gently slopes downward for a few miles until you get to the Oak Creek Vista Point. From this vantage point you can visualize the full spectrum of terrain and colors you will be entering. The timberline drops into recesses of orange, greens, and grays with billowing white clouds forming a backdrop. The road below invites you as it twists and turns down the canyon spine. The only problem with stopping is that you will be so anxious to hop back on your bike, you will forget to snap a picture!

Continue down 89A, relishing the hairpins as the road winds down Oak Creek Canyon. The vegetation changes from pine and aspen to maple and oak. The road hugs the west bank of the creek for about fourteen miles. Mid-October is a great time of year to enjoy the cooler weather as autumn leaves bring even more color to the diverse landscape.

Various campgrounds line the corridor along Oak Creek Canyon. One of the most picturesque is Cave Springs Forest about four miles from the Vista Point. Sites are secluded and away from the main road. There are even coin showers for the discriminating camper. For more info see www.fs.us/r3/coconino/recreation/red_rock/cavesprings-camp.shtml or call 877-444-6777.

THE ROUTE FROM FLAGSTAFF

0	89A and I-40/I-17 Interchange—head south
12	Oak Creek Vista Point
20	Slide Rock State Park
28	89A and Route 179 intersection in Sedona. Turn left for Schnebly Hill Road (unpaved- optional)
32	Turn left on Upper Red Rock Loop Road
37	Red Rock State Park
41	Continue loop and turn left on 89A
56	Take 89A to Main Street intersection in Cottonwood—go straight
59	Tuzigoot National Monument Turnoff
60	Tuzigoot National Monument
61	Turn right back onto Main Street
62	Follow Main to Broadway in Clarkdale to the Verde Railroad
63	Turn right back on Main Street and then left on 11th Street
66	Follow 11th street and then 89A to Jerome
93	Stay on 89A from Jerome to 69 and Fain Road turnoff—turn left
100	Follow Fain Road and turn left on 69
103	Take 69 to 169 and turn left
118	Stay on 169 until I-17—go north (left)
127	I-17 to the Camp Verde Exit (260)
163	Take 260 to 87—turn left
175	Follow 87 to 487 (Lake Mary Road)—turn left
205	Take 487 to the Mormon Lake Turnoff
209	Roundtrip to Mormon Lake—go back to 487
241	Stay on 487 (Lake Mary Road) back into Flagstaff

For those of you traveling in the summer months, stop by **Slide Rock State Park** or **Grasshopper Swim Area** to cool your feet and splash some cold water on your face. Slide Rock is composed of natural chutes of flowing water. Nature's version of a water slide. Stop by for a picnic or use that extra pair of jeans to slip down the creek (the ride is a little bumpy). For more information call 928-282 3034 (www.pr.state.az.us/parks/parkhtml/sliderock.html).

After cooling off at Slide Rock, follow 89A for another 8 miles right into downtown Sedona. Hwy 89A is lined with shops, restaurants, and malls.

Drop by an ice cream shop, wander through town, or just sit on a bench and take a look around. What is truly breathtaking is not the town, but the surrounding landscape. The amber hued monoliths jutting up around the city create a natural contradiction to the residential and commercial structures clustered at their base.

Sedona is the epitome of an "artsy" town. The resplendent scenery gives the city a charm like few other locales. Although the Oak Creek was one of the original reasons fruit farmers and ranchers originally settled this area, it is the red glow of Sedona that really draws the artists and tourists today.

If you have only a short time to stay, I would suggest a couple of options. Firstly, turn left from 89A to 179 at the stoplight and visit the arts and crafts

The sun setting on the Red Rock Loop just south of Sedona creates amazing colors and shadows.

Wow! You can definitely feel the vortex here!

village of **Tlaquepaque.** This is a delightfully recreated version of Spanish villas and narrow alleys of brick and mortar, which are home to various local art studios. Wander through these shops and get a feel for the essence of this town. Restaurants and often live music add to the charm of this hideaway. Check out the website for a host of information, including a calendar of events and times (www.tlaq.com).

For those of you interested in a scenic dirt back road away from the commercialization, hang a left on route 179 off 89A (first stoplight), go down about half a mile (just past Tlaquepaque), and turn left on Schnebly Hill Road. This route is a six-mile detour, climbing up the side of the surrounding mountains to the Schnebly Vista Point. The first mile is paved and then becomes unpaved for the next five miles. Not an option for street bikes. The road is rocky and, in some spots, sandy, but the views are worth it. The road twists and turns as it slices its way up the side of the mountain and takes about one-hour round trip.

After getting your fill of downtown Sedona, drive back to 89A and continue through the several stoplights until you arrive at the Upper Red Rock Loop Road about four miles south of the 89A and 179 intersection. This detour takes you down to Red Rock State Park for some majestic views of Cathedral Rock. The road winds down the side of the canyon through some residential areas that overlook the park. Be careful, as there are few turnouts and residential traffic uses this as an access road. After about three miles, the

There are great views heading up Schnebly Hill Road, but you will need a GS or dual-sport.

road turns into a "primitive" road which sounds scarier then it really is. Take it slow and even street bikes will be fine. The road is well graded fine gravel for just a couple of miles and connects with the other side of the paved loop back out to 89A. Total loop distance is nine miles and the road and scenery are splendid. Try to feel the aura emanating from Cathedral Rock.

At the bottom of the loop is **Red Rock State Park.** Formerly a part of Smoke Trail Ranch, the Oak Creek meanders through this area creating a diverse riparian habitat amidst the red rock. A visitors' center with information about the area is available at the entrance. The smoke trail loop is only four tenths of a mile and, if you are lucky, you may even see a wedding ceremony being performed by the infamous "wedding tree." Can "just married" fit on a motorcycle? (www.pr.state.az.us/parks/parkhtml/redrock.html, 928-292-6907).

The Red Rock Loop connects back onto 89A a few miles south of where you started. Turn left on 89A and follow the signs to Cottonwood. This stretch of road is about fifteen miles and turns into a four-lane highway as it runs through the outskirts of Sedona. Upon entering Cottonwood drive straight on to Main Street. Do not turn left at the posted sign for 89A to Jerome at this point. Main Street leads across a bridge, through old town Cottonwood, and to the Tuzigoot National Monument turnoff. Total miles from the Red Rock Loop to Tuzigoot are about 18.5.

Enjoy this run through small town USA and then turn right at the posted sign to Tuzigoot National Monument. This road is about one mile long and crosses over Oak Creek to the park entrance. The Sinagua Indians built the **Tuzigoot Monument** around 1100 AD (TOO-zee-goot). A two-story pueblo perched on a hilltop once housed over 200 people. A visitors' center and self-guided tours are available to explore these 900-year-old ruins. The views are expansive looking down from the pueblo (www.nps.gov/tuzi).

Another detour in this area (especially for locomotive lovers) is to take a look at the **Verde Canyon Railroad.** To get to the station, return to Main Street, turn right, and go about one mile to Broadway in Clarkdale. Veer right to the Verde Canyon Railroad Station. Touted as "Arizona's Longest Running Nature Show," this wilderness train ride takes you into an area not accessible by vehicles. The steep canyon walls of the Verde are home to bald eagles and various other wildlife. The train meanders across old-fashioned trestles and man-made tunnels as it heads to Perkinsville, an old ghost town and then back to Clarkdale. Vintage Diesel FP7s pull you in restored Pullmans on this four-hour round trip train ride. If you just want to look, stop by, and have lunch at the cafe/grille, you can save this trip for next time (www.verdecanyon.com, 800-293-7245).

Long Valley Cafe at the intersection of State Routes 87 and 487 (Lake Mary Road) is worth a stop.

The dual-sport option allows you to extend the journey.

After a visit to the railroad station, head back on Broadway and turn right on Main Street through downtown Clarkdale (short and sweet). About one-quarter mile up the road turn left on 11th Street. The posted sign reads 89A to Jerome. Go straight at the stop sign and you are now back on 89A heading up to Jerome.

This is where the fun really starts. Enough sightseeing, it's time to ride. The next thirty miles of pavement will get your adrenalin pumping. The road twists and turns through Jerome, climbs up over Mingus Mountain at 7,000 feet and then rolls down the backside of the mountain into the Upper Prescott Valley.

The road begins with sweeping S-curves winding up the slopes of Jerome. Jerome is built like San Francisco back in the 1800s, except this town hasn't changed since then. The town literally clings to the side of Cleopatra Hill overlooking the Verde Valley and appears to be slipping down the hillside. Once a thriving mining community of 15,000 during the late 1800s and into the 1920s, this "wickedest city" in the west faded from memory during the Great Depression and could barely claim fifty people as residents. Starting in the 1960s, artists, tourists, and retirees slowly put

Jerome back on the map. Today, Jerome is a well-know weekend getaway from Phoenix. Driving through the town is like taking a step back in time. The unique setting and early 20th century architecture give Jerome its own character and ambiance. The saloon on the corner at the Connor Hotel (established 1898) is a favorite watering hole for motorcyclists. Stop by and listen to a little music before heading up the mountain.

The switchbacks through town last a few miles as you approach Mingus Mountain. The road is carved neatly from the side of the cliffs as it gently climbs upward. About two miles outside of town, a scenic overlook provides a grand view looking back to Jerome and the valley below. Stop, take a picture, as this is the only turnout available, and then hop back on 89A and start muscling up the hairpins to 7,000 feet that make this part of the trip a motorcyclist's dream. The road climbs and winds from 5,000 feet up and over the top. The switchbacks are tight, so be careful going around the blind corners. Watch the road for slower traffic and don't get too close to the edge. It is a long way down. But in the meantime, drag your pegs, scrape your boots and then roll down the backside toward Prescott. The miles will pass all too quickly!

Autumn at Slide Rock showcases a brilliant array of colors.

Apple orchards at Slide Rock State Park bear fruit in the fall.

The road straightens up about twenty miles outside Jerome on the south side of Mingus Mountain. Look for signs to Route 69 and then turn left at the stoplight on Fain Road. Fain Road is new and may not be shown on your AAA maps. This road bypasses Prescott, and after twelve miles links up with Route 69. Personally, I would avoid Prescott. This area has turned into the closest summer getaway from Phoenix and has more stoplights than I care to count. Fain Road is peaceful and winds around Prescott giving some grand views of the valley and outlying mountains in the process.

At Route 69, turn left and drive about two and a half miles to the Route 169 intersection. As you need to head back north to Flagstaff via Camp Verde, turn left here and go fifteen miles to I-17. This stretch of road is relatively straight and hilly. At I-17, head north (left) for about nine miles to the Camp Verde Exit.

More fun now awaits you. It's time to climb back up the Mogollon Rim toward Flagstaff. Head past the Chevron Station (gas up if you need it) and drive through Camp Verde on Route 260 as it again climbs up some radical elevations. The trip home is high and cool on roads that tempt you along just a little faster (remember . . . self control!). This road is not the rapid-fire switchbacks you encountered in Jerome, but rather gentle sweeping curves that allow the throttle to slip down a few notches. If you can, open your visor and feel the change in temperature while climbing from 4,000 feet to over 7,000 feet on a delightfully long thirty-four miles. The wide open S-curves tempt you to ratchet it up as you fly toward the clouds. The scenery changes from scrubby desert pine to green pastures with ponderosa pine over the course of this road. Even the smell changes! As most tourists drive up I-17 to Flagstaff, this back way is uncongested and wide open.

When you arrive at the top of the rim, the road ends in a T. Turn left on Route 87, which goes up through Long Valley to Clints Well. The road

Take a break and cool off your feet in Oak Creek Canyon.

The autumn colors and evening sun make for a magical ride down Oak Creek Canyon.

swerves gently through pine and meadows. The traffic is usually minimal and the scenery green and blue.

Continue on 87 for eleven miles. On the left side of the road is the **Long Valley Cafe**, a grocery store and service station. Tank up, grab a donut, and enjoy the cool crispness in the air. A meadow sways with the breeze east of the road and occasionally elk or deer will wander into view.

About half a mile further up 87, turn left on route 487 (Lake Mary Road) toward Happy Jack and Mormon Lake. This leg to Flagstaff is one of my favorites. Most travelers veer right to Winslow, leaving this stretch of road wide open as it climbs to 8,000 feet and eventually hugs Mormon Lake and Lake Mary into Flagstaff.

There are several lakes in this area, some of which are accessible only via Forest Trail Roads. For you motorcyclist-anglers, staying in this neck of the woods may be worthwhile. Lakes and reservoirs are dotted throughout this region. Blue Ridge Reservoir, Long Lake, Knoll Lake, Stoneman Lake, Kinnikinnick Lake, and Ashurst Lake are stocked with trout, catfish, bass, yellow perch, and northern pike. From what I hear, an anglers dream!

Campsites are also plentiful and well maintained along this corridor. For more information on this area contact the **Mormon Lake Ranger Station** (928-774-1182) or **Peaks Ranger Station** (928-526-0866). Online access available at www.fs.fed.us/r3/coconino.

Continue winding your way along Route 487 for twenty-six miles. The road is pleasant, gently curving through the pines on top of Mogollon Rim. Between mile marker 317 and 318, the road intersects with the Mormon

Lake turnoff. Turn left for a short rendezvous with the **Mormon Lake Lodge Steakhouse and Saloon** (www.mormonlodge.com, 928-354-2227). This recreational center offers food, outdoor activities, a western-style town, and dinner theater. As you are only thirty miles from Flagstaff, a mesquite grilled steak may be essential to finishing up your trip. If you have the time, chow down and wander around this old western town for a moment.

Returning to Flagstaff via 487 sends you around the North end of Mormon Lake and then hugs the upper edges of Lake Mary. Various side roads are available for picnic areas and campsites. Anglers can often be seen reeling in their catch of the day or barbecuing some rainbow trout. The scenery is green and calm, with afternoon clouds billowing like white cotton candy in the clear azure sky. After twenty miles the outskirts of Flagstaff are visible, and before you know it, the freeway looms ominously overhead. The sounds of the city are close and imminent. But for some reason, the noise and bustle seem quieter and less bothersome. Maybe the gentleness of the last seventy miles has settled your senses, or maybe that Sedona vortex has quelled your spirit (or maybe you are just flat out tired from a long day of driving and the food in your belly is making you drowsy). Either way, a good night's rest is well deserved!

The Secret Garden Cafe at Tlaquepaque is a good choice for dinner.

Taos

A thousand years of history in New Mexico? You have got to be kidding! Well, don't be surprised when you arrive in Taos. This small town in northern New Mexico is home to the oldest continuously inhabited community in North America (Taos Pueblo), Kit Carson's former home, and a host of famous 20th century writers and artists. When the Spanish first arrived in 1540, the Pueblo Indians had already been here for 500 years. These two peoples peacefully coexisted until the Pueblo uprising in 1680 when the Spaniards were driven out. In 1696, Don Diego de Vargas reconquered this territory and brought it back into the Spanish Empire.

As a result, the legacies of these two cultures combined with the likes of Kit Carson and the artist community have created a town with real charm.

Boutiques, shops, and cafes built in traditional Spanish colonial adobe architecture line the streets of Taos.

The streets are well shaded under a canopy of spruce and cottonwoods; boutiques, shops, and cafes built in traditional Spanish colonial adobe architecture line the boulevards culminating in the quiet ambiance of the Plaza at the town center.

Taos (www.taoschamber.com, 800-732-8267) lies at 7,000 feet in the Rio Grande Valley snuggled next to the Sangre de Cristo Range of the Southern Rockies. Its location make it an ideal staging point for several motorcycle journeys through some majestic mountainous terrain. The Enchanted Circle and Jemez Mountain Loops climb high into the crystal air and give you a real taste of New Mexico's grandeur and history. Another

The Taos Plaza is a popular parking spot and meeting place for fellow bikers.

Good places to stay are plentiful in Taos!

journey races high into Colorado's mighty San Juan Range and flies across even more white-knuckle, high-altitude twisties.

Bed & Breakfasts are plentiful in Taos as well as standard motel rooms. A couple of my favorites are the **Old Taos Guesthouse** (www.oldtaos.com, 800-758-5448) situated just outside of town overlooking Taos, or if you want something in town drop by the historic **Taos Inn** (www.taosinn.com, 888-518-8267) located right in the center of town. Both are well managed, enjoyable, and great places to unwind after a long day of motorcycling. Campers can stake their tent at the El Nogal or Las Petacas campgrounds just two to three miles east of town in the **Taos Canyon** (505-758-8268).

And, finally, when the day is done try Taos's best kept secret (until now) and have lunch or dinner at **Orlando's** at 114 Don Juan Valdez Lane (505 751-1450). This family-run New Mexican restaurant dishes up some delicious local cuisine and is about two miles north of the Plaza on US Hwy 64. Last time I went it was cash only and well worth the wait. So be patient (maybe the secret is already out!).

Trip 3   The Enchanted Circle

Distance   *155 miles (medium day)*
Terrain   *See all that is New Mexico on this Scenic Byway through mining towns, river gorges, and mountain peaks with an elevation change of 6,000 to 9,800 feet. Drop by the "World Heritage Site" of Taos Pueblo and the first memorial dedicated to the Vietnam Veterans in Angel Fire on a high altitude circle through the Southern Rockies.*
Highlights   *Twisties, S-curves, and switchbacks. Take a backroad adventure on the Lower Arroyo Canyon Road to the original crossing of the Rio Grande.*

The lush, green countryside on the way to Taos Pueblo leaves no doubt as to why this is called the Enchanted Circle.

The Enchanted Circle in Northern New Mexico is "enchanted" for a couple of reasons. Firstly, this loop traverses through some of the most majestic terrain in the Southern Rockies and, secondly, it exposes you to everything that is New Mexico. From the oldest living Native American Community at Taos Pueblo to the more recent past at the D.H. Lawrence Shrine in San Cristobal and the Vietnam National Memorial at Angel Fire. All of this is juxtaposed within the majestic Sangre de Cristo (blood of Christ) Mountain Range centered around Wheeler Peak at 13,161 feet and then edged by the roaring Rio Grande passing through 800-foot chasms at its western perimeter.

Even though this trek is relatively short at 165 miles, it travels deep into the history and culture of New Mexico, across mountaintops with cool air and clear lakes nestled amidst resplendent wildlife and roads paved in joyously soft, black asphalt. The loop begins in Taos, heads up to the base of Wheeler Peak, straddles the Rio Grande Gorge and then circles back via old mining towns and trout-filled lakes.

THE ROUTE FROM TAOS

0   Start at the Plaza in Taos going north on US Hwy 64
1   Turn right onto BIA 701 to Taos Pueblo
3   Arrive Taos Pueblo, turn around
5   Turn right on US 64
8   Turn right on State Route 150 to Taos Ski Valley
24   Arrive Taos Ski Valley, turn around
40   Turn right on State Route 522
47   Arrive Arroyo Hondo, turn left to the John Dunn Bridge on Lower Arroyo Canyon Rd (unpaved- optional).
59   Arrive Questa, continue north on Route 522 to Cerro
63   Arrive Cerro, turn left on State Route 378 to Wild Rivers Recreation Area
77   Arrive La Junta Campground, continue on loop
91   Arrive Cerro, turn right on Route 522
95   Arrive Questa, turn left on State Route 38
107 Arrive Red River
125 Arrive Eagle Nest, continue southeast on US Hwy 64
134 Arrive Angel Fire Memorial
155 Arrive Taos

Start in Taos and head north on US Hwy 64 and State Route 68. Continue about a mile, and then turn right at the sign to Taos Pueblo. Although this site is just out of town and your ride has just begun, this side trip is worth your time. **Taos Pueblo** is the only living Native American Community in the world and has been designated a National Historic Landmark and World Heritage Site by UNESCO (www.taospueblo.com).

The Pueblo is made entirely of adobe and the main building was constructed between 1000 AD and 1450 AD (exact date is not divulged due to religious privacy). There are approximately 150 people living continuously within its walls. Get a taste of Native American Culture by taking the walking tour, visiting with the local artists, and touring the St. Jerome Chapel built in 1850 (replacing the original church first built in 1619). The Pueblo is generally open to visitors except during traditional tribal rituals and during the late winter and early spring. Parking is available just left of the entrance in an unpaved parking area. Call ahead at 505-758-1028 for more information.

After purchasing some Native American jewelry (your wife will love you), head back to Routes 64/68, turn right, and drive about three miles to the light. Make another immediate right on State Route 150 toward the Taos Ski Valley Resort fifteen miles ahead. This road skirts along the Wheeler Peak Wilderness Area with ample views of these Southern Rockies. Enjoy this approximately thirty-mile round trip to the ski resort at the base of Wheeler Peak. The road winds and weaves through this rugged landscape making this short run fun to drive. Lean into the curves and brush your boots as the road pulls you toward the tallest peak in New Mexico. Park your bike at the **Bavarian Lodge** about one mile past the main ski area on a dirt road and if time permits take the one and a half mile walk to **Williams Lake** set in a glacial cirque at 11,000 feet (trailhead right by the Kachina

Heading back from Taos Pueblo, the Sangre de Cristo Mountains loom large in the background.

chairlift). This hike is moderate, but rewards you with a stunning view of a mountain lake set high in the towering Rockies (helps work off that breakfast, too).

After a quick cup of hot chocolate at the lodge, dash back down Route 150 and then turn right again on Route 522 in the direction of Arroyo Hondo. Just across the bridge, turn left on Lower Arroyo Canyon Road to the **John Dunn Bridge** crossing the Rio Grande. This detour is optional, as the road is paved for about two miles, then turns into a dirt backroad as it meanders down to the Rio Grande. The Hondo Valley envelopes the road alongside its namesake river and ends up at the original Rio Grande bridge crossing at the base of the gorge. This ten-mile round trip detour trickles down to the Rio and cuts through the gorge wall like a tiny rivulet. You seem small and puny driving in this chasm to the shores of the Rio Grande.

The bridge was built in the 1890s by John Dunn, a legend in Northern New Mexico folklore. Dunn was a colorful character who had tried his hand in most everything. From farming and raising cattle, to running from the law and opening two gambling houses in Taos. Eventually, he bought and built the only toll bridge across the Rio Grande into Northern New Mexico. Passengers from the Denver and Rio Grande Railroad had to cross at this

Take a break on your way back from Wheeler Peak and enjoy the great mountain scenery.

This bed & breakfast epitomizes the meaning of "eclectic" in the artsy community of Taos.

spot to get in and out of Taos. He charged $1.00 per person, 50 cents per horse, and 25 cents for sheep. His $5,000 investment turned into quite a profit over the years.

After a brief stop at the Rio Grande, head back up to Arroyo Hondo and turn left on Route 522 toward San Cristobal. If you are a "literature buff," visit the **D.H. Lawrence Ranch and Memorial** (formerly Kiowa Ranch) just outside of town. Lawrence and his wife, Frieda, first came to New Mexico in 1922 and in 1924 spent a total of 11 months here. The memorial is now maintained by the University of New Mexico and open to the Public. Lawrence and Frieda fell in love with this mountain hideaway and when he died, she returned to live here the remainder of her life. D.H. Lawrence's ashes are also kept here. For more information visit the website at www.unm.edu/taosconf/lawrence.html.

Continuing on Route 522, the town of **Questa** looms ahead at the junction of State Route 38. Formerly known as Cuesta, meaning lowering, this town is situated in a recess ringed by steep-sided volcanic cones including Utes Peak, Ortiz, and the San Antonio Mountains. Although boasting only a population of 400, Questa does have a Mexican Restaurant with some volcanic green chile sauce that will sizzle your taste buds. So if you are hungry for a little south of the border cuisine, try **El Seville** for some traditional, *hot* Mexican food.

Before heading east on Route 38, continue north on Route 522 for four miles and then turn left on State Route 378 into the **Wild Rivers Recreation Area** (www.nmblm.gov/tafo/rafting/rio_grande/wrra/wild_ rivers. html, 505-758-8851). This thirty-mile side trip skirts the edge of striking chasms dropping 800 feet to the mighty Rio Grande. A visitors' center, campgrounds, picnic areas, and viewpoints await you on this neat little detour. The road hugs the gorge and the views pull you off the asphalt more times than necessary, thinking that this has got to be the place for the best picture. There are numerous overlooks, but hardly any tourists. The roads are empty and open and . . . I'm not complaining. Be sure and stop at the **La Junta Campground** about fourteen miles down Route 378 for some great views of the confluence of the Rio Grande and Red Rivers. The two rivers converge a thousand feet below between sheer, rock-faced cliffs. I got dizzy just looking at it. This road has recently been paved and winds gracefully through the reserve with Mt. Wheeler and the Rio Grande Gorge in the background. Eventually it will loop back to Route 522 where you turn right and reconnect with Route 38.

Back on Route 38, head east through a narrow valley to the town of **Red River** (www.redrivernewmex.com, 800-348-6444). This area has seen its fair share of mining in the late 1800s and into the early 1900s. The tailings, or wasted materials, are a gruesome reminder. However, the road is a great ride with sweeping turns pushing you toward town. Red River itself is an old restored mining town set in beautiful alpine scenery now catering to tourists. The area has a frontier atmosphere with saloons, daily gunfights, and, yes, the infamous souvenir shops. Grab an ice cream or take the main ski lift from the center of town to the 10,250-foot mountaintop for views of

A sea of American flags dedicated to our veterans wave by the side of the road over Memorial Day weekend.

Get ready for a breathtaking ride in the Wild River Recreation Area. The roadside drops off 800 feet to the mighty Rio Grande below

the entire valley. If you really feel ambitious visit Red River during the annual Motorcycle Rally held every Memorial Day weekend. The rally is well organized and is packed with fellow motorcyclists (definitely having a good time!).

Route 38 continues on over the highest point on this trip at **Bobcat Pass**, 9,820 feet, and offers up some of the best scenery on the Enchanted Circle. The road then drops in a way only motorcyclists would appreciate as it twists into the Moreno Valley's east end. A couple of turnouts are available for views of Wheeler Peak's north face, so have your camera ready.

As you drive down Bobcat Pass, **Baldy Mountain** rises in the not-too-far-distant horizon. In 1866, gold was discovered on its slopes. Elizabethtown to the west of the Highway erected itself overnight to handle the flood of miners and entrepreneurs. The town grew to a rowdy 7,000 residents before shutting down its mining operations in 1871. In 1903, a fire ravaged the city leaving it pretty much empty and forgotten. What was once the county seat and largest city in Northern New Mexico is now a ghost town with only the stone shell of the Mutz Hotel remaining. E-town, as it is often referred to, is located on the west side of Route 38 about one mile north of Eagle Nest Lake.

Recently paved asphalt and virtually no traffic in the Wild River Recreation Area makes this a great ride.

On past Elizabethtown, Route 38 ends at the junction of US Hwy 64 right by **Eagle Nest Lake** (www.eaglenestlake.org). This lake is nestled neatly between Baldy Mountain and Wheeler Peak at 8,300 feet above sea level. The privately constructed dam got its name from nesting eagles on either side of the structure. Salmon and trout are plentiful, and as a result this lake is a haven for the discriminating angler. **Laguna Vista Lodge** (www.lagunavistalodge.com, 800-821-2093) provides a nice break with good food and brew as well. The trout couldn't be fresher!

From Eagle Nest, take US Hwy 64 south through the Moreno Valley. The road gently swerves across the high altitude plains where you may see herds of elk grazing peacefully in the meadows (just don't hit one!). After nine miles, just before the Angel Fire turnoff, the nation's first **Vietnam Veterans Memorial** comes into view.

The catalyst for creating this memorial was the death of Victor David Westphall III on May 22, 1968 in Vietnam. David's father, mother, and younger brother used David's insurance money as the nucleus to construct a monument to the sacrifices made by the Vietnam Veterans. Back in 1968 this was not a popular idea, but due to the family's perseverance the memorial has gained national renown and is now officially recognized by the United States Congress. The visitors' center is compelling and thought provoking. Well worth your time to honor those who served and gave their lives during the Vietnam conflict (www.angelfirememorial.com, 505-399-6900).

Upon returning to Hwy 64, continue to the west end of the valley as the road pulls you upward one more time over the 9,101-foot Palo Flechado Pass and then drops you into the Canyon of the Rio Fernando de Taos. The road meanders beside the Fernando River and the landscape slowly changes from pine and fir to ponderosa and pinion-juniper while approaching Taos. This leg of the trip rolls gently through the hills then winds dramatically up and over the pass. The scenery is green and lush, the skies blue, and the pavement black. These last miles into Taos are like icing on the Enchanted Circle cake. As the sun slowly sets below the horizon, you feel the blood rush through your veins one more time as this trip comes to a close.

The circle ends as you drive your motorcycle along the tree-lined corridor of Kit Carson Road into Taos. The shops and restaurants invite you to take a leisurely stroll on shaded streets amidst traditional adobe architecture. Not too much driving today, just an enchanting look into the colorful past and rugged backcountry of New Mexico and still plenty of time to delve into the ambiance of Ranchos de Taos.

The annual Red River Motorcycle Rally is huge. Motorcycles are parked on each side of the road as well as in the center lane.

Trip 4 Jemez Mountain Trail

Distance *327 miles (full day or maybe two, get up early)*
Terrain *Stark contrasts define this journey. Arid, colorful lowlands to verdant green woodlands and bubbling sulfur-smelling hot springs to pine-scented waterfalls. Elevation change 4,000 to 9,000 feet.*
Highlights *The Jemez Mountain Trail, Bandelier National Monument, Jemez Springs, and the red cliffs of Abiquiu. State Route 4 is a Scenic Byway and wraps itself around the Jemez Mountains with an abundance of twisties.*

New Mexico is a land of enchantment, but also a land of contrasts. On this journey you will see quaint, unspoiled towns exuding a Spanish colonial flair dotting the countryside next to ancient Indian ruins; rugged, pinion-covered mesas leading to mountain peaks covered with fir and spruce; towering cliffs rising above volcanic calderas next to rivers rushing between steep canyon walls. And then you will see the ultimate contrast of all sitting squarely in the middle of this trip, Los Alamos, the birthplace of the Atomic Age, veiled by the opulent magnificence of the Jemez Mountains. Nature's beauty and man's contradictions are majestically threaded together on

When you reach the top of State Route 68 this magnificent view of the Rio Grande Gorge and the Sangre de Cristo Mountains suddenly opens up in front of you.

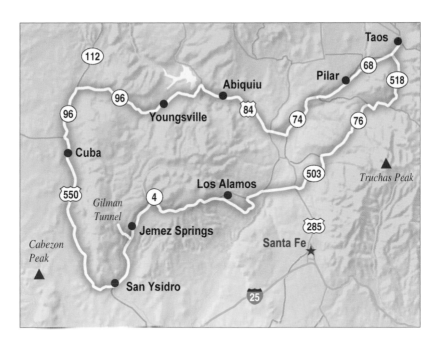

luscious black-topped pavement weaving its way through the landscape in that swaying motion motorcyclists love.

Today's trip takes you on a loop down the Jemez Mountain Trail Scenic Byway from Taos to San Ysidro on State Route 4 and then circles back past Cabezon Peak up to Cuba, through the red cliffs of Abiquiu on Route 84 and then back home to Taos. This journey is approximately 325 miles and takes a full day of driving and visiting Native American pueblos, hot springs, granite-hewn monuments, and mountain lakes. Leave bright and early and plan to stop frequently particularly along New Mexico State Route 4 "The Jemez Mountain Trail." If you want to travel at a more leisurely pace, Jemez Springs make a good stopover. Lodging and B&Bs are available in and around town as well as the recently refurbished **Jemez Springs Hot Bath** to soothe your weary buttocks (www.jemezsprings.org, 505-829-3540)!

Begin this trip by heading south on State Route 68 to Rancho de Taos. Veer left on State Route 518 for about sixteen miles and then turn right on State Route 75 to Penasco. Just outside of town about two to three miles turn left on State Route 76 toward Truchas. This jaunt from Taos to State Route 4 is a great way to get the morning started and unleash some of your pent up motorcycling desires. The road climbs and falls through forested, unpopulated countryside with Truchas Peak (13,102 feet) and Baldy Peak

THE ROUTE FROM TAOS

0   Start in Taos, go south on State Route 68

3   Turn left on State Route 518

19   Turn right on State Route 75

27   Turn left on State Route 76

47   Turn left on State Route 503

64   Turn left then right on State Route 502 to Los Alamos

76   Turn left on State Route 4 to White Rock

81   Arrive White Rock

90   Arrive Bandelier National Monument, enter park, turn left

92   Arrive visitors' center, turn around, continue back onto Route 4

106 Arrive Valle Cardera

126 Arrive Battleship Rock

130 Arrive Soda Dam

132 Arrive Jemez Springs, eat chile cheeseburger at Los Ojos on Route 4

140 Turn right on State Route 485 to Gilman Tunnels

145 Arrive Gilman, turn around

150 Turn right on State Route 4

160 Arrive San Ysidro, turn right on US Hwy 550

202 Arrive Cuba on Hwy 550

206 Turn right on State Route 96

257 Turn right on US Hwy 84

282 Turn left on State Route 74

287 Turn left on State Route 68

327 Arrive Taos (whew!)

(12,622 feet) providing a snowcapped backdrop. It's just you and the pavement as the asphalt tightens its grasp with each passing mile. These thirty to forty miles of riding are some of the best in New Mexico, climaxing as you drive atop the ridgeline on State Route 76 looking down on the valley below.

About forty-five miles into the ride, keep your eyes open for the State Route 503 turnoff. It's just off Route 76 as you descend into the valley. There was major construction on the road the last time I went and the turnoff was partially blocked by concrete dividers. The exit to Route 503 is more like a U turn then a left. Don't miss it! This little gem of a road takes you back in time and wanders through what looks like old colonial Mexico. You feel transported to a different country driving by small Catholic churches, colorful cemeteries, and tree-canopied single-laners. This little undiscovered road emanates its own personality and charm.

After seventeen miles on Route 503, turn left on Route 502, then right toward **Los Alamos**. Travel about twelve miles on this well-groomed four lane blacktop and then turn left on State Route 4 to White Rock. You will pass the Tsankawi Indian ruins on the southeast corner of route 4 and 502. Tsankawi is part of the **Bandelier National Monument**, but is not developed nor fully excavated. Drop by and walk along the one and a half mile trail worn into the rock by the original inhabitants. Pottery shards and petroglyphs are located in haphazard fashion, just where the Pueblo Indians left them over 500 years ago.

Continue on Route 4 and follow the signs to White Rock. At the stoplight hang a left to the overlook situated just outside of town. At the

To sample local taste and culture, try the, rustic little rest stop right next to the church in Trampas.

State Route 503 sometimes winds under an idyllic canopy of trees.

overlook you will be rewarded with some panoramic views of the entire valley. The Rio Grande meanders through **White Rock Canyon** beside two huge plateaus, the Caja del Rio on the east and the Parjarito to the west. Although the area is arid and dry, rock canyons and endless mesas create a colorful vista of breathtaking beauty at this relatively unknown overlook.

Return to Route 4 and turn left toward **Bandelier National Monument** (www.nps.gov/band, 505-672-3861 ext 517). After about nine miles you will see the entrance to the park on your left. Enter the park and drive a few miles through the canyon toward the visitors' center. Bandelier is located in the Santa Fe Forest and is steeped with narrow canyons, wildlife, ancient ruins, and mountain peaks rising over 10,000 feet. Driving along the canyon floor you will notice thick deposits of lava full of natural cavities. These cavities were enlarged by the **Anasazi Indians** 700 years ago to create clusters of dwellings and ceremonial edifices used by these ancient people.

Stop at the visitors' center. If you have time, take the one and a quarter mile hike for some close up viewings of these dwellings. Or continue another half mile to the **Alcove House** used as a ceremonial cave and reached only by climbing a series of ladders 150 feet up the cliff wall. The parking is limited, but motorcycles have a way of sneaking in that tight spot, don't they?

After a quick peek at Bandelier, turn around and head back out of the park on Route 4 toward **Valle Grande** (www.vallescaldera.gov, 505-661-3333). The climb up the steep Jemez Mountains begins as you leave the park. On the right hand side you will notice semi-camouflaged turnoffs to fenced-in areas with signs posted saying, RESTRICTED or NO TRESPASSING. Must be part of the super-secret workings of the Los Alamos Complex. Hope I don't turn a radioactive green after the trip! The road ascends quickly up the mountain slope via a series of several switchbacks. Lean your bike carefully through the corners as loose gravel and dirt were common-place during my last venture up the slope. Ultimately, you will be rewarded with one of the most astounding sights on this trip. As you start to descend, a vast meadowland opens up in front of you. Notice the bowl-shaped nature of the earth's crust. Although it appears to be a valley, this natural phenome-non is actually a caldera, or collapsed volcano. This is the largest volcanic caldera in the country and is seventeen miles in diameter. Redondo Peak in the distance rises about 2,500 feet above the floor and is the plug on top of the volcano. Stop at the Valle Grande Overlook so you can fully appreciate the immensity of this once great volcano.

About ten miles from the overlook, there is a turnoff on the southside of the road to Jemez Falls. A thirty-mile roundtrip detour will take you to a beautiful cascading waterfall feeding into a pine-rimmed pond high in the Santa Fe National Forest. A picnic area makes this a perfect spot to have a snack and unwind a bit. Just don't take a long nap as you still have a long way to go before returning to Taos and this side trip adds about another sixty miles to your 300-mile trip. This is a great detour if you plan to over-night in Jemez Springs.

You'll enjoy the sweeping curves that climb the Jemez Mountain Trail toward the Valle Grande.

Continue back up to La Cueva on Route 4, and then the road doglegs south toward Battleship Rock. A wooded gazebo with tables, grills, and picnic area are available. **Battleship Rock** juts up like the prow of its namesake (www.fs.fed.us/r3/sfe, 505-438-7840). A trailhead to another beautiful twenty-foot waterfall, Hidden Falls, is located here. Or if you feel real daring, hike to the ninety-nine degree **McCauley Hot Springs** set in a mountain meadow (clothing is optional!). Did you at least bring a towel?

About three miles south of Battleship Rock, **Soda Springs** bubbles to the surface. You will smell it before you see it. The Jemez River drops into a deep fault and gurgles back up creating a natural mineral dam and one of several hot springs along this corridor of the Jemez Mountains (type in soda dam at www.fs.fed.us/r3/sfe, 505-438-7840). Bathing is permitted. Or if you are interested in more history, the **Jemez State Monument** is located just a hop and a skip down the road (www.nmmonuments.org, 505-829-3530). A former Pueblo Indian village and ruins from a Spanish Mission are open to the public. There is a visitors' center and exhibits explaining the historic events surrounding this area.

About one mile further on Route 4, the road quickly enters **Jemez Springs** (www.jemezsprings.org). This quaint town of 400 people has several galleries and restaurants, and makes an ideal place to rest your weary bum. If you are so inclined, treat yourself to a mineral bath on the north

The Valle Grande is not really a valley, but a collapsed volcanic caldera. That must've been one big volcano!

Don't miss this side road to the Gilman Tunnels just south of Jemez Springs.

side of town at the restored **Jemez Springs Bathhouse**. Or at the very least, try one of the famous chile cheeseburgers at **Los Ojos** right across the street. Relax and recharge in Jemez Springs as the next part of the journey "brakes" less and covers about 180 miles before returning to Taos.

However, there is one more interesting side trip just south of Jemez Springs that is worth the detour. Continue south on Route 4 toward San Ysidro and about eight miles from Jemez Springs look for the turnoff on State Route 485 to Gilman. This five-mile detour takes you along the Rio Guadalupe past the Guadalpita Mesa to the **Gilman Tunnels**. The tunnels are located at the Guadalupe Box which were originally blasted in the 1920s for a logging railroad. There are numerous turnouts for some striking views of the Jemez Mountains and outlying mesas. Just past the last tunnel the pavement ends and the dirt road continues on to State Route 126 and back to La Cueva. This ten mile round trip takes you alongside an often roaring river and through some single lane tunnels that send chills up your spine!

San Ysidro lies at the junction of Route 4 and US Hwy 550. This small village was named after the patron saint of the farmers and is the only remaining settlement of the seven **"Pueblos de los Jama"** formed under the

The Gilman Tunnels were originally blasted in order to haul timber down to the sawmills. Now they make an exciting diversion for motorcyclists.

Spanish Crown. There is a restored Spanish adobe church still standing, symbolic of the bond between deity and the farmer's harvest. Drive on through and then head north on Hwy 550. The landscape has now changed dramatically. Pine and Ponderosa have been replaced with high desert scrub and juniper. The wide expanse of a more desolate New Mexico unfolds and soon **Cabezon Peak** rises like a giant's head 2,000 feet above the valley's floor. Its commanding presence is another witness to the power of the volcanic eruption eons ago and now plugged by these solitary peaks. A side road about twenty miles north of San Ysidro can take you to the peak where climbers from all over the world attempt to scramble up its vertical cliffs to the summit (www.nm.blm.gov, 505-761-8700).

After passing through the small town of La Ventana, you will arrive in **Cuba**. Not the country, but the town. Although the story goes that the original soldiers named the town after the island (don't ask me why) that is where the similarity ends. No tropical resort here! There is a nice little restaurant that does cook homemade pies and cinnamon rolls, though. You may want to try an apple pie a la mode at **Presciliano's Restaurant** right on Hwy 550.

Continue through town and veer right off Hwy 550 to State Route 96. Sweeping turns carve their way through the Santa Fe Forest and then continue down to Coyote and Youngsville in the Abiquiu Reservation. A nice set of switchbacks end this leg just before intersecting US Hwy 84. Kick your bike in gear on this back road and enjoy the run! At the T, turn right on Hwy 84 and drive through landscape made famous by the artist Georgia O'Keeffe. The multicolored cliffs near **Abiquiu** are on fire with red, orange, and gold. The remoteness gives credence to O'Keeffe's description of this area being the "Far Away" land. It certainly feels that way.

After about twenty-five miles, take a slight left onto State Route 74 and then after five miles turn left on State Route 68. Only another twenty-one miles and you will be back in Rancho de Taos. This final leg is just what the doctor ordered: nice sweepers cut through a rocky canyon before returning you back to civilization. As you exit the canyon, the Rio Grande's jagged chasm swallows you on your left, while dead ahead Mt. Wheeler rises phoenix-like over Taos. Today's journey of 300 miles has probably worn you out, but hasn't been without its rewards. The Jemez Mountain Trail, Valle Grande, Jemez Falls, Soda Springs, Cabezon Peak and the red cliffs of Abiquiu were once strange and unheard of places. Now they have a ring of familiarity as you drive leisurely back to your B&B in Taos with a better understanding why all the license plates read "Land of Enchantment!"

Hope for perfect weather and brand-spanking-new asphalt on US 550 to Cuba.

Trip 5 High Road to Chama

Distance *204 miles (short day)*
Terrain *Cross over a miniature Grand Canyon, the Rio Grande Gorge, and then ride over three 10,000 foot passes in the remote eastern end of the San Juan Mountains in Colorado. Elevation change 6,000 to 10,500 feet.*
Highlights *Mountain passes and river crossings on numerous twisties and S-curves. These roads are yours alone!*

High in New Mexico's northern country you will find roads that carve the edges of fir-covered granite slopes far from civilization. Roads that twist and turn and climb and drop for miles and miles. This loop takes you across an 800 foot gorge on a steel span bridge that shakes with each passing truck and a road that explodes through the southern edge of the San Juan Mountain Range over three 10,000-plus foot passes. The loop winds through Chama in New Mexico, then continues on State Route 17 into Colorado, intersects with US Hwy 285 in Antonito before reconnecting with US Hwy 64 back toward Taos. The area is remote, passing through only five small towns on a loop of 200 miles. No congested National Parks or Monuments, no traffic, and no stop signs; just wide open asphalt paved on New Mexico and Colorado's mountaintops. And the best part is, I haven't got a ticket here yet!

Just over the bridge crossing the Rio Grande, you will see this pink colored residence. Interesting choice of color!

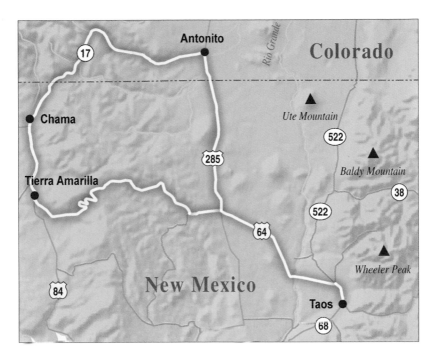

Our journey begins in Taos on US Hwy 64 heading west. Stay on Hwy 64 veering left at the State Route 522 junction and continue ten miles to the Rio Grande Gorge. The road rests comfortably on the plateau and your thoughts focus on the mountains looming on the horizon. And then, without warning, the plateau opens its gaping mouth beneath you as the Rio Grande makes its way to the Gulf of Mexico. Before you know it, you are driving across a bridge peering down at a miniature Grand Canyon.

The second-highest cantilever truss bridge in the United States spans across the Rio Grande in a harmonious way. The bridge seems to fit

THE ROUTE FROM TAOS

0   Start in Taos and head west on US Hwy 64

13   Arrive at the Rio Grande Gorge, continue on Hwy 64

96   Arrive Chama, head north on State Route 17

146   Arrive Antonito, Colorado, turn right on State Route 285

177   Turn left on Hwy 64

208   Arrive Taos

naturally at this particular spot. This will be one of very few stops on this trek, so park your bike at one of the designated areas and then walk across the bridge. The bridge is engineered with tourists in mind and has sidewalks and viewpoints lining both the north and south sides.

Gaze down at the Rio Grande about 800 feet below. The rapids can be seen with the naked eye as can rafters maneuvering through the foaming white water. The gorge reminds you of the Grand Canyon, but is not so overwhelming. It's like the Grand Canyon in its childhood. If you are interested in a hike, try the West Rim Trail which begins on the west side of Hwy 64. The trail follows the "Taos Box" canyon for nine miles to State Route 567. The views down the gorge are spectacular; just be sure and turn around if you get too dizzy.

After a short little hike to wake you up, shake off that dizziness and hop back on your bike for some unmatched riding pleasure. The next stop is sixty miles ahead via pavement that sucks you into that "riding zone." Just after the small town of Tres Peidras, the road starts its magical movements through the fifteen-million-acre Carson National Forest. Sweeping S-curves give way to tight switchbacks finally cresting at 10,500 feet above sea level with views of the **Brazos Cliffs** to the north. The road runs through rolling meadows and next to old abandoned mine shafts. Quaking aspen are intermingled with fir and pine on the steep mountain slopes. And your speed gradually increases as you reach the top of the pass and some exceptionally expansive views.

Nice formation. They must have gone to boot camp together.

This group of bikers is heading east on US 64 to Brazos Cliffs and then on to Chama.

If you packed a lunch or snack, pull out into one of the several picnic spots along the ridge and bask in the beauty of fir-covered mountains sweeping toward the sharp, naked granite Brazos Cliffs forming a curtain-like backdrop. During the spring and early summer, a waterfall plummets down its face created by melting snow and ice. The clear sky and billowing cumulus clouds add the final touches to this unforgettable panorama.

Continue east on Hwy 64 toward Tierra Amarilla. The crushed black rock beneath you curls downward past quaking aspen as cattle graze languidly in alpine meadows. Once again, the motorcycle takes over while winding down the mountain slope. The switchbacks can be tight, so be alert as you rub your pegs around the blind turns.

Just past Tierra Amarilla at Los Brazos, the road starts to hug the Rio Chama as you approach the town of **Chama**. The road and river become one as they cut through the valley toward this old railroad town. Chama is nestled at the base of the southeastern end of the San Juan Mountains. This little village is home to the **Cumbres & Toltec Scenic Railroad Line** built 120 years ago to help service the silver mining mania of the late 1800s and early 1900s. Thousands of miners were transported to the mining fields of Southern Colorado via this route on the Denver and Rio Grande Railroad. Eventually, this narrow gauge rail line was abandoned in 1969 and the last of the "steam locomotives" put out of service.

There's nothing like the feeling of riding high in the Rockies on State Route 17 to Antonito, Colorado.

Due to the efforts of preservationists and with the help of New Mexico and Colorado, the line was refurbished and today hauls tourists on a sixty-four-mile run over 10,000-foot passes to **Antonito** in Colorado. "One of the best twenty railway experiences in the world" as designated by the Society of International Railway Travelers (www.cumbrestoltec.com, 888-286-2737).

Now comes the best part. State Route 17 is the road that links Chama to **Antonito**. It parallels much of the train route north to Cumbres Pass and breaks out on its own across La Manga Pass before heading back south to Antonito. This forty-eight mile ride is probably one of the least-traveled and most-rewarding motorcycle experiences in the Rockies. The scenic, southern San Juans combined with 10,000-foot passes and mile upon mile of sensuously curving asphalt satisfy your motorcycle desires to the limit. Just you, your motorcycle, and miles of uninhabited mountain asphalt. What more could you ask for! As you descend Route 17 toward Antonito, the forest becomes thick and full, the air refreshing and brisk, and the landscape breathtaking. The road hugs the Chama River and the raw beauty of the Rocky Mountains manifests itself in abundance. Just don't do this trek too early in the year; the road is often closed until late spring due to heavy snow and ice.

Upon finishing this non-stop run of S-curves, hairpins, and switchbacks, you are ready for a break when you arrive in Antonito. Located in the San Luis Valley, Antonito sits at 7,888 feet and was once the "mainline" for the Denver and Rio Grande Railroads. The main station for the Cumbres and Toltec Scenic Railroad is housed here as well as some local eateries making this is a good spot to rest, grab a bite to eat, check out the old locomotives, and inform the tourists that State Route 17 parallels much the same route as the railroad . . . and it's free!

After refilling yourself and your bike, head south on US Hwy 285 to US Hwy 64. This thirty-mile run is relatively straight and skirts the edge of the mountains. It can be windy as well! Turn left on Hwy 64 back over the Rio Grande Gorge and head back into Taos about another thirty miles down the road. If you feel like another break, continue past the intersection to the **Old Blinking Light Kitchen & Cocktails** at mile marker one on Ski Valley Road (www.oldblinkinglight.com, 505-776-8787). A roaring fire will keep you warm and local musicians will entertain you while dining on some fine Mexican or American cuisine. A great place to unwind from all those mountain twisties and a great place to kick up your boots after a great day of riding!

Heading back home . . .

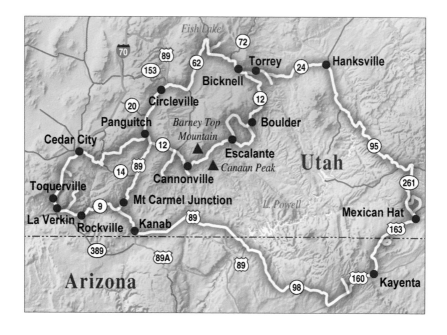

Panguitch

Have you ever wondered if Andy Griffith's Mayberry USA really existed? Well, think no more. When you first drive into Panguitch, Utah, you half expect Gomer Pyle to appear and fill up your gas tank while waiting at the local corner gas station. This small town of around 2,000 people sweeps you back to yesteryear with Mother Main Street and the local five and dime giving Panguitch a quaint, homey quality.

Originally settled by the Mormons in 1864 and then again in 1870 after the Black Hawk Indian War, Panguitch is named after the nearby lake that is a Paiute Indian word for "Big Fish." Driving through town you will notice the architecture is primarily of well made red brick. Panguitch

Panguitch, on US Hwy 89, offers an easy drive to the popular national parks and monuments of the area: Bryce, Zion, Canyonlands, and Capital Reef.

originally had its own kiln and made brick for itself and the surrounding area. Workers at the kiln were paid in brick, as opposed to cash, giving them the ability to build their own houses. The homes and shops lining the streets are mostly made from it, giving the town an almost "eastern" flavor. The older homes are two stories, while the second-generation structures are single story.

Panguitch (www.panguitch.org) is ideally located only thirty miles east of I-15 on Hwy 89 and about 145 miles south of Salt Lake City. Situated at 6,600 feet alongside the Sevier River, the town has ready access to several national parks and monuments in the remote, yet beautiful region of Southern Utah. Bryce Canyon, Zion, Canyonlands, Captital Reef, Escalante Staircase, Cedar Breaks, Lake Powell, and the North Rim of the Grand Canyon are all within driving distance. As a result, Panguitch has a budding tourist industry not yet tarnished by commercialism.

There are several places to stay in town, from standard and inexpensive motels to pricier lodges and inns. My personal favorite is **The Red Brick Inn of Panguitch** (www.redbrickinnutah.com). This bed and breakfast was

Panguitch is a stereotypical western town set in the heart of great riding country. You will drive through many towns like this as you journey in the Rockies.

An old kiln brick home in Panguith looks like something from back East.

built by a local doctor in the 1930s and served as the first hospital in rural Southern Utah. Enjoy the quaint, individually-decorated rooms and then unwind outside on a relaxing deck with a cold cup of lemonade. After a long day of motorcycling, gazing up at Panguitch's clear starlit sky from a wood-fired hot tub with a tray of Peggy's chocolate chip cookies to munch on is nirvana.

For those interested in camping, the **Red Canyon State Park** just up Route 12 has a beautiful campground nestled between pink limestone cliffs and ponderosa pines. The facilities are clean and well kept with showers, flush toilets, horseshoe pit, and volleyball court. The camping is first come, first served. For more information visit the website at www.fs.fed.us/dxnf/recreation/campground/redcanyon.html or call the ranger station at 435-767-9300. If you want to stay closer to Bryce Canyon, **Ruby's Inn** (www.rubysinn.com, 866-866-616) is a full service resort with rooms, campground, pool, and activities. It is set in a beautiful location just outside the park on Route 63.

The town of Panguitch will undoubtedly slow you down a few notches. The pleasant setting and ample natural wonders will help erase your urban sprawl mentality and create fond memories of small town USA when life was a whole lot simpler. Maybe Andy Griffith wasn't so dumb after all!

Trip 6   The Kolob Loop

Distance *259 miles (full day)*

Terrain *Feast your eyes on mammoth rock formations and a kaleidoscope of colors throughout this trip. Start in Panguitch and ascend to the Cedar Breaks natural amphitheater. Take spur roads into the less-visited north and central regions of Zion before visiting a famous ghost town and then heading back on the Zion Mt. Carmel Scenic Byway. Elevation change 3,500 to 11,00 feet.*

Highlights *Mountain curves, switchbacks, tunnels, and sweeping turns. Occasional disrepair and gravel on Kolob Terrace Road to Lava Point. Gravel and dirt on scenic Smithsonian Butte Backway (optional).*

In ancient Hebrew Kolob means "God's dwelling place." Well, the Almighty must drive motorcycles because this part of Southern Utah has roads that are definitely divine. This particular trip winds through scenery etched in pastels of red, blue, pink, and orange. The rock formations lining this loop are hewn from limestone and granite with names like Guardian Angel, West Temple, and Court of the Patriarchs. The scenic, soaring monoliths will dampen your speed and enlighten your understanding of why the early pioneers called this area Zion, or "sanctuary for God's chosen."

The official eastern boundary to Zion National Park beckons you to the "sanctuary for God's chosen."

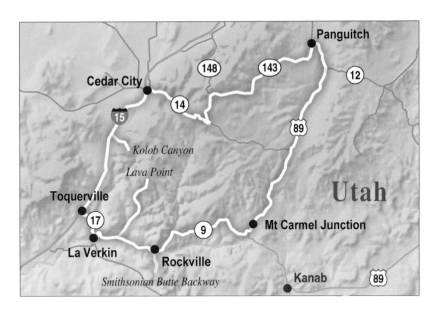

Zion National Park (www.nps.gov/zion, 435-772-3256), like the Grand Canyon, has millions of visitors each year. And most tourists take the Zion Canyon Scenic Drive and Zion Mt. Carmel Scenic Byway (State Route 9) which cuts through the south end of the park. This motorcycle loop takes you away from the crowds and to vistas unfrequented by the average motorist. Zion's northern neighbor, Cedar Breaks, has one-tenth the number of visitors and is just as visually stunning. The north and central regions of Zion National Park also have spur roads rarely traveled which are enveloped by massive cliffs and have views from 7,500 feet peering down inside the park. Ultimately, the touristy Route 9 is taken to complete the loop, but not before one more uncongested detour south and a visit to a famous ghost town. Elevation changes are significant on this run, so be prepared with T-shirts at 3,500 feet and jackets with liners at 11,000 feet.

Starting out in Panguitch, head west on State Route 143 toward the **Brian Head Ski Resort** (www.brianhead.com, 435-677-2035) thirty-two miles ahead. The road quickly leaves the town behind and starts its climb up ribbon-like roads toward **Panguitch Lake** (www.panguitchlake.com). Panguitch Lake sits beautifully at the base of rising mountains and open meadows. A small resort community has developed to take advantage of the fishing and countryside. The road is often closed in the wintertime due to heavy snows, but in the summer wildflowers erupt in a kaleidoscope of colors. So take an allergy pill and enjoy the over 150 species of flowers blossoming along Route 143, particularly in July and August.

THE ROUTE FROM PANGUITCH

0	Panguitch, Utah, at intersection of US Hwy 89 and State Route 143
32	Take 143 to Cedar Breaks National Monument, turn left on Route 148
34	Arrive Cedar Breaks on Route 148
40	Turn right on State Route 14 toward Cedar City
46	Zion Overlook
60	Arrive Cedar City and I-15 interchange, go south on I-15
79	Take exit 40 toward Kolob Canyons
85	Arrive Grand Viewpoint at Kolob Canyons, turn around
91	Arrive I-15, go south
104	Take exit 27, State Route 17 toward La Verkin and Toquerville
110	Arrive La Verkin, turn left on State Route 9
116	Arrive Virgin
117	Turn left on Kolob Road (100 Street East)
137	Turn right on Lava Point Road (gravel road)
139	Return to Kolob Road
159	Re-arrive in Virgin, turn left on Route 9 to Zion National Park
168	Arrive Rockville (Smithsonian Butte Backway optional)
174	Turn left on Zion Canyon Road (may be restricted to open air buses)
186	Return to Route 9, turn left (east)
209	Arrive Mt. Carmel Junction, turn left on US Hwy 89
259	Arrive Panguitch, eat some fresh chocolate chip cookies

At about mile thirty, turn left (south) on route 148 into **Cedar Breaks National Monument** (www.nps.gov/cebr, 435-586-9451). Route 148 brings you into the park and then teeters on the 10,660-foot ridge overlooking a huge natural amphitheater carved into the pink cliffs. This little-known park was originally known as "circle of painted cliffs" by the Paiute Indians and then changed to Cedar Breaks due to the pioneers' inability to take their wagons up the steep Cedar Mountain. The craggy, canyon-filled cliffs reflect numerous shades of colors off rock walls, spires, and columns.

A five-mile road is the main route through the park. Stop at the visitors' center and hike down to Point Supreme Overlook for a view. Three additional overlooks with parking are further down the road. Just remember that the entire park's elevation is in excess of 10,000 feet! Bring a warm jacket and portable oxygen if necessary! Camping is also available for you hardy Alaskan motorcyclists.

Continue on Route 148 heading south for a few more miles and then turn right (west) on State Route 14 toward Cedar City. The road drops coming out of Cedar Breaks and then climbs again on Route 14 to 9,890 feet at Midway Summit. For a panoramic view of Kolob Terrace and the north end of Zion turn right at Zion overlook. Take in the views and then follow Route 14 down into Cedar City.

Cedar City (www.cedarcity.org, 435-586-2950) is best known for the famous Tony-award-winning **Utah Shakespearean Festival** (www.cedarcity .org, 800-PLAYTIX). These plays are performed in the summer and fall and are definitely worth a visit. If you can, make reservations in advance and see one of these very professional productions. This used to be one of the best kept secrets of Southern Utah, but now people from all over the world come to enjoy the very realistic reproductions of Shakespeare at his best. Cedar City is also a great place to stay due to its proximity to Salt Lake City and Las Vegas on I-15.

However, for our purposes just continue through town until arriving at the I-15 interchange. Go south on I-15 for twenty miles and then turn east on the Kolob Canyon Road. This five-and-a-half-mile spur road winds

Looks a little dark. Be on the lookout for any surprises in there.

around the finger canyons of the northern part of Zion and is not nearly as congested as the south end. Drop by the visitors' center and follow alongside Taylor Creek while climbing several switchbacks to the **"Grand Viewpoint"** for an unfrequented and unforgettable view of the finger canyons in Zion National Park. Traffic is minimal and many times I have seen only a few vehicles on this road. So, put your visor up and enjoy this short trip into Zion's northern borderlands. Total drive time is about thirty minutes.

Back on I-15, continue heading south for another thirteen miles and then go east on State Route 17 to La Verkin. At La Verkin turn left again on Route 9 toward Virgin seven miles ahead. When you arrive in Virgin (population 200), keep a lookout for the road sign to Kolob Reservoir (easily missed) on your left. This nineteen-mile spur road is called the Kolob Terrace Road and ventures into Zion's backcountry. Few motorists tackle this road due to its disrepair and steepness. Some spots are unpaved, so be careful climbing from 3,500 feet to 7,890 feet over the course of this detour. Consequently, the road is uncrowded and provides rare glimpses looking down into Zion National Park.

The road starts at 3,500 feet and begins its ascent to the **Lava Point Overlook** as it winds in and out of the park. The vegetation changes from dry brush to grassy meadows with cattle and horses. Eventually at 7,000 feet

This can't be Zion. Where are all the tourists?

Huge rock monoliths rise around you on every side.

the air turns crisp and cool as pine and aspen dot the countryside. At about mile nineteen, turn right on Lava Point Road beside Blue Springs Reservoir and drive about eight tenths of a mile to the overlook. Drive slowly as this portion of the road is gravel. At Lava Point, elevation 7,890 feet, the park spreads out beneath you in all its glory. The domes, spires, and columns give you a sense of gazing inside a huge cathedral.

After getting this grand view all to yourself, head back to Virgin and turn left on Route 9 toward the main entrance of the Park. Drive nine miles to Rockville and if you are up for another backroad detour, head south on the **Smithsonian Butte Backway.** This nine-mile dirt road provides spectacular panoramas of Zion looking up and north. Total round trip time is about one hour. If you want, drop by the abandoned town of **Grafton** (www.americansouthwest.net/utah/zion/grafton_ghost_town.html) and now one of the most photographed ghost towns in Utah. Parts of the movie classic Butch Cassidy and the Sundance Kid were filmed here. Watch for Bridge Road; turn right and go about three and a half miles to the townsite. Great spot for a picnic.

Return to Route 9, turn right (east), and drive about one mile into the outskirts of Springdale. You have now arrived at Zion's official tourist mecca. The next three miles are covered with every tourist trap known to man. Hotels, motels, shops, restaurants, and theaters line the corridor to the park entrance. My advice is to move on and witness the abrupt change from gaudy civilization to pristine nature when you enter the park. If you want a quick bite to eat try a fresh veggie wrap at the **Tsunami Juice and Java** just outside the entrance and sit on the outdoor patio for your own private view of Zion.

The sign said "parking lot full" but motorcycles are everywhere.

The two roads providing access to the park's interior are the thirteen-mile Zion Mt. Carmel Scenic Byway (Route 9) and the six-mile Zion Canyon Scenic Drive. Upon entering the park, drop by the visitors' center, get educated, and then drive a few miles further to the junction for the Zion Canyon Scenic Drive. As you drive further north, the road is literally swallowed by colored cliffs towering beside this narrow valley and the Virgin River. Massive rocks, towering cliffs, and jagged canyons engulf you. Driving amongst these huge monolithic boulders makes you feel puny and small, as if the heavens are merely tolerating your visit to their sanctuary.

Due to congestion and the narrowness of the road, the traffic can be wretchedly slow, particularly in the summer, and access may be restricted to open air buses. Just remember, even though the crowds can be horrendous, they are here for a reason. Zion National Park has a distinct, natural beauty you will find nowhere else in the world. So enjoy, grab a bite to eat with some fellow bikers at the Zion Lodge, kick back, and tell them about some neat, uncrowded backroads you read about in this great book called *Motorcycle Journeys Through the Rocky Mountains*.

Finish your journey through Zion by heading east on Route 9 (Zion Mt. Carmel Scenic Byway) via a lusciously steep ascent on switchbacks through tunnels and gorges to the eastern entrance of the Park. Although the going can be slow, no worries, just more time to take in the views.

The trip back home to Panguitch heads out of the east entrance of the Park to the Mount Carmel Junction. The drive is about ten miles long and makes for a pleasant and speedy run. Gas up at the Mt. Carmel Chevron Station, where you will inevitably meet some other bikers, and then go north up US Hwy 89 to Panguitch.

The fifty-mile trip back, runs along the east fork of the Virgin River. The contours of the road help twist your right wrist a little more than it should. The road is well-traveled and weaves through some gorgeous countryside. The river and road are intertwined hand in hand crossing verdant meadows up and over Mt. Carmel before entering the towns of Orderville and Glendale. The plateaus rise in the distance, beckoning you along, but, *beware* of speed traps! Slow down when approaching these small towns, as the local police have nothing else to do than pick on unsuspecting motorcyclists. So keep your eyes on the speedo, not just the scenery while driving back to your B&B in Panguitch. And, hopefully, Peggy has made some fresh chocolate chip cookies and stoked up the spa by the time you arrive back at the Red Brick Inn.

Our helmets got to enjoy the view while we ate lunch at Tsunami Juice and Java (west entrance).

Trip 7 Up the Staircase

Distance *274 miles (full day)*
Terrain *The ultimate in scenic diversity. Visit Bryce's orange-hued hoodoos, climb up a razor-back staircase, and then visit cool alpine lakes. All in one day! Elevation change 5,500 to 9,200 feet.*
Highlights *Switchback, mountain curves, and a few straightaways. No guardrails on some mountain roads, so stay alert! Backroad detour on Hell's Backbone Road.*

Driving back from Bryce through Red Canyon State Park, you'll go through this perfect rock arch.

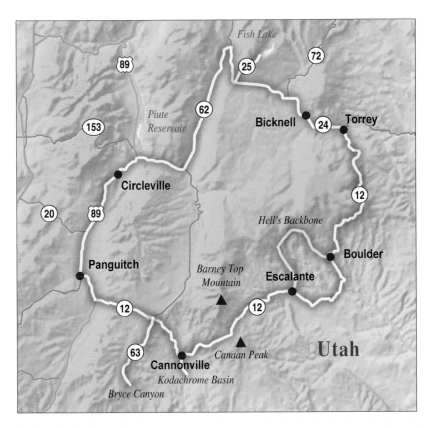

You are about to embark on one of the most enjoyable motorcycle rides of your life. Be prepared for roads that take you through landscape ornate with color and engineered by motorcycle lovers. While driving this loop, you will realize why Highway 12 has been designated a National Scenic Byway and an All American Road by the Federal Highway Administration. This road is indeed a "destination unto itself." And for even further driving pleasure, the route is one of the least traveled in the United States. Most motorists get as far as Bryce National Park and then turn around not realizing that the red canyons only mark the beginning of an unfrequented Scenic Byway. I have made this trip annually for several years over Memorial Day Weekend and am always surprised by the lack of motorists. So listen up and then pack your bags before the word gets out about this little known motorcyclist's dream road.

The trip starts in Panguitch and heads south for seven miles on US Hwy 89 to the State Route 12 turnoff. Go east on Route 12 and immediately the fun begins. Red Canyon State Park opens in front of you like a miniature

THE ROUTE FROM PANGUITCH

0	Start in Panguitch on US Hwy 89 going south
7	Turn left (east) on State Route 12
20	Turn right (south) on State Route 63 to Bryce
23	Arrive entrance to Bryce Canyon
28	Continue to Inspiration Point, turn around
36	Turn right (east) on Route 12 to Cannonville
48	Arrive Cannonville, turn right on Kodachrome Road
55	Arrive Kodachrome Basin State Park, turn around
62	Turn right (east) on Route 12
95	Hell's Backbone Road Turnoff (for backway detour)
96	Arrive Escalante
124	Arrive Boulder
150	Turn left (north) on State Route 24
151	Arrive Torrey
181	Turn right on State Route 25 to Fish Lake
190	Arrive Fish Lake, turn around
199	Turn right on Route 24
203	Turn left on State Route 62
242	Turn left (south) on US Hwy 89
246	Arrive Circleville
274	Arrive Panguitch

Bryce Canyon. The spires and colors are identical to its big brother Bryce, except this park is far less visited. Trails and camping are beautifully situated below red-crested towers and a bike path skirts the edge of Route 12, so mountain bikers can also enjoy the surroundings. This seven-mile canyon drive sweeps you through smooth, black-topped asphalt amidst towering spires and overhanging arches. Two miles up the road is a visitors' center providing information on camping and hiking trails. If you are up for some morning exercise, both the Bird's Eye Trail and Pink Ledges Trail are short (less than one mile) and end with grand overlooks of the park. For more information on this little jewel, call the **Powell Ranger Station** at 435-676-9300 or visit the website at www.utah.com/nationalsites/redcanyon.htm.

Continuing east on Byway 12, turn right on State Route 63 to **Bryce Canyon National Park** (www.nps.gov/brca, 435-834-5322). This well-known and highly-photographed park is really not a canyon at all. No major river runs through the park, but rather the hoodoos were created by the passage of wind and rain. This, combined with freezing and thawing (and a million or so years), have resulted in an exuberance of colors unlike any place in the world.

The park's entrance is about three miles down Route 63. Bryce Canyon can be extremely congested during the summer, so an earlier arrival is better. To really enjoy the park, you need to spend several days exploring, hiking, and driving. For our purposes, a couple of hours will have to do. In order to do this and get a good feel for the park, drop by the visitors' center about one mile from the park entrance. Watch the movie and get educated and then drive to one or all of the major overlooks just two to five miles away. You can loop around to Sunrise Point, drop by the Historic Lodge for some hot chocolate, and then swing by Sunset and Inspiration Points as well. The roads and paths are well marked and easily accessible. If you arrived really early and the park is uncongested, drive to the southernmost end, but plan

Bryce Canyon National Park can be extremely congested during the summer, so arrive early in the season to enjoy it relatively tourist-free.

on at least another one to two hours as the road is about twenty miles one way (forty miles round trip). The drive is beautiful and the road is windy as it makes its way to Rainbow and Yovimpa Points.

Morning is a good time to see the colors and shades as the light shimmers off hoodoos and slowly changes hues from a rusty gray to brown to yellowish gold. On clear days you can see three states and over 200 miles. Much has been written on Bryce Canyon National Park, so I won't say anymore.

After this unforgettable interlude to Bryce, head back up to Route 63 and head east once more on State Route 12. The Byway passes through the north section of Bryce National Park and then drops into Bryce Valley and the small town of Tropic. Continue on to Cannonville about five miles further down the road. Cannonville is the gateway to **Kodachrome Basin State Park**. Turn right at the sign and then drive seven miles south of town. This state park is made up of "sandpipes," or petrified geysers. Named by the National Geographic Society, this basin is a photographer's dream. Hiking trails and a small campground with a store are all available at this state park. Well worth the detour if you have time. For further information visit the

During the 1930s the Hell's Backbone Road was the only access to Boulder from Escalante.

The Red Canyon campground has clean facilities and is a nice place to camp.

website (parks.state.ut.us) or drop by the Cannonville visitors' center (435-679-8981).

Back on Route 12, Table Cliffs Plateau and Powell Point rise up ominously as you weave along Route 12 toward Escalante. This road climbs past a rocky area emanating a variety of bluish colors from the clay-covered hills. The colors quickly change to more stark browns as the road enters the upper valley of the **Grand Staircase**. This valley is sandwiched between Barney Top Mountain (elevation 10,571 feet) and Canaan Peak (elevation 9,293 feet). The road runs gently through the valley as if teasing you in preparation for the **Haymaker Bench Switchbacks** and **Hogback Ridge Trapeze** just ahead.

The town of Escalante, thirty-three miles from Cannonville, is considered the "Heart of Hwy 12." Not only is the town at the midpoint of the Scenic Byway, but named to honor the Franciscan monk who was the first recorded explorer in this area as he searched for a route from Santa Fe to California. Drop by the Escalante Interagency visitors' center (BLM Information Center) located at 755 West Main or call 435-826-5499 for more information about this remote, yet historically significant area.

One side note at this point: There are several scenic backways (dirt roads) crisscrossing this corridor of Utah that are well worth a visit. Most have historical significance and played a key role in the original settlement

The Aquarius Inn in Bicknell, Utah is a good spot for lunch.

of Southern Utah. One particular loop that I enjoy and is convenient to this trip is the "**Posey Lake Scenic Backway**" and the "**Hell's Backbone Road**." This U loop connects the town of Escalante with Route 12 about three miles west of Boulder. The Backway is not for the faint of heart as it stretches along a road with sheer drops on both sides. Hell's Backbone Bridge, built in 1935, was an engineering feat at the time and is still a marvel. This thirty-eight-mile loop follows the Pine Creek Drainage on the Aquarius Plateau eventually reaching 9,000 feet in elevation. Ultimately, the backroad crossed a huge chasm at Death Hollow and Sand Creek ending up in farmlands about four miles south of Boulder. If you are interested, take the Scenic Byway north (left) at Escalante (Forest Road 153). It is paved for a couple of miles and then veers east just south of Posey Lake to Boulder. It was well-groomed dirt and gravel last time I took it.

Continue on Hwy 12 between Escalante and Boulder on what many refer to as Utah's version of their "million dollar road." For many years, Boulder, Utah, was accessible via Hell's Backbone only and was the last town in the United States to have mail delivered by mules. Parts of this road were only paved in 1971 and now provide striking views of the Escalante Basin.

About fifteen miles east of Escalante, Hwy 12 descends to **Calf Creek Recreation Area** (www.americansouthwest.net/utah/grand_staircase_ escalante//lower_calf_creek.html). This spot is a perfect area to have a picnic, wade in the creek, or just cool your feet. For you more serious hikers, a six-mile round trip hike takes you to the lower 120 feet Calf Creek Falls. A deep pool with shade trees makes this a great respite away from civilization. A BLM campground and picnic area are available.

After the Calf Creek Recreation Area, Hwy 12 climbs up some glorious switchbacks called Haymaker Bench and then crosses the Hogback Ridge on to Boulder. The road and scenery intertwine into one natural thread driving atop the pinnacle like ridge. There are no guard rails and the steep drop-offs on either side make your heart skip a beat while peering down into the ravines and canyons below. Catch your breath at one of the several pullouts along the way and pinch yourself to be sure you aren't dreaming. This stretch of road from here on out defines motorcycle nirvana. A combination of switchbacks, narrow, ridge-like roads, and sweeping curves culminating in an alpine pass at 9,200 feet with sweeping vistas are why this road is a destination "unto itself." Words don't do it justice.

This little building is an old meeting place for daughters of the pioneers in Bicknell, Utah.

Hwy 12 veers north from Boulder to Torrey and twists through the Dixie National Forest over the 9,000-foot summit. The road was paved for the first time in 1985 and is a motorcyclist's delight. The traffic is minimal, the curves are tight, and the scenery breathtaking. As you scratch your pegs, take time to pull out at the overlooks and absorb the endless horizons. Views of the Henry Mountains, Capital Reef National Park, and Circle Cliffs are painted like watercolors before you. The hardest part about getting to Torrey is that you will want to turn around and repeat this journey immediately!

Scenic Byway 12 comes to an end upon intersecting State Route 24. The town of **Torrey** (www.torreyutah.com) is one mile west and is a great stop to tank up and grab a well-deserved bite to eat. Although the town is small (pop. 120), it caters to tourists visiting Capital Reef and Bryce Canyon. For some good food with great views try the **Rim Rock Restaurant** at 2523 E. Hwy 24 (435-425-3388) or **Cafe Diablo** at 559 West Main (435-425-3010). If you spent too much time getting here or want to spend some more time exploring the backways, the lodge at **Red River Ranch** is homey and set amidst a natural backdrop making it a perfect place to unwind (www.redriverranch.com, 800-205-6343).

Colors line the landscape heading toward Fish Lake outside of Torrey on Hwy 24.

Some of the finest fishing in the West is found at Fish Lake, and the Lakeside Resort is often full as a result

The return trip from Torrey to Panguitch is about 120 miles and takes you through small town Utah via gently sweeping curves and high mountain passes. I have always enjoyed this run back to Panguitch due to its remoteness and the scenic diversion to Fish Lake Lodge on Route 25 high in the Wasatch Range.

Heading north on State Route 24, you will drive through the towns of Bicknell and Lyman about fourteen miles ahead. Whatever you do, don't blink! The road follows the Fremont River as it meanders alongside the slopes of Thousand Lake Mountain. As you climb toward Fish Lake, the scenery will quickly transition from red rock plateau to wooded alpine valleys. The breeze will cool and suddenly the sculptured sandstone gives way to green forested watercolors.

After approximately thirty miles from Torrey, turn right on State Route 25 through the Fish Lake National Forest toward Fish Lake Lodge. The pavement ascends to 9,000 feet and is gentle and sloping as it slowly climbs to the lake. Be cautious as wildlife is abundant and deer will often dart along the side of the road. Elk and moose are also sighted on this short diversion, so stay attentive and alert.

When you arrive at the lake, the setting is tranquil and quiet. Stop at the historic **Fish Lake Lodge** (www.fishlake.com, 435-638 1000) built between 1928 and 1932 of native spruce logs. Lakeside Resort overlooks the lake and gives you an opportunity to admire its crystal 160-foot deep waters. Some of the west's finest fishing is done here. As the local fishermen say, a Mackinaw Lake trout under ten pounds is just a "pup" and not worth keeping!

After a pleasant break at Fish Lake, backtrack on Route 25 to Route 24, and head north for another four miles until arriving at the Route 62 junction. At 62 go south toward Burrville and then head on down past Otter Creek State Park. The road veers west through Kingston on some nice twisties and then reconnects up with US Hwy 89 about two miles outside of town.

Go south on 89 as the road hugs the Sevier River toward Panguitch. The gentle curves and flowered meadows help ease you back home as your full

This KOA on US 89 has fantastic views of red rock cliffs, and all for a great price!

The view back toward Fish Lake from Hwy 25 is worth a stop.

day of riding ends. There is one more stop, however. For those of you who remember the movie *Butch Cassidy and the Sundance Kid* with Paul Newman and Robert Redford, a diversion to Butch Cassidy's boyhood home just south of Circleville may be in order. The son of Mormon Pioneers, Butch Cassidy turned into one of the most famous outlaws of the Old West. His home is located near the **Butch Cassidy's Hideout Motel** at 339 S. Hwy 89 in Circleville (butch@color-country.net 888-577-2008)

Back on 89, Panguitch is about twenty-eight miles south of Circleville and definitely a pleasant sight after 275 miles of riding. It is time to unwind, reminisce, and wonder how those early pioneers managed to ride these same distances and more on horseback. If anybody deserves an Iron Butt Award, it's the early pioneers!

Trip 8   The Grand Circle Loop

Distance   *705 miles (three days, two nights)*
Terrain   *Take a journey through alpine meadows, sunbaked canyons, and the soaring buttes of Monument Valley. This trip will make a grand circle around Lake Powell from Capital Reef in the north to Hite Crossing in the east, Monument Valley in the south and Glen Canyon Dam in the west. Three days of motorcycling bliss! Elevation change 3,500 to 9,200 feet.*
Highlights   *You name it, you got it! One dirt road portion for three miles on sharp mountain curves with no guard rails (street bikes ok). Valley of the Gods backcountry byway on well-maintained sand (dirt optional).*

Can there be too much of a good thing? What could be better than starting on an All American Byway over alpine mountain passes and then twisting your way through sandstone gorges toward Monument Valley? Only one thing: Having the road all to yourself. The most enjoyable aspect of this trip is the absolute isolation you will feel driving along State Route 95 and the

Park your bike at the main overlook for Monument Valley, and you'll get a perfect photo for the folks back home.

THE ROUTE FROM PANGUITCH

Day One

0	Start in Panguitch on US Hwy 89, going south
7	Turn left (east) on State Route 12
20	Turn right (south) on State Route 63 to Bryce Canyon
23	Arrive entrance to Bryce Canyon
28	Continue to Inspiration Point, turn around
36	Turn right (east) on Route 12 to Cannonville
48	Arrive Cannonville, turn right on Kodachrome Road
55	Arrive Kodachrome Basin State Park, turn around
62	Turn right (east) on Route 12
95	Hell's Backbone Road Turnoff (for backway detour)
96	Arrive Escalante
124	Arrive Boulder
150	Turn right on State Route 24
152	Arrive Best Western Capital Reef Resort, continue on Route 24 to Park

160   Turn right on Capital Reef Road (visitors' center)
171   Arrive Stop 11 on "Scenic Drive," turn around
182   Turn left on Route 24
190   Re-arrive at Best Western

Day Two

190   Start at Best Western Capital Reef Resort
235   Arrive Hanksville, head south on State Route 95
326   Turn left on Route 275 to Natural Bridges National Monument
334   Arrive Natural Bridges, take loop road
343   End of loop road; take Route 275 back to Route 95
351   Turn left on Route 95
353   Turn right on State Route 261
377   Arrive Moki Dugway (dirt road)
381   Valley of the Gods backroad turnoff—left (optional)
380   End Moki Dugway, continue on 261
386   Turn right on State Route 316 to Goosenecks State Park
390   Arrive Goosenecks, turn around
394   Turn right on Route 261
395   Turn right on US Hwy 163 to Mexican Hat and Monument Valley
418   Turn right on Monument Valley Road to Gouldings Lodge
420   Arrive Gouldings Lodge

Day Three

420   Start at Gouldings Lodge; turn right on Monument Valley Road
424   Arrive Navajo Monument Valley Park, turn around
426   Turn left on US Hwy 163
450   Turn right on US Hwy 160
469   Turn right on State Route 564 to Navajo National Monument
478   Arrive Navajo National Monument, turn around
487   Turn right on US Hwy 160
500   Turn right on State Route 98
564   Turn right on US Hwy 89 to Glen Canyon Dam
639   Arrive Kanab, stay on US Hwy 89 North
705   Arrive Panguitch

"Trail of the Ancients" past desolate mountains and sandwashed gulleys. Once past Bryce, your fellow motorists become scarcer and scarcer the further southeast you drive. When you arrive at the east end of Lake Powell, you begin to wonder if anybody knows about this scenic route down the Moki Dugway to the Valley of the Gods. How could anyone not know about it! Oh well, just be sure your gas tank is full and camera loaded before heading out on the Grand Circle Loop.

One quick note before getting started: This is one of the longest journeys taken through the Rockies, totaling around 700 miles. You can do this run in two days, but I would recommend three days to truly enjoy it. The first leg heads up Scenic Byway Route 12 past Bryce and then up and over the Escalante Staircase to Torrey and into Capital Reef National Park. At the intersection of Routes 12 and 24 head east (right) on State Route 24 (not north to Fish Lake) to the Park. Overnight just outside the park at the Best Western Capital Reef Resort or camp at the Fruita Campground inside Capital Reef. On day two continue to Monument Valley via the Moki Dugway and Trail of the Ancients and spend the second night at Goulding's Lodge at Monument Valley. On day three circle back to Panguitch through Kayenta and Glen Canyon Dam. Remember things are just bigger and longer out here in the West, so pack your pajamas and plan on the overnighter of your dreams.

Highway 12 is one of the most beautiful roads in the Rocky Mountains. Don't miss it.

Look where you lean—there are no guardrails on Hogsback Ridge!

DAY ONE

Begin in Panguitch on US Hwy 89 going south to Route 12. Turn left (east) toward Bryce Canyon National Park. Please refer to Chapter 3, Trip 7 "Up the Staircase" for details on this leg of the journey. Just remember that State Route 12 is an All-American Byway and a destination "unto itself." So read the previous chapter and when you arrive in Torrey skip back over to this trip and be sure and turn right on State Route 24. Enjoy this run on Route 12. Spend some time at Bryce and Kodachrome Basin, take the **Hell's Canyon Backroad**, cool your feet at Calf Creek Recreation Area and be careful on the Hogsback ridge!

About one mile outside of the park on Route 24, you will see the Best Western Capital Reef Resort on your left. This is a perfect location to stop and then take a short excursion into the Capital Reef to explore the park's very own ten-mile "Scenic Drive." The views are also great from this hotel as all the balconies face north toward red sandstone cliffs. So check in and then unpack before continuing on for a short thirty-mile loop visit to Capital Reef.

Back on Route 24 head toward **Capital Reef National Park** (www.nps.gov/care, 435-425-3791) on a smooth snaking road. This park is a gem and one of the least known and, consequently, least visited in our National Park System. As a matter of fact this whole loop is one of the least traveled in the Rocky Mountain Region due to its remoteness, and Capital

Reef to some degree epitomizes the isolation of this entire area. The earth's crust appears to have folded and unfolded, creating a seventy-mile mohawk down the center of the park as if purposefully discouraging travelers to transit this area. As a result few settlers have braved this isolated frontier.

As you drive into the park, the road winds and weaves through martian-like landscape, tempting you to nudge the throttle down a little bit more with each turn. However, resist the temptation (that can wait until tomorrow), and turn right at the visitors' center about six miles into the park. A beautiful ten-mile spur "Scenic Drive" detour into the heart of the park awaits you. So, stop for a minute at the visitor's center to learn about the geology, culture, and history of the few settlers who did brave this terrain. Over 1,000 years ago, the Fremont Indians settled here and left, and then the Pauites and Navajos came and left. And finally the Mormon Pioneers attempted a settlement. All eventually abandoned. The Mormons finally left around 1940, leaving a one-room schoolhouse and orchards of peaches, apricots, and cherries along the Fremont River (which for a nominal fee are available to the public for picking).

The road in front of the visitors' center continues through an oasis of green grass and fruit trees along the Fremont River. A beautiful picnic area and campground are available here. For those of you interested in camping,

Wow! The views from Hwy 12 looking down at Capital Reef are spectacular.

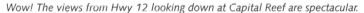

this is the place. Cool shade on a blanket of green grass next to a flowing river makes this an ideal campground for you more hardy camping types.

Upon continuing down this road you begin what is called the Capital Reef "Scenic Drive." This ten-mile spur road takes you deep into the extraterrestrial terrain for close up views of places like Grand Wash and Capital Gorge. There are eleven stops along this scenic tour. All are very informative. However, being on a motorcycle is not always conducive to frequent stops. So, drive slowly, watch out for sand in some of the gulleys and just enjoy the leisurely ride. If you do want to stop, pullouts two and eleven are worth a few minutes. Stop Two provides panoramic views of the western face of Capital Reef. The layers of rock bands are painted on the cliff canvas in distinct contrast marking differing sediments and geologic time periods. Stop nine takes you into the heart of Capital Gorge via the towering Wingate Sandstone walls on a two-mile dirt road. Before Route 24 was completed in 1962, this road cleared by the early pioneers in 1884 was the only access through Capital Reef. The canyon walls, petroglyphs, and pioneer inscriptions make Stop Eleven a fascinating flashback to times past. One word of caution, stay clear of the gorge road during rainstorms. As the early pioneers learned, this area is subject to severe flashfloods.

This is why I like to drive a GS. The pavement ends and the dirt track continues to Capital Gorge at Capital Reef Park.

The Rim Rock Restaurant is right across the street from the Best Western Hotel and is a great place to have dinner.

Heading back around on this spur road, pass the visitors' center again and turn left back onto Route 24 toward the Best Western Resort. As the sun may be setting your stomach may be growling so drop by the **Rim Rock Restaurant** across from the Hotel for some fine dining, music, and more great views. Sleep soundly as another big day awaits you in the morning.

DAY TWO

Start your morning by refocusing on the ribbon-like road in front of you heading toward the Park. The run from Capital Reef to Hanksville hugs the Fremont River and winds along with it. The road at first twists through tight turns cutting across the park (beware of blind corners), and then drops and ascends, then turns and drops again, then changes again as it passes by the river and more orchards. The landscape also changes from fruit trees and meadows to moonish hills and craters and back again to greenery and fertile soil. It is as if the road and terrain are trying to define themselves, but got confused in the process. As you approach Hanksville, the Henry Mountains rise to the south, desolate and lonely, wanting to keep their distance from this pocket of earthly upheaval.

When you arrive in Hanksville, be sure to tank up, as gas stations are few and far between along State Route 95 heading south to **Hite Crossing** at Lake Powell. Mexican Hat is about 130 miles down the road and is the next town to stop for fuel. Don't want to run out of fuel on this road, you may not see another car for hours!

Continue south on Route 95 for a joyous and exhilarating ride to Hite Crossing. The road is relatively straight coming out of Hanksville, but after several miles enters a lush canyon and winds nicely through this oasis before

Beneath the Moki Dugway the Valley of the Gods stretches to the horizon.

continuing its swinging motion alongside towering cliffs to the east end of
Lake Powell. The expanse is spacious and the roads well marked on soft
black asphalt. The beauty of this run lies in its wide vistas and desolate solitude. The turns can be tight, yet the views are all laid out in front of you
without fear of any blind corners. So let the tire bite the asphalt as you dash
toward the Colorado and San Juan Rivers.

A bridge carries you over the confluence of the Dirty Devil and Colorado
Rivers. Pull over on the south side of the bridge and take a stroll to the canyon edge. Peer down at the river and you will be amazed at how far the waters have receded. The canyon appears empty except for the muddy waters
languidly flowing into the lake. What lake? Just a few years ago Lake
Powell's eastern edge lapped below the bridge at Hite Crossing. Sun wor-
shippers and boaters would roam these once water-filled canyons. Nowa-
days, due to the ongoing drought, the water has receded dramatically and
the high water mark reminisces of times past about a hundred or more feet
from the mud-filled bottom. The lake, once filled to capacity in 1980, is
now less then half full and these eastern shores are waterless.

Regardless, the views are just as magnificent. As most water lovers now
depart from the western edge of Lake Powell at Wahweap, this end is even
more desolate. Over Memorial Day weekend as my brother and I hiked below the bridge, we counted five cars passing in about forty-five minutes.
The road truly belongs to you.

Back on Route 95, the road's sweeping turns and the terrain's sun-baked
grandeur seem to swallow your movements as you drive further along toward Monument Valley. After about 100 miles from Hanksville, the

entrance to **Natural Bridges National Monument** (www.nps.gov/nabr, 435-692-1234) appears on your left. I know it will be difficult to break from the "zone," but this National Monument is worth a short visit.

Turn left into the park on State Route 275 and drop by the visitors' center for some general information and a map. The bridges are stream carved and can be seen from several overlooks on a nine-mile loop road through the park. Drop by some of the pullouts and witness some of the largest natural wonders in the world. Hiking trails are also available for even closer views of the multi-colored bridges. The road is one-way and a pleasure to drive as it bends above and around the washed-out streambeds below.

Back on Route 95, head east another few miles to the State Route 261 turnoff. Turn right and enjoy another pleasant run through the edges of the Grand Gulch and Kane Gulch Primitive Areas. These two remote areas are divided by Route 261. The road elevates slowly to about 7,000 feet and the landscape changes to pinion and ponderosa pine, while the air cools and the road stretches ahead toward Cedar Mesa. Your love for motorcycling will be reconfirmed along this empty ribbon of tar and crushed rock smoothly passing beneath you.

After twenty-four miles, you will arrive at one of the most fascinating roads on this entire journey, the **Moki Dugway**. Although the road is unpaved, it is well graded and drops 1,200 feet in three miles. Before starting this dramatic leap to the plateau below, stop at the first overlook just half a mile after the pavement ends. You can see most of the four corners

The Moke Dugway is cut right into a cliff and rises 1,200 feet in just a few miles.

including Shiprock in New Mexico and Monument Valley at the Utah/Arizona border. Right beneath the dugway, the Valley of the Gods awaits enticingly for your arrival. Although not for the faint of heart, the Moki Dugway is streetbike-accessible (I have even seen Harleys on it) if taken slowly. So go slow and easy and have the time of your life gazing down at the grandest scenery you have ever seen. The surreal landscape is, indeed, more picturesque then any postcard. Even those "Old West" movies and car commercials don't do it justice!

After a safe journey down Moki Dugway, you are now 1,200 feet lower on pavement that stretches over even more isolated terrain. About half a mile down the road a sign on your left directs you to the Valley of the Gods. This seventeen-mile dirt backroad takes you to a miniature monument valley and is well worth the detour if you have time. Isolated pinnacles and buttes dot the landscape away from all the tourists in what seems like a lonely, solitary planet. If you want to get away from it all, take this road. Turn left at the sign (Forest Road 242) and after driving through this remote valley connect with US Hwy 191. At the intersection turn right and rejoin this journey to Monument Valley at US Hwy 163 (in the direction of Mexican Hat). By the way, a quaint B&B, the Zippity DoDah, is located at the Valley of the Gods turnoff and offers overnight facilities for those interested (www.zippitydodah.com/vog, 970-749-1164).

Riding south on US 163 just north of the Monument Valley turnoff leaves you time to ponder what you just winessed.

This dirt track affords even better views.

Otherwise, just continue on Route 261 for another five miles until you see a sign on the right labeled **Goosenecks State Park** (www.utah.com/stateparks/goosenecks.htm, 435-678-2238). Turn right on State Route 316 and drive about three miles to the park entrance. Continue on to one of the overlooks and you will be amazed at yet another geological wonder. The San Juan River snakes through eroded limestone and shale twisting and turning like Mother Nature's own intestine. What should have taken one mile, has taken five miles over the course of 300 million years. Looking down over 1,000 feet, the river loops back and forth endlessly creating "goosenecks" before entering Lake Powell.

Continue on Route 261 for one more mile and then turn right on US Hwy 163 through scenery made famous by many Hollywood directors starting with John Ford's "Old West" movies starring John Wayne. The road winds gently up and down and around a narrow canyon into Mexican Hat and the San Juan River. Tank up here and then drive down to the bridge and the **San Juan Inn** (www.sanjuaninn.net, 800-447-2022). This lodge is perched precariously alongside the river on top of the canyon's edge. Drop by the **Olde Bridge Bar & Grille** for some nourishment and take a table next to the window overlooking the river. Good food, great view.

After a bite, cross over the bridge and climb gently out of the river canyon to more vistas of Monument Valley. The reddish black asphalt winds tantalizingly in front of you and weaves across the tabletop plateau like a thread in a colorful Navajo blanket. Sandstone spires and box-like buttes are the images sewn on this rug of haunting beauty.

Various pull-outs line Hwy 163 as you draw nearer the park. Many of them are on unpaved shoulders or via short dirt tracks, so be careful. Stop

Monument Valley is picture postcard perfect.

and spend some time not only taking pictures, but visually painting this image in your mind. The stark, yet grand majesty of Monument Valley testifies to you why the Navajos consider this land sacred and have named these formations reverently. A downpour once caught me unawares, but the summer thunderstorm only added to the brilliance of colors.

Upon arriving at Monument Valley, turn right toward **Goulding's Lodge** (www.gouldings.com, 435-727-3231). Drive past the High School about two miles and then make a sharp left up toward the hotel lobby. Goulding's was established as a trading post and eventually started to cater to tourists in the 1930s. The story goes that Mr. Goulding went to Hollywood in order to promote the relatively unknown area of the "Old West" for movie producers. The director John Ford was so enthralled with its beauty that many of his films were made here . . . and the rest is history.

Goulding's is a great place to stay with clean, comfortable rooms not outrageously priced. The camping facility is also well-kept with showers and an indoor pool. Be sure and dine on some Navajo Fry Bread in the restaurant overlooking the valley. Mr. Goulding's original home is now a museum and well worth a visit. You could easily spend two nights here playing tourist and going for a jeep tour through various areas within Monument Valley. For our purposes, dine with a view, go for a swim, rest up, and then get up early for the ride back to Panguitch.

DAY THREE

In the morning, head over to the actual park located on the **Navajo Tribal Land** (www.navajonationparks.org/monumentvalley.htm). The park is on the east side of Hwy 163 about three miles from the intersection. The overlook at the visitors' center is a great spot for more photos. For you more daring souls on a dual-sport bike, take the land tour via a seventeen-mile dirt road. One word of caution, the road is unpaved and *sandy.* If you feel comfortable taking on sandy gulleys behind slow-moving cars, this ride will take you right to the base of the spires and buttes for a real close-up feel of this valley. If sand gives you the jitters, then park up top and take in the views. Guided tours in four-wheel drive vehicles are also available.

After your Monument Valley viewing, drive back to Hwy 163 and turn left (south) toward Kayenta. The road takes you through the southern outskirts of the park unfurling even more sandstone monoliths such as Agatha Peak and Owl Rock. The twenty-four miles to Kayenta winds around these statuesque sights as the morning light reflects off their surface. No better way to start a morning ride!

In Kayenta, get some gas and then turn right (west) onto US Hwy 160 toward Tuba City. Continue on about twelve miles, and if you are interested in some well-preserved Indian Cliff dwellings head right (north) on State Route 564 for nine miles to the **Navajo National Monument** (www.nps.gov/nava, 928-672-2700). The cool, dry air has preserved the

Riding a GS or dual-sport on the loop around Monument Valley is fun. Some spots are very sandy, so be careful.

remains of some Anasazi villages situated in canyon walls built 700 years ago. There is a visitors' center and two short self-guided tours. Camping and picnicking are also available.

Head back to Hwy 160 on Route 564 and then turn right back toward Tuba City. Be sure your tank is full as we will be taking a shortcut to Glen Canyon Dam on State Route 98 through the heart of Navajo land. This road is about eight miles from Route 564 and will be yours alone as you travel across this moon-like landscape toward Lake Powell. This isolated cut of Navajo Tribal Land speaks with ageless tranquility and solitude. Man appears to be of no consequence here. And then the paradox begins. A power plant looms in the foreground and the man-made majesty of Lake Powell and Glen Canyon Dam strike a conflicting chord within you. Turning on US Hwy 89 north and crossing the arch-spanned bridge over the mighty, yet tamed, Colorado River pricks your conscious and makes you wonder just who is in charge here? Man or Nature. Hmmm . . .

At Glen Canyon Dam at Lake Powell, the white-colored band indicates the high water mark from several years ago. The lake is currently about 100 feet below capacity.

The Parry Lodge in Kanab was once the place to stay for movie stars making Old West films.

Drop by the visitors' center for some info on the dam and Lake Powell. A tour of the dam is available certain times of the day as well. This engineering marvel is quite a feat. For more info and details see my chapter on the North Rim, visit the Glen Canyon Dam website at www.nps.gov/glca, or call 928-608-6404.

The trip back to Panguitch from Glen Canyon Dam is roughly 140 miles. The first leg toward Kanab runs through the Vermilion Cliffs and the southern edge of the Grand Staircase-Escalante National Monument. Kanab is about seventy-three miles down the road and is a great spot to have dinner. My personal favorite is **Houston's Trails' End Restaurant**. The servings are plentiful and the price is right. This restaurant is located just across the street from Parry Lodge on Center Street.

Panguitch is sixty-seven miles from Kanab. US Hwy 89 runs alongside the Sevier River through red rocks, ponderosa pine, and grassy meadows. The ride is a pleasant and gentle end to a three-day extravaganza of out-of-this-world motorcycling. As you drive into town, the Red Brick Inn B&B is a welcome sight. Time to unwind and digest some of those famous chocolate chip cookies. The trip you only dreamed of is now tucked into the "been there, done that" compartment of your brain. No more need to dream of this one, only memories to come back and do it all over again.

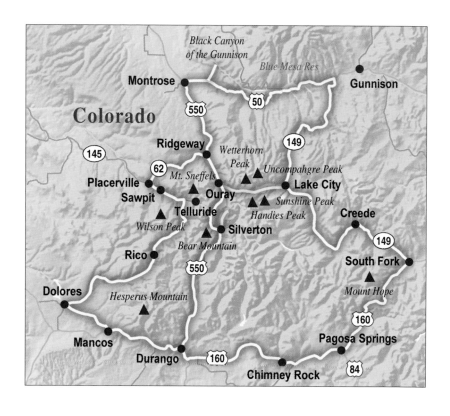

Durango

It's amazing the little tidbits of information you pick up on motorcycle trips. Not too long ago I was walking down Main Avenue and turned the corner just past the Strater Hotel and saw a huge mural of a boxer painted on the corner building's exterior wall. Apparently, Jack Dempsey was from Southern Colorado and fought Andy Malloy in Durango on October 7, 1915. Dempsey eventually went on to become the World Heavyweight Champion. Another tidbit I learned at the museum: When the railroad company heard that Animas City had jacked up the price for the railroad site, they said "to heck with ya" and situated the depot two miles south in the box-tent town of Durango. The railroad then spawned a whole new community that quickly overshadowed Animas City. Durango may very well not have come into existence had it not been for this. A good choice as far as I am concerned!

Durango's main street is a beautiful place to stroll on a summer's day.

Durango was founded as a result of the gold and silver strike. Although no gold or silver was actually found in Durango, the Denver and Rio Grande Railroad built its depot here. A narrow gauge railroad connected the town with Silverton in order to haul the mineral to the smelter operations. The railroad has been in operation for 122 continuous years and now carries tourists through Colorado's scenic mining country. The **Durango & Silverton Narrow Gauge Railroad** is one of the top-ten railroad journeys in the world as rated by the Society of American Travel Writers (www.durangotrain.com, 970-247-2733).

The town now caters to tourists providing a host of recreational activities for all seasons. Even motorcyclists are popular, particularly around Labor Day weekend when the locals sponsor the **"Rally in the Rockies"** (www.rallyintherockies.com). Its location is ideal, situated at the base of the San Juan Mountains and the intersection of US Hwy 550 and 160. This gateway to the San Juan Mountains provides all the amenities necessary as a staging point for two of my favorite rides in the Rockies—The San Juan Parkway and The Silver Thread. Visit the city's own website at www.durango.com for information on lodging, food, entertainment, and

Don't forget that cup of coffee or hot chocolate before heading out!

Jack Dempsey is pictured on the wall of an old building in Durango. Apparently, he started his career in southern Colorado. You learn something new on every trip!

activities. Personally, I stay at the Best Western Rio Grande Inn at 400 E. 2nd Ave 800-245-4466 located in historic Durango. Downtown is just minutes away and you are just steps from the Durango & Silverton Railroad Station.

There are more then enough restaurants and coffee shops on Main Street to appease your appetite after a long ride. Just remember the **Old Tymer's Cafe** (1000 Main Ave) has a nice back patio and makes a mean breakfast burrito. The **Jean Pierre Bakery** (601 Main Ave) will dazzle you with assorted delicacies as well—can you tell I like pastries? Oh, and don't forget, the town has more then twenty thriving bars and pubs for those seeking nocturnal entertainment. One thing is for sure, the Old West is alive and well in Durango, Colorado!

Trip 9 San Juan Scenic Byway

Distance *233 miles (full day)*
Terrain *Rocky Mountain scenery at its best. Start in Durango, visit the old mining towns of Silverton and Ouray, drop by a ghost town via a dirt road, and then head back to Durango through Telluride. From grasslands to mountaintops you will see sweeping panoramas with every color imaginable. Elevation change 5,500 to 11,000 feet.*
Highlights *Endless twisties and mountain curves. Short dirt backway to Animas Fork. No straightaways on this run!*

Colorado. The name itself epitomizes what is the very best in Rocky Mountain motorcycling. Close to half the state is covered with cloud-draped mountain peaks. Literally a thousand miles of roads crawl and wind through mountain passes, over river gorges and through alpine meadows. The air is crisp and clear. The views are heavenly. And the roads are clean, narrow, and windy. A motorcyclist's paradise. Driving through Colorado can almost be surreal—like you have been transplanted into a picture postcard, moving from one photograph to another and not wanting the ride to end.

The Million-Dollar Highway cuts through the San Juan National Forest on the way to Silverton and Ouray.

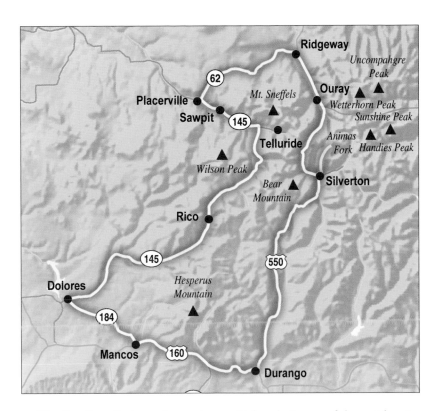

The San Juan Parkway in southwest Colorado is one of those rides. An All-American Scenic Byway lasting roughly 230 miles. The best of what the Rocky Mountains has to offer. Very few rides can even compare. I remember coming down from the Canadian Rockies one summer and driving through the San Juans on my way home. The mountains are as striking as any location in the Rocky Mountains, or for that matter, anywhere in the world. If you are going to do just one ride, this one should be at the top of the list.

But, you say, everyone knows about the San Juan Scenic Byway and the Million-Dollar Highway. Too many cars and RVs. Too much traffic. Too many tourists. Not worth it.

You couldn't be further from the truth. Sure, there can be a lot of tourists, but timing is everything. And, actually, coming down the backside through Telluride is often wide open. Traveling on the off holiday weekends and heading out in the early morning leaves the roads wide open and clear. My wife and I rode from Rico to Delores early one Sunday morning and saw three other vehicles. Don't let the tourists scare you; otherwise you'll be missing a ride of a lifetime.

THE ROUTE FROM DURANGO

0   Start in Durango

36   Coal Bank Pass on US Hwy 550, elevation 10,640 feet

42   Turnoff for Andrew Lake, turn right

44   Molas Pass Summit, 10,910 feet

50   Enter Silverton on State Route 110 (Greene Street). Continue straight to Animas Fork (unpaved- optional)

60   Red Mountain Pass, 11,108 feet

74   Arrive Ouray on 550

86   Arrive Ridgeway, turn left on State Route 62

109   Arrive Placerville, head south on State Route145

124   Arrive Telluride

136   Lizard Head Pass, 10,222 feet

152   Arrive Rico

189   Arrive Delores

190   Turn left on State Route 184 to Mancos

207   Arrive Mancos, turn left on US Hwy 160

233   Arrive back in Durango, go to sleep

Before you begin this 230-mile loop through the Rockies, a couple of housekeeping items need to be addressed. Firstly, take some raingear. Afternoon showers are quite common. And secondly, take your swim trunks. If you have time, a relaxing dip in the Ouray hot pools may be in order. Not only are the hot springs soothing, but the views are to die for.

They don't call this place "Little Switzerland" for nothing.

This journey starts in the old railroad town of Durango at the intersection of US Highways 160 and 550. Founded in 1880 by the Denver and Rio Grande Railroad Company, the town has seen over 300 million dollars in precious metals transported through its historic depot. The downtown area on Main Avenue appears similar to the town established over 100 years ago. It centers around **The Strater Hotel** (www.strater.com, 970-247-4431) built in 1887 by a pharmacist and is still in use today. Most of the buildings are built with brick due to a city ordinance resulting from fires that destroyed the city in 1889. As a result, the structures are still standing and evoke their colorful past as you explore downtown.

To get to the historic downtown, start on Highway 550 going north and make an immediate right on College Drive, go over the railroad tracks and then turn left onto Main Avenue. Main Avenue runs about one mile before hooking up to the 550 again. Since you got up nice and early, grab a cup of coffee at the Durango Coffee Company, or sit in the patio at the Old Tyme Cafe for a breakfast burrito. Store up your energy for the upcoming climb over the San Juan Mountains. This trip will take all day. When you come back, take an evening stroll down Main Avenue and leisurely peruse the shops, restaurants, and historic landmarks.

Now that the coffee has kicked in, finish driving down Main Avenue and hook back into US Hwy 550 heading north. This seventy-six-mile stretch of Hwy 550 from Durango to Ouray is more often referred to as the Million-Dollar Highway. It cuts through the San Juan Peaks across three 10,000-foot passes before entering the Ouray basin. The road got its name from low-grade gold ore used in its construction, but the real value is in its

Someone forgot their coffee this morning but found the perfect spot to recover with a snooze.

million dollar views! This marvel of road engineering slices through rugged mountains as it follows old stagecoach and pack trails. What took weeks to traverse now can be done in two hours (maybe a little faster on a motorcycle)!

The 550 outside Durango is nicely paved and has passing lanes for several miles toward the **Durango Mountain Resort** (www.durango mountainresort.com). The road flows gently from left to right giving you time to gaze up at the mountain peaks and down into the river valley. The scenery is breathtaking as you climb up to Coal Bank Pass at 10,640 feet. The Animas River flows between the peaks on the east side and Engineer Mountain juts up in the background with its barren, yellowed rock face. The contrast set with the blue sky and white clouds forces your eyes to wander and bask in the picture perfect scenery—and just think, the trip has just begun!

The summit at Coal Bank Pass is about thirty-six miles outside of Durango. Watch out for snow pack in late May and into June, and sometimes July. Stop at the scenic overlook on your right. Walk down the trail a few hundred feet and the views and valleys open up in grand opulence. There are some picnic tables if you want to stop for a snack. For further views looking back, cross the road to the dirt trailhead for Coal Miners Pass. Climb up the trail a short distance and look south across the tundra-like meadow. These fields are colored with wildflowers during the summer and make for some more great pictures.

Hiking down the trail is as rewarding as hiking up, especially when your bike awaits.

*You can get off
the beaten track
by taking this dirt
road just across
from Coal Bank
Pass.*

Heading down Coal Bank Pass, the road hairpins dramatically downward on its way to yet another summit crossing at Molas Pass about eight
miles further on. Throttle back and enjoy this run. A neat diversion before
the Pass is **Andrew Lake**. The Andrew Lake turnoff is about six miles from
the Coal Bank Pass Summit. Follow the narrow one laner all the way around
to the lake; don't bother with the side road to the overlook. The views are
more open right by the lake. There is a walking bridge on the eastern edge
over the water and Engineer Mountain looms spectacularly in the background. My brother and I made this detour over Memorial Day Weekend
and the snow packs were three feet high! Should have brought snowshoes.

Continue on to Molas Pass. The road is a combination of open curves
and hairpins. Passing lanes open up about every two to four miles. At Molas
Pass Summit, elevation 10,910 feet, there is parking and a great overlook.
This one is especially sweet as it peers down on Molas Lake. A dirt road on
the west side of 550 weaves down to the lake for you more daring souls. The

views are expansive and encompass a host of peaks and ridges surrounding the turquoise lake below.

After about six miles, Hwy 550 winds down from Molas Pass right into **Silverton**. You will see the town laid out like a grid as you scurry down the switchbacks. In most cases, the hairpinned road is open and visible, giving you time to anticipate the next turn. Follow the signs to Silverton (Route 110) and ride into one of the highest towns in the Rockies.

Coming into Silverton on Greene Street is like entering an old west time warp. You'll feel like kickin' your bike rather then grippin' your throttle! Find a parking spot to tie up your mount and then take a walk through old town Silverton. Apparently the name of the town got started when miners were searching for gold in this area and instead they discovered silver—by the ton. Various shops and restaurants line the street with Old West flair—Victoria-style antique shops, art studios, restaurants, and saloons, all reminiscent of times past.

If you are hungry, drop by one of Silverton's many restaurants. For a quick bite and some good conversation drop by **The Rocky Mountain Funnel Cakes and Cafe**. Carolyn and Richard Wilcox are retired schoolteachers and now make tasty concoctions on Funnel Cakes. The Mexican Style Funnel Cake is particularly good. While waiting for your order, stick a pin on the visitors' map to mark your hometown and chat with Carolyn as she tells

Heading down a single-laner to Andrew Lake, the views are great.

A neat diversion before Coal Bank Pass is the Andrew Lake turnoff.

you the latest "happenings" in this old mining town. A couple of dates to remember are the "Step Back in Time Historical Celebration" from June 3rd to 6th when the whole town dresses in authentic 18th century attire (apparently, Carolyn dresses up as Miss Kitty in the local bordello). Another date worth noting is the annual motorcyclist's **"Rally in the Rockies"** (www.rallyintherockies.com) over Labor Day Weekend. This rally starts in Ignacio, Colorado, rides into Durango, and continues on to Silverton and other popular riding destinations. Talk to Carolyn, she will tell you all about it!

Old mining towns abound in and around Silverton. A quick introduction into this part of Colorado is just up the road from Silverton. If you want to see a relatively intact ghost town, continue on **Greene Street** (Hwy 110) northeast of town to **Animas Fork** about twelve miles outside of Silverton. There are several buildings clustered around the mill, which are still open to the public. Climb around the interiors of the old miners' boarding houses and try to visualize the living conditions in those days. Rangers roam these parts and are more then helpful to fill you in on all sorts of historical tidbits. Just remember before heading out of town, that Hwy 110 turns into an unpaved back road as it climbs into these old mining areas. Loose dirt and rocky terrain make it difficult for street bikers (particularly the last half mile), but a blast for dual-purpose bikes!

As you can tell, there is much to do in the Silverton area and you could

Time for a break in colorful Silverton.

spend days exploring, hiking, and hitting a few washboards. If you want to stay awhile, check out more activities in Silverton by visiting their website at www.silvertoncolorado.com, or call 800 752-4494.

For those continuing on, head back on Greene Street to the 550 intersection and turn right toward the Red Mountain Pass and Ouray. Red Mountain Pass takes you through unmatched Rocky Mountain scenery. The road from Silverton twists and turns up and down through the majestic peaks and shallow valleys. Red Mountain Pass Summit is the highest point on the ride at 11,108 feet. Breathtaking vistas take in Bear Mountain as the skyway continues to weave its path through the Rockies. Eventually the road cuts a tortuous path from the sheer side of the mountain and leads into Ouray twenty-four miles to the north. This stretch of road between Silverton and Ouray is the portion most referred to as the Million Dollar Highway. The old toll road now runs like a threading terrace along the mountains' edge. The views are definitely worth a million dollars, but remember the guardrails are few and far between. The cliffs plummet to distant valleys below you, so keep your eyes on that million dollar two-laner!

As you approach Ouray, the road disappears into tunnels and emerges under cascading waterfalls. During spring runoff, countless streams create a picture postcard view of alpine-like scenery. One mile outside of town there is a scenic turnout overlooking a roaring waterfall during spring runoff and the town of Ouray spreads out below like a Swiss village. No wonder this area is called the "Little Switzerland" of the Rockies. You'll feel like wearing lederhosen driving into town (do they come with knee pads?).

Ouray (www.ouray.com) was founded in the 1870s, originally by farmers and ranchers who coexisted peacefully with the Ute Indians. The rich soil and Uncompahgre River provided fertile territory for all to enjoy. In 1875 precious metals were discovered in the San Juan Mountains and this sleepy backcountry town turned into a rowdy mining camp overnight. Over time, a more "proper" community evolved with its own school district, waterworks, and opera house. Today, Ouray's Main Street is still lined with old Victoria-style buildings. It's just that the miners have moved out and restaurants, art studios, and hotels have moved in.

When you arrive, drive down Main Street and park in front of the newly restored **Beaumont Hotel** (www.beaumonthotel.com, 888-447-3035). Walk across the street and have a treat at the ice cream parlor or have lunch at one of several eating establishments. If you have time, take an hour and indulge yourself by taking a soothing soak in the hot springs at the far end of

They don't call it the Million-Dollar Highway for nothing.

The road to Ouray is literally cut right into the mountain. Guardrails are few and far between.

town. The pools are separated by temperature, gradually increasing to 100-plus degrees Fahrenheit. While relaxing in the pool, gaze up at the mountains and bask in an alpine setting that looks almost surreal. Who knows, you may quit your job and call this idyllic place your new home!

For those of you who want to stay overnight in Ouray, there is a range of places to stay from the pricier Beaumont Hotel to a very scenic **KOA Campground** (www.koa.com) just north of town. While in town, hike to Bridal Veil Falls or Box Canyon Falls. Go to the local theater on Main Street, enjoy the art display, or go horseback riding in the backwoods. This "jeep capital of the world" has more back roads than you can count and you could literally spend weeks exploring all the old mining areas and ghost towns.

From Ouray, follow the 550 north past the KOA Campground for eleven miles into Ridgeway. This road drops from Ouray on some gentle S-curves and then opens up just before arriving into town. Enjoy this short stretch of straightaway as it is about the only one on this trip.

In Ridgeway, turn left on Route 62 heading west to Placerville about twenty-four miles down the road. After a few miles, the mountains again loom in the background in a row of sharp, rugged, snowcapped peaks. In the foreground, the meadows roll along with you while climbing upward toward this imposing wall of mountains. Mt. Sneffels at 14,150 rises as its centerpiece. This return trip to Durango is full of dramatic landscapes, yet the sweeping curves make it seem gentler. After the harrowing hairpins coming north on 550, this road heading south soothes the nerves and allows your eyes to wander toward the horizon.

At Placerville, head south on Route 145 for fifteen miles to Telluride. The road follows a narrow canyon along the San Miguel River. Watch for animal life, as I have been surprised several times when suddenly passing deer feeding along the road's shoulder. The road continues to hug the river with offshoots along the way to various camping and picnic areas. One word of advice: don't blink at Sawpit, population twenty-five, you just might miss it!

"Thumbs up" for this beautiful ride near Placerville.

Main Street in Telluride is filled with interesting shops and restaurants.

Telluride is a different story. You can't miss this old mining town turned Hollywood Ski Resort nestled at the base of the mountains. A quick visit to Telluride involves two things: One, take a look at the old Main Street with its restored Victorian-style architecture and, two, hop on the free gondola ride up and over the ski runs to a restaurant and shopping center. In summer, the gondola operates free of charge in order to entice tourists to spend a little (or a lot) on fine dining and shopping. I'll just say I did the free part and loved the views from the gondola. If you are interested in staying in Telluride, there are more websites then tattoos on a sailor. Try www.telluride.com for starters.

The next part of the loop up to Lizard Head Pass and Dolores is my favorite. Lizard Head is twelve miles south of Telluride on Route 145. The summit is 10,222 feet in elevation. The views encompass all that you could imagine in a Rocky Mountain setting. The ribbon-like road carries you up the plateau where the afternoon sun adds a shadowy effect to the mountain crevices and valleys unfolding before you. Aspens and meadows flank the forefront of Wilson Peak and Sunshine Mountain. The road eases up and rises above Trout Lake reflecting the mountains and clouds in the background. At the summit of Lizard Pass an overlook invites you to take one last look before heading down glaciated valleys into Rico. Accept the invitation. I guarantee you will meet some fellow bikers doing the exact same thing!

Thirteen miles farther south on 145 is Rico, an old miner's camp with a population of 500 (200 in the winter). If you are tired and want a nice quiet spot to spend the evening, this is the place. The **Rico Hotel** (www.ricohotel.com, 800-365-1971) is a restored boarding house for miners and offers a quaint, rustic appeal. The rooms are reasonably priced and the hotel offers four-star cuisines in the **Argentinean Grill.** Enjoy a nice meal and then unwind with your book in the homey common room before heading out in the morning. The spa out front will soothe your sore muscles just before bedtime.

From Rico to Dolores, the road sweeps through the valley following the Dolores River. The mountains become less mountain-like as lush green meadows open up periodically on either side of the river. The run is steady and quick as your bike takes on a life of its own coasting down the snakeish road to civilization. Vehicles are few and far between.

Stop on Main Street in Telluride to explore its unique architecture.

The scenery changes slowly, yet unmistakably, from high alpine aspen to ponderosa pine and reddish rock of the high altitude Colorado Plateau. The thirty-six miles from Rico to Dolores will remind you why you love riding motorcycles!

Swing through Dolores and then head east on Colorado Route 184 toward Mancos. Mancos is seventeen miles from Dolores on state route184 and twenty-seven miles to Durango on US Hwy 160. The road winds through farmland and ranches heading back toward the La Plata and San Juan Mountains. The scenes are pastoral as the road lazily runs along fence posts and barns. A variety of aromas tickle your nostril along the way—some good and some not so good. Cattle roam the open fields gnawing on the grass. Horses trot through the meadows, their skin shimmering against the setting sun. With the mountains in the background, this short road typifies your mind's view of what "Colorado" should look like.

In Mancos, head east on State Route 160 to Durango. This is the last leg of your journey home. As the road climbs toward Durango, Mt. Hesperus

A nice sweeper brings you from Silverton to Ouray.

The old mining town of Ouray, is Colorado's very own little Switzerland!

rises majestically amongst the La Plata Mountains. Hesperus, Greek for "spirit of the evening star," seems the perfect name for this mountain as the sun reflects off its slopes in hues of green, orange, and gray. You're tired but the briskness in the air and the mountains looming in front of you have a rejuvenating effect. The wonder and beauty of the last eight hours start to return to you. Thoughts of alpine passes, mountain curves, and river valleys flood back into your mind: When can I do this again? I wonder what this loop looks like heading in the opposite direction? Hmmm . . . maybe, I'll call the office and tell them I'm going to be a day late.

Trip 10   The Silver Thread

Distance   *402 miles (two days)*
Terrain   *Visit the Old West mining towns of Creede and Lake City surrounded by five of Colorado's fourteeners. Race adjacent to the Gunnison Gorge alongside Colorado's largest manmade lake and then complete the loop by taking the southern route on the San Juan Parkway back to Durango. Elevation change 5,500 to 11,000 feet.*
Highlights   *Six 10,000-foot passes on the eastern and western legs and then rolling, gentle S-curves on the north and south runs. Scenic Alpine Loop dirt road available at Lake City. The eastern San Juan Mountains along the Silver Thread to Creede and Lake City, the Black Canyon of the Gunnison National Park, and then south on the San Juan Parkway All American Byway.*

Uncompaghre Peak, Handies Peak, Redcloud Peak, Wetterhorn Peak, and Sunshine Peak all have two things in common: First, they are all over 14,000 feet and, second, they can all be seen from the saddle of your motorcycle while driving along the "Silver Thread" Scenic Byway. Be sure your heated handgrips are working properly as this two day journey will take you over six 10,000-foot passes through unparalleled Rocky Mountain Scenery.

Blue Mesa Reservoir is a pleasant place to take a break on your way to Montrose.

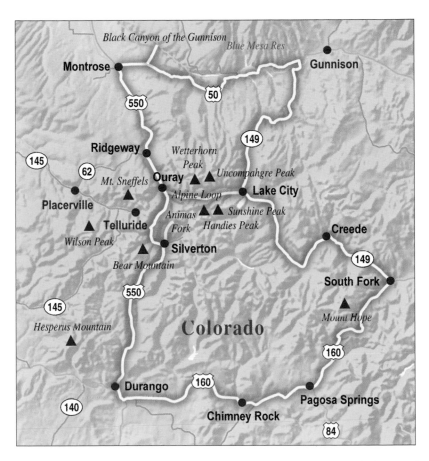

Total mileage is close to 400 miles on this trek and even a little longer if you detour up to Black Canyon of the Gunnison National Park. The trip starts in Durango, heads east through Pagosa Springs, climbs north over Wolf Creek Pass, and on to Lake City. Lake City is a good midpoint and a nice spot to overnight before continuing on to Blue Mesa Reservoir and Montrose. The final leg delivers you back on the San Juan Parkway for southern views of this All American Byway.

Our journey starts from Durango and heads east on US Hwy 160 to **Pagosa Springs**. The road gently sways through meadowed ranchlands and the small towns of Gem Village and Bayfield before crossing the Piedra River. The lush San Juan Peaks loom invitingly to the north, while high arid mesas dominate the southern horizon. About forty-three miles ahead at the State Route 151 intersection, you will see Chimney Rock rise on your right, its rigid outline blocking the horizon like a decaying tooth. After seventeen more

THE ROUTE FROM DURANGO

Day One

0   Start in Durango at the intersection of US Hwy 160 and 550, head east on 160

60   Arrive in Pagosa Springs, continue north on 160 to South Fork

102 Arrive South Fork, turn left on State Route 149 to Creede

123 Arrive Creede

172 Turn left to Lake Cristobal, loop around lake

176 Reconnect with Route 149, turn left

177 Arrive Lake City, spend the night

Day Two

177 Start in Lake City, continue on 149 or head west on Alpine Loop (dual sport only)

222 Turn left (west) on US Hwy 50

262 Turn right on State Route 347 to Black Canyon of the Gunnison National Park

269 Arrive visitors' center at Black Canyon of the Gunnison National Park, turn around

276 Turn right on US Hwy 50 to Montrose

291 Arrive Montrose, turn left (south) on US Hwy 550

319 Arrive Ridgeway, continue south on 550

330 Arrive Ouray

354 Arrive Silverton

402 Arrive Durango

miles, you will arrive in Pagosa Springs (www.pagosaspringschamber.com, 800-252-2204) the home of the sacred spa.

Over 150 years ago, the first white man discovered the bubbling springs at Pagosa. However, Native Americans had been bathing in its wondrous healing powers for centuries beforehand. They called the area Pag-Osah, or sacred place of Healing Waters. A beautiful resort now exists at this spot with breathtaking views. Definitely worth a stay if you have the time (and money!). For now, grab a cup of coffee and a donut at **Daylight Donut and Cafe** just after the Golf Club (2151 W. Hwy 160) and settle in at the city park. The views are just as grand and it's a whole lot cheaper!

As you leave Pagosa Springs your riding anticipation will be rising with each passing mile. You are now heading north on Hwy 160 directly into the southeast corner of the San Juan Mountains. The road soon begins its gyrating motion upward through the San Juan River Valley toward Wolf Creek Ski Resort. Mount Hope juts up to your left. Greyback Mountain and Del Norte Peak rise to the east. The road's gentility quickly disappears as you begin to crest the pass at 10,850 feet and cross the Continental Divide. A rest area with a sign commenting on the divide is located at the top of the pass.

Cruising down **Wolf Creek Pass** is a blast as the road winds to South Fork through crevices carved by glaciers eons ago. Spruce covered mountains show periodic bald rock faces created from this glacial action. The forty-two miles from Pagosa Springs to South Fork will fly by all too quickly! What took two to three weeks for the first pioneers is now completed in little over an hour.

South Fork is the official gateway of the **"Silver Thread" Scenic Byway**. The route was originally built in the 1870s from portions of two toll roads used to exploit the mining boom in the San Juans. Eventually, these toll roads merged creating one of the most spectacular byways in the entire Rocky Mountain Region. The terrain is formidable and the last stretch of seven and a half miles was finally paved in 1984. Traveling along this byway is also like traveling back in time. Creede and Lake City are both historic sites and haven't changed much over the last 100 years. As ninety-six percent of the lands are federally owned, views are expansive, pristine, and remote.

At the intersection of Hwy 160 and State Route 149, turn left on 149. You will be heading northwest and will cross the Rio Grande within half a

The road seems to climb up to the clouds just outside Lake City.

mile. The road runs along the bottom of a deep canyon and adjacent to the **Collier State Wildlife Area**. Elk use this spot as a staging area in November before migrating to the northeast. Don't be surprised to see herds of Elk grazing off in the distance.

After about seven miles from South Fork, you will notice cliffs of volcanic tuff on the east side of the Rio Grande called the **Palisades**. The ragged edges jut up abruptly in stark contrast with the gentle lush valley to your left. These ghostly rock formations were created by earth shattering volcanic activity thousands of years ago.

About eleven miles up Route 149, the canyon begins to narrow and then after two to three miles the road suddenly turns into a slot with towering cliffs on one side and the river on the other side. This area is called the "Wagon Wheel Gap." Folklore says this is where Charles Baker, a miner, lost a wheel while fleeing from the Ute Indian, Colorow. The wheel was later found stuck in the mud, hence where the canyon narrows became **"Wagon Wheel Gap"** (might help in a game of trivial pursuit).

The "Gap" soon opens up into an expansive valley. Views of alpine meadows, running rivers and towering snowcapped mountains epitomize the Rockies at their best. The road eventually pulls into the historic mining town of Creede about twenty-one miles from South Fork.

In 1889 Nicholas Creede discovered silver in North Willow Creek. By

It's "Home Sweet Home" at the G & M Cabins in Lake City.

This is one of my favorite lakes in the Rockies, Lake San Cristobal.

1892 more then 10,000 people had settled here and at one point this boom town was shipping in excess of $1,000,000 worth of silver per month. Now it boasts a more manageable 500 people and its major attraction is tourism.

Creede (www.creede.com, 800-327-2102) is a great place to stop and stretch your legs. The entire town has been declared a National Historic District. So park your bike in front of the Old Firehouse Restaurant and take a stroll down Main Street. Mosey into one of the several galleries and jewelry shops lining the street. The architecture is an eclectic mix of Victorian and Old West. If the weather cooperates, grab a "dog" at the **Best Little Dog House in Creede** (719-658-3000) and enjoy the Old West atmosphere of this former mining town. For dessert walk back to your bike and have a cone or sundae at the **Old Firehouse Ice Cream Parlour**. You may not want to leave!

As you exit Creede, Route 149 will swing south and then quickly twist back to a northwesterly direction. The valley widens as the Rio Grande loops lazily downward from its headwaters at Stony Pass. Continuing along, the mountains slowly envelope you as the multiple fourteeners rise up in all directions. At the first hill's crest, stop and take a picture from the overlook. Hermit and Brown Lakes double the pleasure with their mirrored reflections.

About twenty-seven miles from Creede, look for Forest Road 510 and the signs to **Clear Creek Falls**. Don't miss this! The detour is only half a mile off the main drag and the falls drop a stupendous 100 feet. Views to the south and east open us as well. Watch out for moose, as they were

Creede, Colorado, an old mining town gone bust, is a great place to have lunch and do some window shopping.

introduced to this area in 1991 and often are seen standing beside water coming off the falls.

The next seven miles climb rapidly up the mountain slope until you reach the 10,898-foot Spring Creek Pass. The pass sits right atop the Continental Divide. Empty your bottled water and watch half of it flow down the Colorado to California and the other half down the Rio Grande to Mexico. This is also the trailhead for the **Continental Divide Scenic Trail** that stretches from Canada to Mexico. The forest service has developed this rest area as an informational site with explanatory placards showcasing its history (restrooms also available!).

The road then descends into another majestic valley for about six miles before ascending over the 11,361-foot Slumgullion Pass. About two miles before the summit, stop at the Windy Point Scenic Overlook for views of five fourteeners. There are signs at the overlook pointing to and naming the locations of these peaks. Continue over the pass (the result of two mudslides several hundred years ago) and close to the bottom of the slide, just south of the Lake Fork crossing, is another bit of trivia. A historic marker commemorates Colorado's infamous **Rocky Mountain Cannibal, Alfred Packer.** The story told by Packer differed from the evidence later found by the Sheriff and the rest is history. So be sure to stop and read the plaque for the whole story (you won't miss it now, will you!).

Continue north and the road winds through pine and aspen, making its way to Lake City.

About one mile before **Lake City**, make a left to Lake San Cristobal for a view of one of the most scenic and unspoiled spots in Colorado. Drive the three to four miles around the lake (part of the road is gravel) and enjoy this spectacular setting high in the Rockies (camping is available). After the short detour, continue back to Lake City on Route 149. Lake City is another one of Colorado's unmistakable historic mining towns dating back to the late 1800s. The town is filled with Victorian style homes and buildings from over a century ago.

When you arrive in Lake City, you will need to make a few decisions. If it is a reasonable time and you feel ambitious continue on Route 149. There are a few more towns along the way to overnight if you need to (Montrose is 100 miles). Otherwise, just spend a relaxing evening in Lake City, have dinner, and head out in the morning. For those on a dual sport or GS, I would seriously consider spending the night in Lake City and then continuing in the morning on one of the most scenic backways in the Rockies, the "Alpine Loop" to Ouray. The Alpine Loop is about twenty-five miles one way to Ouray. In Ouray catch US Hwy 550 south back to Durango. One word

Clear Creek Falls just outside of Creede, Colorado is magnificent.

of caution, although most of the Alpine Loop is well groomed hardrock, the passes are formidable and require high-clearance mounts. For more information read my section on "The Ultimate Scenic Backway" at the end of this chapter.

There are several places to stay and dine in Lake City. Some of my favorites are **The Cinnamon Inn Bed & Breakfast** with separately unique rooms (800-337-2335) and the **G & M Cabins** in the center of town for a more rustic atmosphere (866-204-6344). There are also several lodges and campsites in and around town. Restaurants are plentiful, just be sure and drop by the **Lake City Bakery** at 922 Hwy 149 for some fresh baked pastries in the morning (970-911-2613). For more information on Lake City visit their website at www.lakecityco.com, 800-569-1874.

In the morning, continue north on Route 149 for forty-five miles to US Hwy 50. Route 149 rocks like a pendulum as it weaves its way north. The panoramas continue to enthrall as the cold air brushes your face. It seems each day keeps getting better on this trip!

At US Hwy 50, turn left toward Montrose. This next stretch of fifty-five miles is one of my favorites. The road skirts the Blue Mesa Reservoir, the largest lake in Colorado, swaying rhythmically alongside the shoreline to

The land around Lake San Christobal at Lake City is scenic and unspoiled.

Wagon Wheel Gap just south of Creede cuts an impressive path.

the south and the unseen Gunnison Gorge on the right. The landscape is drier, providing unobstructed views for miles. The river or car's motion and clear views pull your wrist downward and the fifty-five miles to Montrose fly by all too quickly.

If you want to visit a narrower version of the Grand Canyon, turn right on State Route 347 to **Black Canyon** of the **Gunnison National Park** (www.nps.gov/blca, 970-641-2337). The turnoff is about fifteen miles east of Montrose and seven more miles to the gorge itself. The Black Canyon is a schism cut 2,700 feet into the earth's crust by the Gunnison River. Thirty million years of river flow has created a gorge of stark yet magnificent beauty.

At the visitors' center walk over to Gunnison Point for vertigo inducing views deep into the schist. For more views drive down the South Rim Drive to Chasm Point about three to four miles further into the park. The side trip to Black Canyon of the Gunnison National Park totals twenty to twenty-five miles round trip and you won't regret it.

After your head stops spinning hook back into Hwy 50 and at Montrose, turn left on US Hwy 550 to Ridgway. Before you know it, you are in familiar territory. The remaining eighty miles to Durango are covered in my earlier chapter on the San Juan Parkway (only in reverse order). What a grand way to end a grand journey! The stupendous Silver Thread, the gorgeous Gunnison Gorge, and the unmatched beauty of the San Juan Parkway rolled into one of the best motorcycle journeys in the Rockies—for that matter, in the world!

Trip 11   The Alpine Loop Backway

Distance   65 miles for the entire loop (plan on a full day).
        22 miles from Lake City to Ouray (allow 1/2 day)
Terrain   Visit the heart of the San Juan Range via two, 12,000-foot passes
and explore the ruins of abandoned ghost towns on a solitary backroad
adventure through the Colorado Rockies.
Highlights   From Lake City the road starts out smoothly and after about 10
miles deteriorates to potholes and rocks as you climb over the passes. Dual-
sport only.

THE ROUTE FROM LAKE CITY

This loop between Lake City, Ouray, and Silverton was built by miners in
the late 1800s for hauling equipment and ore by mule wagons. The journey
takes you deep into the soul of the San Juans, passing ghost towns, old mining conveyors, and blossoming wildflowers along the way. Most of the trip
is on groomed dirt and gravel, but the passes can be dicey, requiring high
ground clearance and a focused mind.

The Alpine Loop is one of my favorite backroad adventures in the Rockies.

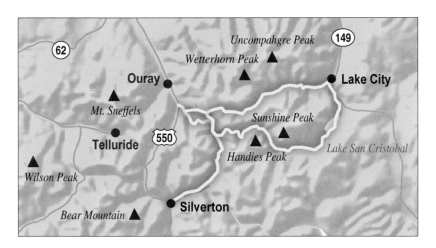

The entire loop is sixty-five miles round trip, but the portion to Ouray is only about twenty-five miles. I would suggest heading east on the loop and then connecting with US Hwy 550 just south of Ouray. The run from Ouray to Durango is on blacktop and covered in my chapter on the San Juan Parkway. Plan on a full day, as the going can be slow on the Alpine Loop, not only because of the road, but because this trip offers all that is best in the Rockies. Majestic views, ghost towns, and alpine lakes all surrounded by towering peaks.

Start in Lake City and look for the blue columbine sign that indicates the route. You won't miss it. Continue on this road for eighteen miles to Engineer Pass. Don't be fooled by the well groomed appearance of the road, because after about twelve miles the road degrades to a rockier surface until it becomes very jagged as you climb over the 12,800-foot pass. Along the way you will pass the **Old Capital Homestead** and the **Thoreau Cabin**. Continue over the pass and veer right toward Ouray (follow the blue columbine signs). As you climb down the narrow shelf road from Engineer Pass, the scenery is littered with remains from old mining operations. The last mile back through the tree line is a little rough and eventually reconnects with US Hwy 550 about three miles south of Ouray.

For more detailed information on the Alpine Loop contact the BLM San Juan Public Lands Center in Durango and ask for the "Alpine Explorer," a twenty-page guide to the area (970-247-4874, 15 Burnett Court, Durango, CO 81301).

Good luck and bring lots of film!

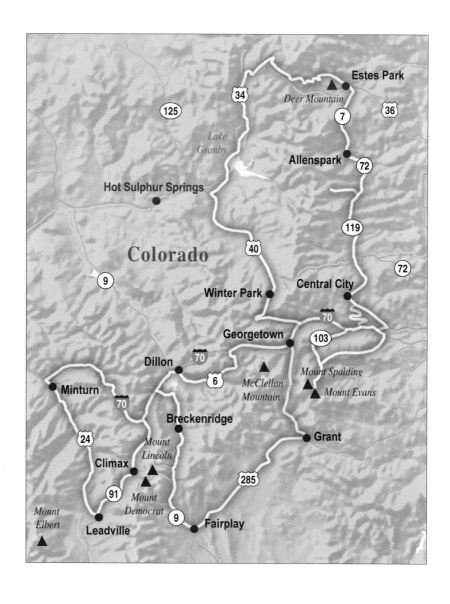

Georgetown

Located about forty miles west of Denver, **Georgetown,** (www.george towncolorado.com, 800-472-8230) just off I-70, makes an ideal base for exploring the Rockies of North Central Colorado. Three Rocky Mountain Journeys are easily accessible from this historic town. The Peak to Peak, Guanella Pass and the Top of the Rockies, and the Mt. Evans Scenic Byway are just a kick start and throttle turn from here.

Nestled at the base of Mt. McClellan, Georgetown was one of the few historic communities not ravaged by fire during the 1800s. As most mining towns were wood constructed, accidental fire caused the demise of many

The upscale New Prague in Georgetown, has a great reputation for its food.

old, historic towns along the Colorado "mineral belt." However, due to the well trained and brave "fire ladies" of Georgetown, this area is the only surviving wood constructed mining town that has not been ravaged by fire. As the honorable Senator from Colorado said in 1882, "The red devil fire has destroyed every other town in the state. Thanks to the bravery and training of our teams, our town never burned." The original 100-plus year old Victorian-style architecture gives Georgetown an atmosphere reminiscent of times past and contributes to its local charm.

Shops, boutiques, and restaurants now line the center of this once-booming mining town. Old homes meticulously restored surround the small downtown area at 6th and Rose Street. A good place to stay is the reasonably-priced **Georgetown Mountain Inn** (www.georgetownmountain inn.com, 800-884-3201) located on Rose Street. The rooms are large and it is conveniently located in the older part of town. If you prefer camping, head on up Guanella Pass Road (Rose Street) to the **Clear Lake Campground**

Georgetown is the only surviving wood-constructed mining town that has not been ravaged by fire.

Old Victorian homes like this one line the streets of Georgetown.

(www.fs.fed.us, 303-567-3000). The rugged beauty of this area will enthrall and make you wonder why everyone doesn't camp here (lack of showers, maybe?).

Georgetown offers several dining establishments from fast food to sit down eateries. My favorite is the **Red Ram Restaurant & Saloon** on 6th Street (303-569-2300). The interior is similar to an old mining town saloon and the meals are great. Another more upscale restaurant is the New Prague just past 6th Street on Rose. Or if you just want some ice cream, try "End of the Line" on 6th north of Rose Street. It's a small town, but you definitely won't go hungry.

This historic little mining community is like an Old Western town without the wild action of Gunsmoke or Wyatt Earp. A relatively mild town for the Old West, but a great place to relax after a long day of mountain twisties.

Trip 12 Top of the Rockies and Guanella Pass

Distance *206 miles (full day)*
Terrain *Eight 10,000 feet passes and five crossings of the Continental Divide all in one day. Old ghost towns and colossal peaks, from which fortunes were made and lost, line the way along the Top of the Rockies. For the adventurous, a gorgeous span of backroad takes you deep into the heart of the Rockies on the Guanella Pass. Elevation change 8,500 to 12,000 feet.*
Highlights *Narrow mountain passes, switchbacks, a beautiful piece of Interstate, and twenty-two miles of semi-paved and dirt backroad over the Guanella Pass (optional).*

This inverted figure eight loop takes you on two of Colorado's most scenic byways through the heart of the Rocky Mountains. The "Top of the Rockies" was designated a National Scenic Byway in 1999 and rarely drops below 9,000 feet. The old mining town of Leadville lies at the hub of the byway sitting at 10,430 feet between towering fourteeners. The other scenic byway at Guanella Pass links the two mining towns of Georgetown and Grant via an old wagon route built during the 1860s. Both routes combine into an unforgettable journey through pristine natural wonders and rustic, Victorian style mining camps.

Both signs say Guanella Pass thataway. Let's go!

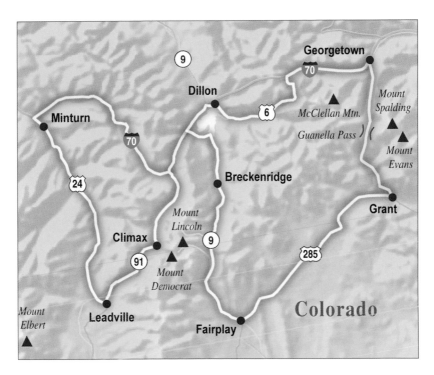

One question and one word of caution before we get started: Are you feeling adventurous today? The Guanella Pass Scenic and Historic Byway is twenty-two miles long with about ten miles of pavement or oiled backroad and another twelve miles of well-groomed dirt. The well groomed part can be subject to debate depending on recent weather patterns and road maintenance. The run from Georgetown to the pass summit is usually well maintained, but the backside to Grant can sometimes require navigating through various and sundry potholes. Ask about conditions in Georgetown, and if at all possible try to complete the entire twenty-two miles to Grant as it ties in well with the "Top of the Rockies" loop. If I did it on a Yamaha FZ-1, then no doubt you can do it as well! Otherwise, just head up as far as you can to get a taste for some beautiful backcountry solitude and then return to Georgetown. Connect up with I-70 west to Exit 195 on State Route 91 toward Leadville for a shortened version of this loop.

For you daring souls, start this journey in Georgetown and turn right on Rose Street. This will take you to **Guanella Pass Road** (route 381 on your map) and on to Grant. The road is well marked and paved as you climb toward Clear Lake. Several pullouts line this stretch providing panoramas of Georgetown and South Clear Creek Valley. Have your camera ready as you

THE ROUTE FROM GEORGETOWN

0   Start in Georgetown. Take Guanella Pass Road (State Route 381) toward Grant.

22   Arrive Grant. Turn right (west) on US Hwy 285.

50   Arrive Fairplay. Turn right (north) on State Route 9 toward Breckenridge.

71   Arrive Breckenridge. Continue on Route 9.

81   Arrive Frisco. Continue on to I-70.

82   Merge onto I-70 west.

87   Take Exit 195 onto State Route 91 to Copper Mountain/Leadville.

110   State Route 91 becomes US Hwy 24.

111   Arrive Leadville. Then head north on US Hwy 24 to Ski Copper/Camp Hale.

141   Arrive Minturn. Continue onto I-70.

143   Merge onto I-70 east.

177   Take Exit 205 State Route 9/US Hwy 6 to Dillon.

178   Arrive Dillon. Continue on US Hwy 6 toward Keystone and Loveland Pass.

194   Merge onto I-70 East just past the Ike Tunnel.

206   Take Exit 228 to Georgetown.

will be passing numerous lakes and meadows set between mountain peaks. Soon Clear Lake appears on the east side of the road and you will pass the Lower Cabin Creek Reservoir. The road hugs the creek as willows, meadows, and beaver ponds create a rich green blanket framed by snowcapped Gray's and Torrey's Peak in the background. The road snakes up the mountain slopes on to Guanella summit at 11,666 feet.

Descending the backside of the pass requires your full attention as the road may deteriorate. The natural solitude surrounding you, however, seems to rejuvenate and refresh as the road passes Duck Lake and follows another creek toward Grant. Just north of Geneva Park Campground, stop at Duck Lake Picnic Area to recharge and enjoy the beauty of this historic backway. The road soon descends (now Route 67) more quickly through a series of switchbacks to Falls Hill and then drops through Geneva Creek Canyon to the town of Grant. The trek may have been challenging, but you will not regret it!

At Grant, turn right on US Hwy 285 toward Como and Fairplay. The road feels heavenly after the washboards on Guanella Pass. Enjoy the smooth pavement as you accelerate to your normal cruising speed. But don't go too fast, because **Kenosha Pass** at 10,000 feet quickly lifts you up and gently sweeps you down in that "I want to do it again" kind of ride. And you *will* do it again on this ride, I promise. About six more times, so just hang on.

The town of **Como** soon approaches. Once housing over 500 people, Como suffered a fire in 1909 and then in 1937 the railroad shut down, leaving little behind. There are a few buildings and just off the road an old railway roundhouse. This roundhouse is now considered a "holy" spot for narrow gauge railroad worshipers and is being restored to its original state.

And then it starts again. Although not excessively high for this journey, about five miles outside of Como you begin another ascent over **Red Hill Pass** at 9,993 feet. Certainly not the most remarkable pass on this trip as the average elevation is around 8,500 feet, but nonetheless a definite kick as you ascend and then descend into the old mining town of Fairplay. A nice way to prepare as you approach the switchbacks at Hoosier Pass and the precipice at Loveland Pass.

Soon after Red Hill Pass, turn right on State Route 9 at Fairplay and head toward Alamo and Breckenridge. Although you appear to be in a valley, the elevation is around 9,000 feet! The towering peaks help reinforce the "

Most of the twenty-four miles to Grant is unpaved.

*It's a good idea to
check weather
conditions
beforehand on
Guanalla Pass,
even in the
summer.*

valley" illusion. Fairplay and Alamo are both old mining towns and still just barely alive. Be sure and drop by the grave of Prunes, the Burro, next to the Hand Hotel in Fairplay. Apparently, this burro worked sixty-two years in the mines and his owner Rupert Sherwood requested they be buried together at this grave site. Like I said, you learn all sorts of interesting tidbits on these motorcycle journeys.

Continue on Route 9 past Alma and you are in store for another treat. Mounts Lincoln, Democrat, and Bross loom ahead as you ascend **Hoosier Pass** toward Breckenridge. The summit at 11,542 feet lies atop the Continental Divide (again) and is about eleven miles from the ski resort. The rolling motion up the pass is fun and can be done at a relatively quick pace. Descending toward Breckenridge is another story. Three miles of switchbacks indulge your every fantasy as creeks run alongside the road with views of mountains in every direction. Scrape the pegs and then continue toward Blue River. As you approach Breckenridge, a small lake with cabins is nestled to the right. If your timing is right (mid-July), the summer flora will add colorful accents to this picture postcard scene. Resist the temptation to race by; slow it down a notch and enjoy the kaleidoscope of colors flowing by.

The road weaves gently through the countryside and follows the Blue River just south of town. This area was once heavily mined in the 1800s and into the 1900s. **Breckenridge** boasted a population of 2,000 by 1882 and secured the depot for the Denver, South Park and Pacific Railroad. However, by 1945 the population had dwindled to 242 and many historic buildings were demolished. And then "white gold" was discovered in them thar hills! Starting in the 1960s, the Breckenridge Ski Resort was opened and another boomtown was born. The town now boasts a population in excess of 30,000 and vacationers flock to this summer and winter getaway.

Situated at the base of two thirteeners and two twelvers, Breckenridge is indeed picturesque, but also touristy. If you like to people watch and hang out at some eclectic restaurants, this is a convenient place to grab a bite before moving on. For more info visit one of their numerous websites such as www.breckenridge.snow.com or call 800-789-SNOW. Personally, I prefer the smaller town of **Frisco** about ten miles north of Breckenridge because all the restaurants are right on Main Street and the town seems to fit more with the biker aura. If you stop in Frisco, try the **Moose Jaw Restaurant** for some reasonably priced burgers and then head over to the **Butterhorn Bakery** for some dessert. Frisco is about one mile from I-70 and makes for a nice break before starting the official "Top of the Rockies" byway.

After lunch, merge onto I-70 heading west. This short stretch of double-wide is gorgeous. The 12,000-foot peaks surrounding the super slab turn the tankers into Tonka Toys and motorcyclists into puny little ants. At Exit 195 turn south on State Route 91 to Copper Mountain and Leadville. For those of you who decided not to take the Guanella Pass route this is where our paths meet (a good meeting place is in Frisco at the Moose Jaw). Now our third crossing of the Continental Divide lies just ahead. As the road winds its way past Copper Mountain Ski Resort dramatic views open up

Although this part of Guanella Pass is paved, the road deteriorates rapidly.

approaching **Fremont Pass**. The scenery unfolds just like that postcard you bought in Denver. If you want to actually touch it and get some dirt on your soles rather then just scuffing your toes, stop at the Mayflower Gulch trailhead about five to six miles from Copper Mountain. An easy two-mile hike leads to the Old Boston Mine with various mining ruins strewn along the way. Good way to work off that high cholesterol burger you ate in Frisco!

Continue up Route 9 past Clinton Reservoir toward the pass. The road carves its way through the granite and weaves uphill to the summit at 11,318 feet. And then nature's beauty shows a smear the size of Rhode Island at the massive mining facility of **Climax**. Probably on a snowy day the scar won't look so bad all covered up, but during the summer it is quite

Don't motorcyclists always travel at their own risk? This sign was posted just before Guanella Pass.

visible. Stop for a quick look, discuss the impact of man's handiwork on nature and then continue on to Leadville. The minimal descent takes you into a valley high in the Rockies. Leadville is the highest incorporated town in North America at 10,400 feet and is surrounded by a host of thirteeners and fourteeners. Mt. Elbert at 14,433 feet is the highest in Colorado.

Looking down at **Leadville** (www.leadville.com, 800-933-3901), the contrasts are markedly visible. The rugged peaks and scenery are blemished with open sores from the mining boom and bust cycles over the last 100 years. The town was home to various mining magnates such as "the invincible" Molly Brown, the Guggenheims, and Horace Tabor. Leadville boasts numerous historic buildings from the 19th century now filled with restaurants and boutiques. The majority of these buildings are located on Harrison Avenue, the city's main street.

So, park your bike by the Silver Dollar Saloon on Harrison Avenue and West 4th Street, grab a drink, hear some stories from the bartender, get some green chile at the "Golden Burro," and then take a walk down Harrison Avenue and the "miner's" version of memory lane. Leadville is a National Historic Landmark District and you could easily spend the whole afternoon visiting the **Tabor Opera House**, the **Annunciation Church**, various museums and/or just window shopping.

After a short walk, continue north on US Hwy 24 toward **Camp Hale**. Camp Hale was the training site for the 10th Mountain Division during World War II. The camp was finished in 1942 and housed as many as 14,000 troops by 1943. The troops trained in the nearby mountains under harsh winter conditions and many eventually saw action in the Apennine Mountains of Italy. A memorial to our WW II veterans is located at the entrance of Ski Copper and well worth a stop to pay our respects to those who lost their lives in combat.

Now, I want you to guess what is just up the road. You got it! Another pass over the Continental Divide. **Tennessee Pass** (10,424 feet) is located at the headwaters of the Eagle and Arkansas Rivers. Get that bottle of water ready for your half and half routine or just continue on over and enjoy the grand vistas as you wind up and over the divide. About ten miles ahead the old mining towns of Red Cliff, Gilman, and Minturn come quickly into view. **Gilman** was active through the 1950s, but was closed by the EPA for pollutants from its zinc and lead operations. There are NO TRESPASSING signs posted around the area, and beware, they apparently are well enforced. **Minturn** is a sleepy little town that has survived the closing of the Gilman mine and now caters to tourists visiting the local ski resorts at Vail and Beaver Creek (and summer motorcyclists riding the Top of the Rockies).

Even the interstates in Colorado are spectacular.

Minturn sits on the west bank of the Eagle River and the town is lined with shops and restaurants. From what I understand, it's also a great place to do some fishin'.

US Hwy 24 connects with I-70 about one mile north of town. Merge onto the Interstate and head east on some of the most gorgeous pieces of super slab in the world. I-70 starts by running adjacent to the Vail Ski Resort and then climbs over the 10,666-foot Vail Pass. This engineering marvel weaves like an overweight, drunken sailor on top of the Rockies. The billowing white clouds, blue sky, green timbered slopes, and snowcapped peaks make this a rare and unforgettable golden nugget of Interstate.

One slight detour on this return trip takes you over yet another pass across the Continental Divide with views looking down onto I-70. Don't miss this final pass! Instead of taking the Ike Tunnel on I-70, exit to US Hwy 6/State Route 9 Exit 205 to Dillon and then head east on State Route 6 over the 11,990 foot **Loveland Pass** (toward Keystone). This road is a kick and reconnects with I-70 as you descend down the pass. The switchbacks combined with the "Top of the Rockies" vantage point at almost 12,000 feet make this one a doosey. This is well worth the effort as the road takes you up and over with nerve-wracking views looking down on I-70. Hang on!

Heading east once more on I-70, the wide pavement again cuts through more pristine Rocky Mountain Scenery. I don't care much for Interstates, but this portion to Georgetown is just as panoramic and makes for an easy, yet scenic ride home. And by the way congratulations! Today you have taken a dirt backroad, driven a full day for the most part above 9,000 feet, conquered eight passes all over 10,000 feet (Red Hill was close enough!) and crossed the Continental Divide five times. No wonder they call this the "Top of the Rockies!"

Trip 13   Rocky Mountain High

Distance   *204 miles (full day)*
Terrain   *Travel through old mining camps on the Peak to Peak Scenic Byway and then ascend to 12,000 feet on the highest continuously paved road in North America. Return through Old West ranchlands and one final pass at 11,000 feet. Elevation change 5,500 to 12,000 feet.*
Roads   *Switchbacks, hairpins, S-curves, and ridgeline roads. If you want, take the dirt "Oh My God" road to Central City for even more riding pleasure. Rocky Mountain National Park, Grand Lake, and the Berthoud Pass.*

"He climbed cathedral mountains, he saw silver clouds below. He saw everything as far as you can see" (from the song "Rocky Mountain High" by John Denver). I think John Denver wrote the words to this song while riding a motorcycle on the Trail Ridge Road through Rocky Mountain National Park. Who knows, you may even get inspired and write your own song as you embark on a journey along the highest continuously paved road in North America. All directions lead to soaring peaks and July snowdrifts.

A combination of blue sky, billowing clouds, green forests and black asphalt is a typical view heading to Rocky Mountain National Park.

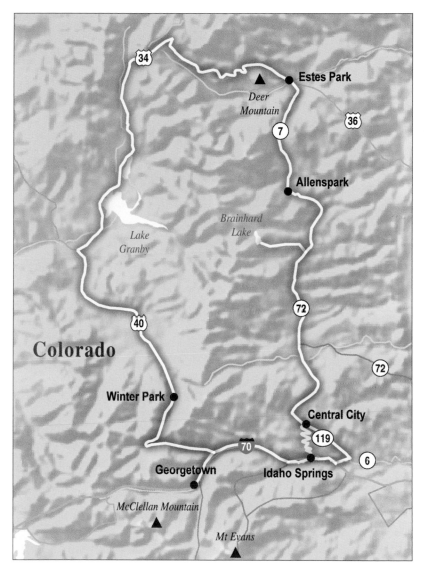

Mile-high valleys resplendent with arrowheads and columbine ultimately give way to barren, half-frozen tundra 12,000 feet about sea level. Don't be surprised to see three-foot-high snow banks as you peel around that mountain curve in the middle of July, and don't be surprised if you start humming a few bars from John Denver's "Rocky Mountain High" (thank goodness no one can hear you!).

Colorado is truly the state closest to heaven as you drive this loop up the

THE ROUTE FROM GEORGETOWN

0   Start in Georgetown, Colorado

16   Turn on exit 244 to US Hwy 6 to Blackhawk/Central City (use exit 240 for the "Oh My God Road")

19   Turn left on State Route 119

46   Head north on State Route 72, the Peak to Peak Hwy

58   Turn left on Brainhard Lake Road

63   Arrive Brainhard Lake, turn around

68   Reconnect with Route 72

78   Turn left on State Route 7

93   Arrive Estes Park, turn left on Marys Lake Road to connect with US Hwy 36

96   Turn left at stoplight onto US Hwy 36

140   Arrive Grand Lake Lodge, continue on Hwy 34

155   Turn left on US Hwy 40

201   Arrive I-70, head west

204   Take exit 228 to Georgetown

Peak to Peak Scenic Byway, through Rocky Mountain National Park on the Trail Ridge Road, and then south past Grand Lake and Granby. The final leg of this journey winds up and down Berthoud Pass to I-70 and then back home to Georgetown. Be prepared on this trip! I have seen motorcyclists start in T-shirts and end up on the side of the road caught in furious rainstorms. The weather can be very unpredictable. Count on afternoon showers and beware of fierce winds, especially on Trail Ridge Road.

This trip starts from Georgetown bright and early on a typical cool, crisp summer morning. Head east on I-70. At exit 240 you need to make a decision, so I hope you had that cup of coffee and are wide awake! You can either take the "**Oh My God**" road (groomed dirt with washboards) from Idaho Springs to Central City or continue on to exit 244 and US Hwy 6 and Blackhawk/Central City. Since I usually ride a GS, I prefer exit 240 and definitely recommend it if you are on the right bike. This dirt road was once the major thoroughfare between Central City and Idaho Springs, transporting both miners and their supplies in 1865. However, once the railroad was completed in the late 1860s, traffic dwindled, leaving the road for tourists to enjoy. The road is about nine miles long and the views are heavenly (hence the name!). Head west through town and look for signs to Virginia Canyon Road (State Route 279). Follow this about one mile north of town and then turn right on a dirt road directing you to Central City. This is the "Oh My God" road. Eventually you will reconnect with State Route 119 at Blackhawk.

For those of you interested in "lady luck," **Central City** (www.central citycolorado.com) and **Blackhawk** (www.blackhawkcolorado.com), once former mining towns, are now full of high-tech gambling casinos. Personally, I speed right on by. What was once the "richest square mile" on earth now caters to a different type of gold miner—the gambler. You can almost hear that great big sucking sound as you drive through town!

Route 119 continues to climb through a magnificent gorge opening into the **Roosevelt National Forest** (www.fsfed.us/r2/arnf/index.shtml, 970-498-1100). The byway flows over hills and ridges, weaving its way up toward aspen, fir, and spruce. The scenery is rugged yet lush, with several

These stunted trees in the Rock Mountain National Park are misshapen primarily because of howling winds and a short growing season due to very high altitudes.

A converted caboose and train car make for a nice touch at this restaurant while driving toward Estes Park.

slopes marred with tailings from old mining camps. Man's scars are slowly being overwhelmed (again) by the inevitable cycle of nature.

At Nederland, Route 119 veers right through the **Golden Gate Canyon State Park** (parks.state.co.us/default.asp, 303-582-3707). Maintain a northerly course onto State Route 72 to Ward. The pavement pounces and weaves lulling you forward more and more quickly. The rhythm and scenery are mesmerizing along this stretch. Just past Ward turn left on Brainard Lake Road. This short detour takes you to two picture postcard lakes set high in the Rockies. After about three to five miles you will see Red Rock Lake and then Brainard Lake. Floating amidst the Indian Peak Wilderness Area, the barren peaks reflect off these looking-glass lakes. There are picnic areas and tables to enjoy that Snickers bar (or beef jerky) you brought along or take a short hike to the Trailhead for even more views.

Back on Route 72, the road continues its joyous movements as you drop into Peaceful Valley. Don't miss the church set up on the mountain crag to your right—bet that took a while to build. As you approach Raymond, a granite slot-like canyon surrounds you, then opens up on State Route 7 heading west. Continue on Route 7 toward Allenspark and after about three miles look for the Mt. Meeker Pullout. This scenic overlook provides great views north and west to Rocky Mountain National Park. Continue north and about three to four miles outside of Allenspark you can see Long's Peak (elevation 14,255 feet) to the west.

Soon you will enter **Estes Park** (www.estespark.com, 800-44-ESTES), the gateway to Rocky Mountain National Park. Turn left on Marys Lake Road toward the Highway 36 intersection about three miles ahead. The town is touristy, but is a convenient spot to relax before tackling Trail Ridge Road. If you want some nourishment, there are numerous eating establishments from fast food to sit down steak restaurants. Usually, I just grab a sandwich at the **Country Market Deli** on the corner of Marys Road and Hwy 36; check out the tourists, chat with a few fellow motorcyclists, be sure the rain gear is handy, and get set to go.

You are now ready to begin a trek along one of the most phenomenal roads ever built in the U.S., for that matter in the world. Started in 1929, the next forty-four miles to Grand Lake was finally completed in 1938 and climbs to over 12,000 feet, eleven miles of which hover precariously above tree line at over 11,000 feet above sea level. No need to drive to Alaska. The permafrost is alive and well in Colorado. As mentioned earlier, be prepared on this road. Winds, rainstorms, hail, and summer snow flurries are the norm at these altitudes. And don't forget the shades and sunscreen—the ultraviolet rays are a killer!

Begin by taking US Hwy 36 from Estes Park to the **Rocky Mountain National Park** visitors' center (www.nps.gov/romo, 970-586-1333). Get acquainted with the history, geology, and nature surrounding this park. With more than twenty peaks over 12,000 feet, 150 lakes, and hundreds of

With more than twenty peaks over 12,000 feet, 150 lakes, and hundreds of miles of trails, you could easily spend days roaming the Rocky Mountain National Park wilderness.

miles of trails, you could easily spend days roaming this vast wilderness. This brief motorcycle trip barely scratches the surface and really doesn't do justice to this great and historic park.

As your anticipation mounts, be patient with summer traffic (this is a popular destination) and plan to stop frequently and even take a hike along the road. This is a once in a lifetime ride that should be savored patiently. You can make up time when you fly down the western edge of this loop.

Upon leaving the visitors' center, Hwy 36 intersects US Hwy 34 after about five miles. The road soon climbs Deer Mountain and meets with Hwy 34 at the Deer Ridge Junction. This is the official start of the historic Trail Ridge Road. The road twists up the mountain slope like a snake. At Many Parks Curve Observation Point, the town of Estes Park and rolling meadows flanked by craggy mountains fill the horizon. Soon you will pass the two-mile elevation sign posted alongside Hwy 34 and Rainbow Curve. The views continue to take your breath away—and that may be a problem at this altitude.

Continue on Hwy 34 toward Forest Canyon Overlook and more noticeable changes begin to unfold in the scenery and vegetation. Aspen and Ponderosa are left behind and the fir and spruce evolve into mutant tree aliens. Due to the fierce winds, trees struggling for life adapt to the short summer season and grow into contorted, misshapen phantoms. Stop at the overlook to fully appreciate what nature has created at this high altitude. View the valley below and witness the power of slow-moving glaciers as they carved their way between the mountain slopes.

A definite stop is the overlook at Rock Cut. Rest a minute to catch your breath (remember, the elevation is about 12,000 feet) and walk the half mile Tundra Nature Trail. The permafrosted tundra chills you to the bone. You feel transplanted to the Canadian Arctic. The wind can be nasty, so grab hold of that baseball cap and don't lose those $200 sunglasses! Climb the boulders at the end of the trail for unimpeded views of the park.

Back on your bike, the road continues to balance itself on the mountain ridge as it weaves toward the summit at 12,180 feet. Continue on to the Alpine Visitor Center perched high aloft Trail Ridge Road and usually surrounded by snowdrifts (even in the summer). After a brief stop, Trail Ridge descends to Medicine Bow Curve overlooking the Cache La Poudre River. Soon the descent returns you to vegetated civilization and crosses over Milner Pass atop the continental divide. You know the routine: grab your water and pour half into the Mississippi and half into the Colorado!

About two miles farther at Fairview Curve, the road resurrects itself into a series of excellent switchbacks descending quickly to the marshy floor of the Kawuneeche Valley. Your mind refocuses on the blacktop as your pegs scrape the asphalt. Watch for gravel and loose dirt on those turns!

The road toward Grand Lake is lined with thick, green spruce and fir. It's like driving your bike in a green corridor or hallway, except this one makes wide, sweeping turns. Hang a left at the **Grand Lake Lodge** (www.grandlakelodge.com, 970-627-3967) and bask in stately, old-time elegance from times past. This resort was once (and still is) the summer getaway for the well to do from Denver. The Inn is timbered and nestled on a hill overlooking Grand Lake, Colorado's largest natural lake. Destroyed by fire in 1973, the lodge was painstakingly restored over seven years by the James Family and is now a National Historic Landmark. Grab a drink and sit on the patio (if you can find a spot), and let the ambience and beauty of this area sink in. My last visit not only treated me to a Grand View, but also a bride and groom taking their vows on the front lawn. I would love to see those wedding pictures!

The views are truly expansive at Rocky Mountain National Park.

The next part of this journey will race by as you leave Grand Lake and head toward Granby. The western edge of Rocky Mountain National Park is less traveled and the roads run more gently beside the towering peaks on your left. Put your bike in gear and refine those motorcycling skills as you drive by Lake Granby and enter the **Arapaho National Recreation Area**. US Hwy 34 joins US Hwy 40 just north of the town of Granby. Turn left (south) and follow the Fraser River toward Tabernash.

The Fraser River Valley is open and serene with grasslands dominating the landscape. Snowy peaks lined atop the Continental Divide border the ranchlands. You feel transplanted into an old "Bonanza" film clip. Don't be surprised if one of the Cartwrights come riding up beside you (probably on a Harley)! An interesting bit of trivia about this area is that during World War II the town of Fraser housed a German POW camp. These prisoners were captured at the battle of Anzio in Italy and were transplanted to the main Colorado Camp in Greeley. During the wartime years, these POWs provided labor for lumber production. They earned 75 cents a day, which they could spend in the PX. Apparently, letters received after the war from

It's like clockwork! Right around 2–3 pm the clouds turn grey and that pitter patter turns into a deluge!

One of these days I'm going to spoil myself and stay at the Grand Lake Lodge.

ex-POWs spoke favorably of life in Colorado and helped change their misconceptions about the U.S.

Continuing south on Hwy 40, the mountains tighten their grip around the Fraser River and you enter the resort town of **Winter Park** (www.winter-info.com, 970-726-4118). The town is a popular ski destination, located at the base of Berthoud Pass, but originally was settled by ranchers and loggers. Eventually the railroad came to town and built one of the longest railroad tunnels in the world. Moffat Tunnel runs for six miles under the continental divide on its way to Salt lake City. You can still see the tunnel from Winter Park.

This journey ends with one last adventure over the continental divide via **Berthoud Pass**. The wide, smooth, black tar begins its twisting motion from Winter Park and rises to a summit of 11,307 feet. Stop for more views if you like, but at this point you can smell home just around the corner and may just want to continue down the winding slope for more marvelous motorcycling. The road was recently widened and repaved a few years ago but the winters are harsh so don't be surprised if some lanes are closed for construction. Regardless, existing passing lanes are well-marked, providing a boot-scraping good time. Enjoy this final rollercoaster ride and then re-connect with I-70 back home to Georgetown.

Trip 14   Mt. Evans Scenic Byway

Distance   *95 miles (half a day)*

Terrain   *Visit the highest paved parking lot in America at 14,100 feet then climb to the summit of Mt. Evans at 14,264 feet. Let your motorcycle do the work as you conquer one of Colorado's mighty "fourteeners." Elevation change 8,000 to 14,000 feet.*

Highlights   *Mountain twisties and high-altitude switchbacks. Mt. Evans Scenic Byway*

Ride high in the Rockies and enjoy some challenging switchbacks.

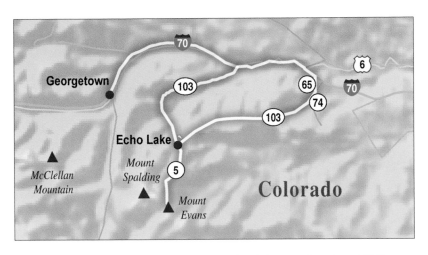

Your butt a little tired? Been driving too hard the past few days? Well, stop your whining and sleep in this morning! Enjoy a leisurely breakfast and then plan on a late lunch at Echo Lake Lodge on your return from the highest paved summit in America. Today's 100-miler gushes through the gateway of the Rockies on an ascent of **Mt. Evans** and doesn't stop until you reach the summit parking lot at 14,130 feet. Walk another quarter mile from the pavement up the trail and you have just conquered one of Colorado's famous "Fourteeners." Not bad considering you had a late start!

In 1888, Pike's Peak toll road was opened endearing many tourists to the beauty and majesty of the Colorado Rockies. There was one problem though: Pikes Peak was near Colorado Springs and Denver wanted its share of tourists too. So in 1917, Denver's Mayor Speer procured state funds to build a road to compete with Pikes Peak. Mt. Evans Scenic Byway was completed in 1927 and takes you to the only known permafrost south of the Arctic Circle. The road is only open from Memorial Day through Labor Day and rides like a rollercoaster through Colorado's Front Range.

Since this ride is relatively close to Denver, the byway can be busy, particularly on weekends and holidays. Mid-week passage makes all the difference in the world. One Tuesday in July I enjoyed this run with few intervening vehicles. Divine. Just be sure the raingear is handy as the weather is extremely unpredictable and the road may close from Summit Lake to the Peak even in the summer. Call in advance or check at **Echo Lake Lodge** for conditions (www.echolakelodge.com, 303-567-2138).

Start by taking I-70 east for twelve miles to the State Route 103 Exit 240 toward Echo Lake and Mt. Evans. State Route 103 is accessible all year and runs gently through the frontal range as it gradually ascends to the lake at

THE ROUTE FROM GEORGETOWN

0   Start in Georgetown. Merge onto I-70
12   Take exit 240 onto State Route 103 toward Mt. Evans
25   Arrive Echo Lake, continue on Route 5 (Mt. Evans Road)
39   Arrive Mt. Evans Summit, climb to top, turn around on Route 5
53   Turn right on State Route 103 (Squaw Pass Road)
70   Turn left on Evergreen Pkwy (Route 74)
71   Turn left on State Route 65
74   Turn left on US Hwy 40 to I-70
75   Head west on I-70
94   Take exit 228 to Georgetown
95   Arrive Georgetown

10,600 feet. The scenery is genteel and peaceful as the road cuts through the green and fertile landscape at the base of Mt. Evans.

Echo Lake is located at the junctions of Route 103 and Mt. Evans Road about thirteen miles from I-70. Stop for a minute and admire the mirrored reflection of the mountains off the lake. A trail circles the lake and makes for an easy three-quarter-mile walk. Drop by the lodge for some homemade pie or come back for lunch on your way back down from the summit.

Mt. Evans Road is a fee road and costs $3 for motorcycles. From here, it is around another fourteen miles to the summit. This section of road will eventually take you past mountain lakes, a variety of vegetation, and, if you are lucky, some ptarmigan (new word!), the bighorn sheep, and white mountain goat.

As you begin ascending Mt. Evans, the road invites you to quickly accelerate (especially on weekdays), but resist the temptation (do it on the way down) and enjoy the scenery as it transitions from sub alpine to alpine to arctic. There are several pullouts along the way and a good first stop is the **Mount Goliath Natural Area** between Echo and Lincoln Lakes. Located at timberline, the spruce become scarce and are replaced with groves of bristlecone pines, sometimes called "flag trees," as their limbs grow away from the prevailing winds. A twenty- to thirty-minute interpretive walk provides some general information as well as some nice views of the surrounding area.

Continuing on Mt. Evans Road you will soon see Lincoln Lake 800 feet below the road on the right. The road is well above timberline at this point and on a clear day mountain peaks stretch endlessly on the western horizon. While carving your bike through the barren rock on wide, sweeping S turns, don't slip off the mountain slope, and keep an eye out for marmots as they have been known to frolic by the side of the road.

About nine miles from Echo Lake and five miles from the peak, you will come to the **Summit Lake** turnoff. Take a minute and enjoy this stereotypical alpine lake set between Mt. Evans and Mt. Spalding. The only known area of permafrost south of the arctic is located just east of the Lake at Summit Lake Flats. There is also a quarter-mile hike to the Chicago Basin overlook for another great view.

Some of the hills look like they are covered with dark green velvet.

The final miles to the peak start out climbing a ridge then turn into a quick set of switchbacks just before reaching the summit. On weekdays parking is usually not a problem. However, parking alongside the road at the entrance is allowed if the parking lot is full. Looking south to Pikes Peak, north to the Rocky Mountain National Park, west to Torrey's Peak, and east to Denver, the panorama of Colorado unfolds like a National Geographic photo album. Take the quarter-mile hike to the "official" summit and congratulate yourself on conquering a mighty "fourteener!" thanks to you and your motorcycle.

Now that you are familiar with the terrain, quicken the pace and drag your pegs as you head back to Echo Lake. Keep an eye out for wildlife as well as that RV entering your lane from the various pullouts. At Echo Lake, grab some lunch or pie to recharge and then turn right on State Route 103 toward Bergen Park. This is another fireball of a road, taking you up and over

The higher you climb, the better the views.

Wonder how much I could buy that house for. Note the 360-degree views even without the windows!

Squaw Pass at 9,807 feet past Blue Valley and down to Bergen Park, about twenty miles west of Denver about sixteen miles east of Echo Lake.

In Bergen Park, connect with US Hwy 40 and then merge with I-70 west to Georgetown. Take exit 228 about nineteen miles down the superslab and you are back in familiar territory. This quick trip up Colorado's one and only paved fourteener is a treat to be savored—and you're still back in time for your afternoon nap.

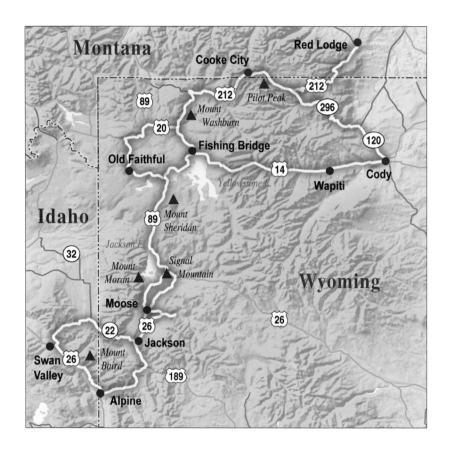

Jackson

Home to the rich and famous. Yes, I know that is what everyone says about Jackson Hole, Wyoming. Elegant boutiques display dazzling (and expensive) merchandise and avant-garde restaurants boast entrees that cost more than my rear tire! My advice, unless you want to hobnob with the local "royalty," is to stay clear of establishments with names you can't pronounce and chow down at places like "Bubba's Bar-B-Que" for lunch. Jackson may be a little snobbish, but it is also a lot of fun for the mud-splattered motorcyclist.

Wagon Wheel Village is the place to stay while exploring the Tetons and Yellowstone National Park.

Although Native Americans have long inhabited this area of Wyoming, one of the first white men to explore Jackson Hole was John Colter around 1807. Returning from the Lewis and Clark Expedition, Colter wanted to set up a fur trapping company to profit from the lucrative trading of beaver pelts. Several famous mountain men such as Jedediah Smith trapped successfully in Jackson Hole for many years. It was the French Canadian trappers who ultimately named the peaks "Les Trois Tetons" or the three breasts (why am I not surprised the French came up with that?). However, when silk replaced beaver pelt as the material of choice for hats, ranching took over and made the area around Jackson a more permanent settlement. In 1929, the Grand Teton National Park was dedicated and since then tourism has become the focal point of this community.

Jackson's streets are lined with restaurants, shops, bars, and ice cream parlors. Walking on the wooden sidewalks, window shopping, or just sitting on a park bench in the town square people-watching is a great way to spend an evening. You'll see the "elite" dressed to the hilt, families with strollers, and freckle-faced teenagers, cowboys, and maybe a celebrity or two!

There are numerous places to stay in and around Jackson. The city's official website at www.jacksonholechamber.com (307-733-3316) is a good

The entrance to Jackson's downtown park is a real marvel. Wonder how many antlers this took to make?

I was a frequent visitor to Bubba's while staying in Jackson, Wyoming.

starting point to begin your search for lodging and eating establishments. Personally, I prefer to stay in town within walking distance to town square. A convenient spot located close to downtown is the **Wagon Wheel Village** (www.wagonwheelvillage.com, 800-323-9279) about one quarter mile from historic Jackson located at 435 N. Cache. The cabins are clean and reasonably priced. There is a campsite on the premises but only 8 sites are available for tents, the rest are for RVs. It's first come, first served, so get there early if you want a campsite. If you are really into camping, though, sites are plentiful in **Grand Teton National Park** (www.nps.gov/grte.pphtml/camping.html, phone numbers listed for each campground) or as mentioned in the chapter "Teton Rendezvous" take the backroad to Spalding Bay for your own personal campsite and views of the Grand Tetons.

A quick note on eating in Jackson: You can find the whole gamut from fast food to elegant dining. I spend most of my time eating breakfast, lunch, and dinner at **Bubba's Bar-B-Que** at 515 W. Broadway 307-733-2288. Just remember the waiting list is not there to irritate you—it means this is the restaurant of choice for locals and frugal motorcyclists. The food is great and the portions are large. What more could you ask for!

Trip 15 Teton Rendezvous

Distance *206 miles (full day)*
Terrain *Visit the Grand Tetons and explore the park on some less-frequented backroads. Head south on another loop over the Teton Pass into Idaho before returning to Jackson via the Snake River and Palisades Reservoir. Elevation change 5,000 to 8,500 feet.*
Highlights *Gentle S-curves, river crossings, and a couple of mountain passes. A few short gravel backways thrown in to get you away from the crowds.*

There are certain images that don't fade with time. Gazing at the Grand Tetons from Oxbow Bend as the sun slipped below the western horizon a few years ago was one of those images. A late winter storm had just left a dusting of snow on the towering Tetons, adding a fresh white blanket to their surface. As dusk fell, the light played games with my eyes, casting shadowy figures within mountain crevices and bouncing ultraviolet rays off jagged slopes. In the foreground, the lush thicket at Oxbow Bend had more

Here's a peek into Teton National Park from the North Entrance.

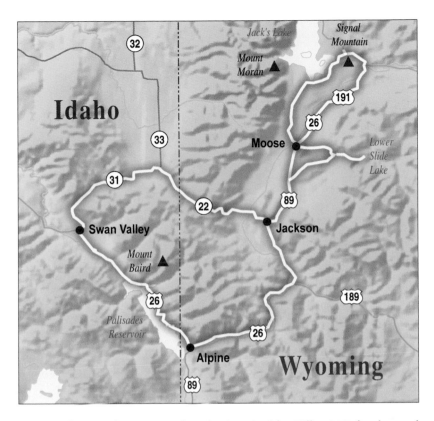

shades of green than I ever thought imaginable. Billowing clouds raced across the blue, azure sky framing a motion of colors I will never forget.

There are not enough superlatives to describe the rustic, natural beauty of the **Grand Teton National Park** (www.nps.gov/grte, 307-739-3300). And what better way to see it than on a motorcycle. The park is located just south of Yellowstone on the triple combo 26-89-191 roadway. In its center, eight peaks over 12,000 feet rise suddenly over a glacial moraine. The ragged, sharp edges of this mountain range grab your attention immediately. This is not like Colorado where endless rows of thirteeners and fourteeners line the horizon. Rather, a jagged, isolated strip similar in appearance to the Italian Dolomites cuts through the landscape with such an immense presence you can't take your eyes off it. The alpine lakes, meandering rivers, and abundant wildlife make this one of the most beautiful parks in our National Park System.

This journey can be broken into two separate and distinct loops if you like. The first loop takes you from Jackson through the south end of the park at Moose Junction, north on Route 26-89-191, and then moves in a

THE ROUTE FROM JACKSON

0   Head north on the triple combo US Hwy 26-89-191

5   Turn right on Gros Ventre Road to Kelly

10   Arrive Kelly, turn left

11   Turn right on Bridger-Teton National Forest Access Road to Lower Slide Lake

16   Arrive Lake, turn around

21   Turn right at junction

24   Turn left on Antelope Flats Road

28   Reconnect with 26-89-191, turn right (north)

45   Turn left into the Moran Entrance Station

50   Turn right on US Hwy 89-191-287 to Jackson Lake Lodge

51   Arrive Lodge, turn around

56   Turn left on Signal Mountain Road

61   Arrive summit, turn around

66   Turn left on Teton Park Road

74   Turn right on Jenny Lake Drive

78   Reconnect with Teton Park Road, head south

86   Turn right on Hwy 26-89-191

98   Arrive Jackson

99   Turn right on State Route 22

117   State Route 22 becomes State Route 33

122   Turn left onto State Route 31

143   Arrive Swan Valley, Route 31 connects with US Hwy 26

171   Arrive Alpine, Wyoming. Turn left onto US Hwy 26-89

206   Arrive Jackson

counterclockwise motion down Teton Park Road past Jenny Lake back to Jackson. This loop is about 100 miles in length and can take all day if you want to stop at all the turnouts, have lunch at the fabulous Lodge, enjoy a boat ride on the lake, and hike around a bit.

Personally, I prefer about a half day riding the "park loop" and then heading west from Jackson over Teton Pass into Idaho for phase 2 of the "Teton Rendezvous." This run takes you to the southeastern edge of the Tetons and then loops farther south to Swan Valley past Palisades Reservoir and the

Snake River back to Jackson. Open roads and fewer tourists are a perfect balance to your morning encounter with the busier National Park.

Begin your journey early in the morning and head north on the 26-89-191 combo through the **National Elk Refuge** (www.national elkrefuge.fws.gov). Some antlered beasts may still be grazing in the wee morning hours. Established in 1912, this 25,000 acre wildlife refuge was created for the sole purpose of preserving the Jackson elk herd. In the 1800s there were as many as 25,000 elk in the valley, but due to the influx of farms and ranches, livestock competing for the scarce winter fodder diminished the elk population substantially. As a result this refuge was created. An eight-foot-high fence prevents the elk from moving into town or private land.

This road skirts the western edge of the refuge and you can occasionally see moose and their calves grazing in the distance. About three miles outside town a pullout is available with informational placards. Take a moment and read the history and purpose of this meadowed refuge.

Just two miles north of the National Elk Refuge pullout, head east at the Gros Ventre Junction. This twenty-five-mile side trip is not well-traveled and gives you an opportunity to see part of the park overlooked by many

A magnificent panorama awaits you at Jackson Lake Lodge.

tourists. Head east toward the town of Kelly and then one mile north of town turn right to Lower Slide Lake on the Bridger-Teton National Forest Access Road. About eighty years ago a layer of sandstone broke off from Sheep Mountain damming the Gros Ventre River creating the lake. The road is narrow and winds gently through groves of quaking aspen and fir for about five miles. This is a neat little motorcycle ride just minutes from the main park thoroughfare.

Enjoy the ride and the view, then turn around and instead of going back to Kelly, turn right at the junction and then left on Antelope Flats Road back to the 26-89-191. Turn right and you are back on the main road again. Drift slowly up the black asphalt, keeping an eye on the Grand Tetons hovering on the western horizon. There are numerous overlooks, but I prefer the Teton point, Snake River, and Oxbow Bend pullouts. Each provides an informational outline unique to that area. Ansel Adams took his famous photo of the Tetons from the Snake River Overlook. At this point the river makes a nice bend adding a unique touch to your photograph.

Another neat stop is the **Cunningham Cabin Historic Site** north of the Snake River Overlook on an unpaved road heading west. You can see the remains of an early pioneer's sod-roofed homestead in which they struggled to

Take your pick. You can get around on your own or take the public transportation. I choose to ride.

From the top of Signal Mountain you can see from the Tetons all the way to Yellowstone.

survive from 1890 to 1928. The Cunningham's finally gave up and sold out to the Rockefeller Land Co. in 1928.

Continue north and soon the road veers west toward Oxbow Bend. This is my favorite turnout. The slow moving river has created a wetland of plant and wildlife. Glimpses of eagles, elk, pelicans, otters, and moose are frequently seen here with Mt. Moran making a perfect backdrop. Just watch out for that bull moose as he may mistake your motorcycle for a cow!

At the junction just past the pullout, make a quick detour right to the **Jackson Lake Lodge**. The parking lot will be busy, but just take a few minutes, go inside, and bask in the fantastic view afforded through the huge paneled windows. Walk in front of the Lodge for even more unobstructed views of the Park. Benches line the front veranda and a patio with tables is available if you want to buy a drink or a sandwich at the deli inside. Relax a moment and enjoy the glorious surroundings.

After a quick look, head south on Teton Park Road to **Jenny Lake**. This road flanks the Teton Range and provides unparalleled views of the mountains. Although in the summer months the road is congested, the beauty outshines any driving inconvenience. I almost look forward to a traffic jam, so I can just sit on my bike and enjoy the views. Those poor motorists in that shell of a car don't have nearly the 360 degree view I do. No roof or side paneling to block any of the panorama unfolding around you.

A few miles south of the Jackson Lake Junction, turn left on Signal Mountain Road. About a half mile short of the summit at Jackson Point

Overlook, a sweeping vista awaits you. Continue to the summit and the horizon extends all the way to Yellowstone. This road is fun to drive, but can also be a pain as many tourists take this side trip.

However, if you are looking for your own private views and your own campground, head down Signal Mountain, turn left on Teton Park Road and on the west side before the **North Jenny Lake Junction** (about two miles south of the Mount Moran turnout) is an unmarked dirt road. This little back way takes you to **Spaulding Bay** where there is a boat launch and a primitive restroom. If you are lucky no one will be there, and for you campers this makes a perfect spot to camp and get away from all the tourists. Mountains and lake views all for the price of a park permit!

Continuing south on Teton Park Road you will arrive at the North Jenny Lake Junction. Veer right (west) onto the scenic one way loop beside the lake. This four-mile lakeshore drive attracts more than its fair share of tourists, but rightly so. The mountains and lake are but a stone's throw away. The parking lot may be full of cars, but being on a motorcycle has its benefits. A short hike around the lake (two miles) will take you even closer to the rough-hewed stone outcropping of the Grand Teton.

Grab a drink at the general store after your hike, and then reconnect with Teton Park Road and make one final stop at the Teton Glacier Turnout for a look at a shrinking glacier. Only twelve glaciers remain in this once oasis of ice and they are shrinking fast, so be sure to savor it.

Smooth asphalt, sweeping bends and towering mountains greet you in Grand Teton National Park. Have I got your mouth watering yet?

Jackson Lake sits still and quiet at the base of the Tetons.

Another nice detour is the Schwabacher Landing Road which leads to the river on a gravel road. This well groomed gravel backway is about a two mile round trip and takes you for a close up look at the river far from the crowds. The turnoff is about 4.5 miles north of Moose Junction. Maybe this is what it was like 150 years ago when the pioneers first started to settle this valley.

Just before the junction of Teton Park Road and the 26-89-191, stop at the Moose Visitor Center. Good information, literature, and photographs are provided at this facility. Nice restrooms, too!

Head south again on 26-89-191 through the Elk Refuge and back to Jackson. Now you can either call it a day and take a nap in your room with plenty of time to explore the town, or continue west on State Route 22 toward Wilson for the second phase of the Teton Rendezvous. Just remember this next phase might be longer, but goes a whole lot quicker. If you feel like scrapin' the pavement, hop back on your bike and prepare to roll back the throttle a few notches. After the slow pace through the park this morning, this may be just what you need.

So, for those continuing on, head west on State Route 22 toward Idaho and the Teton Pass. Leaving Jackson, you will notice the traffic becoming less and less congested. Most tourists enter the Grand Tetons from the south or the north via Yellowstone National Park. This loop is less traveled and is used mostly by locals on their way to Palisades Reservoir for some "fishin'" or "waterskiin'."

Cross over the Snake River as Route 22 passes Wilson and then over the **Teton Pass** (elevation 8,431 feet). If you haven't had lunch drop by **Nora's Fish Creek Inn** (307-733-8288) in Wilson for some of the best cooking this side of the Rockies. Numerous celebs have eaten here and you will soon find out why. Good prices and great food! Continuing on Route 22, the road starts to climb quickly over the Snake Range through the Caribou National Forest into Idaho. The twists and turns become tighter as you ascend the pass and your pegs continue to brush the pavement upon descending into some of the most scenic areas of Southeastern Idaho on what is now State Route 33.

After twenty-six miles and dropping a few thousand feet, the vegetation changes from green forests to golden prairies. Victor is situated in the high plateau of southeastern Idaho and set in the middle of some of the loveliest farmlands I've ever seen. Turn left on State Route 31 toward Swan Valley to view rolling hills, wheat fields, and fence-lined meadows. Settled well over 100 years ago, red toned barns and old farmhouses transplant you to what you think are the farmlands of Iowa and Pennsylvania. This can't be Idaho!

A few miles outside Victor the pavement starts to climb once more as the scenery quickly changes and forests replace this gentle farming community. Traffic is mild so drive to your heart's content over the next twenty miles.

At the summit of Teton Pass, a "local" welcomes you to Jackson Hole.

Farmlands cover the countryside on the Idaho side of Teton Pass.

Soon more rolling hills covered with quaking wheat fields cover the landscape. Barns, tractors, and ranches with combines attest to this area being one of the breadbaskets of our nation. At the junction near Swan Valley, stop at the gas station for a break and some "square" ice cream. A perfect way to cool off. Try the chocolate or chocolate mint.

Right after the junction the road again changes its name to US Hwy 26 and close to the town of Irwin the road begins to ride tandem with the Snake River to the Upper Palisades Lake and Palisades Reservoir. The black asphalt cuts a nice groove beside the lake and Mt. Baird rises 10,025 feet on your left. This is a beautiful ride. The reflection off the lake of the surrounding mountains and forests is as refreshing as the breeze blowing through your visor. Campgrounds and boat docks line the eighteen-mile run alongside the lake.

Continue on Hwy 26 through Alpine and soon you will re-enter the ranchlands of northern Wyoming. The high altitude grasslands sway gently with the wind. Picturesque ranch homes and summer cabins dot the countryside. The blacktop loops lazily along, skirting the fenceposts and weaving gentle S-curves toward Hoback Junction and back home to Jackson.

Trip 16   Yellowstone and Beartooth Loop

Distance *542 miles (three full days)*

Terrain *This journey takes you on some of America's most scenic mountain highways. Start by driving through historic Yellowstone National Park, then climb the Beartooth Mountains to Red Lodge, follow the Nez Perce National Historic Trail to Cody, and then head back to Jackson through the east entrance of Yellowstone alongside its namesake lake. Elevation change 5,500 to 11,000 feet.*

Highlights *Endless S-curves, mountain passes, twisties, and switchbacks. Never a dull moment on this run.*

Yellowstone emanates more natural wonders per square mile then any park in the nation. In 1872, President Ulysses Grant designated the northwest corner in Wyoming the first National Park in the United States. Why our forefathers arbitrarily chose the square, linear shape of Yellowstone, though,

Is perfect weather guaranteed?

is beyond me. An abundance of natural beauty continues to overflow from Yellowstone into borderlands, lush with remarkable and wild landscape. Mountain roads lead to deep canyons, lazy rivers, azure lakes, open grasslands, and alpine passes. The panoramas of the Tetons to the south, Beartooth to the north, and Cody to the east unfold like the palms of a fan creating a trip of seemingly never-ending grandeur. The roads intertwine this fan with the finest precision, making each piece fit snugly next to the other. On most trips there is a portion of pavement that is just tolerated so you can connect with the good part. Well,there is no such portion on this trip. It is a never-ending loop of pure motorcycling nirvana.

This journey is over 500 miles long and requires at least three days and two nights to enjoy. It begins in Jackson, heads north past the Tetons, into Yellowstone through the south entrance, veers northwest past Old Faithful, and then makes a giant S-curve past the Grand Canyon of Yellowstone before exiting the northeast corner of the park at Cooke City. Overnight in

THE ROUTE FROM JACKSON

Day One

0	Start in Jackson, head north on US Hwy 26-89-191
30	Turn left on US Hwy 89-191-287 into Grand Teton National Park. Continue on US 89 to West Thumb, Old Faithful, and Madison
112	Arrive Madison, turn right on Grand Loop Rd US Hwy 89 to Norris
125	Arrive Norris, turn right on Norris Canyon Rd to Canyon Village
137	Turn left on Grand Loop Rd to Tower Junction
156	Turn right on Northeast Entrance Rd US Hwy 212
188	Arrive Cooke City, spend night

Day Two

188	Leave Cooke City, continue east on US Hwy 212. Stay on 212 to Red Lodge.
252	Arrive Red Lodge, have lunch, turn around
302	Turn left on State Route 296 (Chief Joseph Scenic Byway)
348	Turn right on State Route 120 (Belfry Hwy)
365	Arrive Cody, spend night, see rodeo

Day Three

365	Leave Cody, head west on US Hwy 14-16-20
442	Arrive Fishing Bridge Visitor Center in Yellowstone National Park
443	Turn left on Grand Loop Rd US Hwy 20
464	Turn left on South Entrance Rd US Hwy 89. Continue through Tetons to Jackson
542	Arrive Jackson

Cooke City and then shoot up the Beartooth Highway to Red Lodge, Montana, for lunch and then turn around and have double the pleasure of cruising down the Beartooth as you connect with the Chief Joseph Scenic Byway to Cody. See a rodeo (every evening in the summer) and spend the night in Cody, then head back to the eastern entrance of Yellowstone on the curvaceous US Hwy 14. Cruise by Yellowstone Lake and exit the park south of West Thumb, back past the Tetons, and home to Jackson.

Billowing clouds provide an ideal backdrop to scenic farmland just north of Yellowstone.

DAY ONE

Begin this journey by heading north on the triple combo 26-89-191 through the Teton National Park. Although discussed in more detail in the "Teton Rendezvous," this trip north to Yellowstone provides another opportunity to enjoy the Tetons one more time (I promise you won't get tired of this run). This time enjoy the morning ride without all the stops.

At the Mt. Moran entrance pull out your park pass, officially enter the Grand Teton National Park, and continue north on the John D. Rockefeller Memorial Parkway. This section of road is named after him to honor his philanthropic efforts in support of various national parks. The Parkway lies atop a mountainous plateau with views stretching east of the Tetons before entering the volcanic upheaval of Yellowstone National Park.

Now comes the hard part. Driving through Yellowstone is a dream—and a nightmare. **Yellowstone** (www.nps.gov/yell, 307-344-7381) is without a doubt the most-visited-, most-discussed-, and most-written-about-park in the United States. Typing in "Yellowstone" in any internet search engine will result in more hits than Harleys at a Sturgis Rally. The traffic can be horrendous and aggravating. Be patient and take a leisurely ride through the park. If you really want to enjoy Yellowstone, stay at a lodge or camp at one of the many sites available within the park's boundary. You can literally spend weeks exploring this great park. What is a trip through the Rockies without visiting our nation's first park? I gotta tell you, though, by the time I reach Cooke City, I'm ready to leave the tourists behind and enjoy the semi-solitude of the Beartooth Highway and Chief Joseph Scenic Byway. To each his own, I guess.

I will give you a very succinct tour through Yellowstone with some of my favorite "must see" stops. This is a day trip only, but does cover a lot of ground. Continue to head north on the John D. Rockefeller Memorial Parkway into the park. The Memorial Parkway does not officially end until West Thumb, which is twenty-two miles into Yellowstone. The elevation at the entrance is about 6,800 feet and gradually climbs to 8,000 feet at West Thumb.

The two-laner weaves neatly through the forested hills and hugs the Lewis River for several miles. Mt. Sheridan at 10,308 feet rises to the northeast and soon thereafter Lewis Lake sparkles just to the west of the road. Camping, boating, and picnic tables are available at the lake. As you cross the river, Lewis Falls appears on your left. For a closer view, park at the turnout and walk only a short distance to the Falls. This turnout is about ten miles from the south entrance.

Maybe I'll wait and have my lunch later. I didn't bring enough to share.

Montana's famous Beartooth Highway promises fantastic riding.

Continue on through Grant Village and at West Thumb veer left in the direction of Old Faithful. The pavement continues to ascend over the Continental Divide at Craig Pass (elevation 8,261 feet). Isa Lake straddles the divide, giving it the unique ability to have part of its icy waters flow to the Pacific and part to the Atlantic. The scene is beautiful, as you can tell from the numerous motorists parked along the shoulder.

The road wanders and is sometimes congested on its way to Old Faithful, so be patient and take a gander at Kepler Cascades just two miles south of the famous geyser. Continue to the huge parking lot and park by the visitors' center to see when the next eruption is scheduled. The visitor center has a great bookstore and good all around info, but I prefer strolling around the Upper Geyser Basin and watching the eruption from a distance without all the heads blocking my view. If the weather is cold, walk over to the Old Faithful Inn just west of the visitors' center and warm up in front of the huge stone fireplace built in this historic landmark.

The next leg of this journey continues to follow the Yellowstone Grand Loop to Madison sixteen miles north of Old Faithful. Numerous pullouts line the road. About five miles north, pull over at Grand Prismatic Spring which radiates colors like a submerged rainbow and then take Firehole Lake Drive, a one-way, three-mile northbound loop by the Great Fountain Geyser and the White Dome. If your timing is right you may see an even more spectacular gushing then Old Faithful.

At Madison, turn right, in the direction of Norris fourteen miles ahead. The road meanders beside the Gibbon River and a little less then halfway to

Norris, the eighty-foot Gibbon Falls drops off the escarpment into the Yellowstone Caldera. You can see the falls from the road, but for a closer look take the short hike to the viewpoint.

About three miles past Steamboat Geyser, turn right at Norris toward Canyon Village. Divert to the short one way Virginia Cascade loop soon after Norris and keep a lookout for wildlife in the surrounding meadows. Elk and moose are regularly seen here. Soon you will arrive in Canyon Village, which is twelve miles from Norris.

To me, the awesome grandeur of Yellowstone is best made manifest from Canyon Village to Tower Falls. Along this nineteen-mile stretch to Tower Junction, the Yellowstone River has eroded a band of soft rock creating a canyon eighty- to 1,200-feet deep with widths to 4,000 feet. The river acts like a knife slicing the heart of Yellowstone and then flowing through it like its own pulsating artery. There are numerous waterfalls to be seen. The Upper, Lower, and Tower Falls are the most well known. If you are planning on spending an extra day in the park, a nice detour is the turnoff to Mount Washburn after the Dunraven Pass and the three-mile hike to the summit. Views from the summit are worth the effort as you will be rewarded with the best panoramas of the entire park.

State Route 296 to Cody is not only scenic but far from fellow tourists.

You are close to the top of the world on the Beartooth Highway.

At Tower Junction, turn right toward the northeast entrance of Yellowstone about twenty-nine miles ahead. This piece of pavement rides pleasantly across high plateaus and is less crowded then the Grand Loop. Your hand will start to twitch as the asphalt beckons you past Abiathar Peak, into the Beartooth Range and Cooke City.

Shoofly, now known as Cooke City, is just outside the park and was originally part of the Crow Reservation until 1882. The boundaries of the reservation were shifted eastward to allow mining claims soon thereafter and a mini-mining boom put Cooke City on the map. Most of the claims lapsed after a year and this town now has approximately 100 residents year around. During summer the population explodes to over 300!

Although small and rustic, Cooke City is nestled beautifully in the Beartooth Mountains making it an ideal stopover on the way to Red Lodge. After a rather hectic day in Yellowstone, this small community offers a nice respite deep in the wilderness of Montana.

As **Cooke City** (www.colorado-west.com/cooke) caters primarily to tourists, the area has several lodges and eating establishments. The **Super 8 Motel** on 303 E. Main St. (406-838-2070) is brand new and offers clean affordable rooms. Have dinner at the **Beartooth Cafe** in the center of town and if the sun is still shining, relax on the view deck for an evening drink. If

The summit of the Beartooth Highway is at 10,947 feet.

you really want to get away from civilization, try the **Big Moose Resort** located near the Colter Pass at 715 Hwy 212 (www.bigmooseresort.com, 406-838-2398).

DAY TWO

Dress warmly in the morning, as the chill may not wear off climbing toward Red Lodge. Warm your belly with some hot brew, wrap your legs around your bike, and then tuck your knees in tightly because today's ride is taking you deep into the Beartooth Range and down **Chief Joseph Scenic Byway** on what Charles Kuralt says is America's most beautiful highway.

In 1882, General Philip Sheridan, the famous civil war veteran, was on a scouting mission in and around Yellowstone National Park. Tourists were starting to flock to the wonders out west and the General had led 120 men from Fort Washakie on an inspection. Instead of circumventing the Beartooth before returning to Billings, an old scout by the name of Geer convinced the General to take a more direct route through the mountains. Two days later, they arrived near present day Red Lodge and, voila, fifty years later in 1936, the **Beartooth Highway** opened along the same route.

Begin today's trek climbing **Colter Pass** (elevation 8,066 feet). Pilot Peak at 11,708 feet appears sharp and ragged on your right, easily identifiable and used by the early scouts as a landmark. Coming down the pass, you re-enter Wyoming and the Shoshone National Forest. Most of the tourists are still in Yellowstone, leaving you to enjoy your own personal views of this great wilderness area.

At the State Route 296 junction, stay left on US Hwy 212 and just a mile or so on the north side of the road is a dirt road leading up to an old fire tower on top of Clay Butte. Hopefully it is still accessible, as the views provide an unobstructed panorama of the Absaroka, Bighorn, and Beartooth Ranges. The jagged mountain tips give credence to its namesake of "Beartooth" Highway.

Another few miles up Hwy 212, Beartooth Lake lies tranquil yet foreboding beneath a fanged butte colored in shades of gold and yellow. Beartooth Falls on the opposite side of the road cascades rapidly down a stone staircase. The scene is lonesome and wild.

The road then ascends over 2,000 feet with more S-curves and switchbacks then a drunken snake to **Beartooth Pass**. The air is chilled with snow lingering in high drifts just off the shoulder. The crest reaches 10,947 feet and the views paint an unforgettable kaleidoscope of forests, mountain peaks, and glacial valleys. Beartooth can be seen northward, its craggy slopes outlined sharply in the azure sky. Stop at "Top of the World" for something hot before continuing on to Red Lodge—you're not there yet!

Just think, you get to do this twice in one day— going up and going down!

Beware! The Beartooth can be closed at anytime, even in the summer.

WARNING
Road Subject To Sudden Closures. Gate May Be Locked During Storms Without Notice.

Twin Lakes Headwall just north of the pass is almost always covered with snow. Turn off at the pullout and you may see some summer skiers training for the Olympics. The ribbonesque road teeters on the mountain's edge as it drops to Rock Creek Vista Point for views of Rock Creek Canyon and sage covered terrain.

Continue through the gouged canyon and then descend via a series of switchbacks to the old mining town of Red Lodge. Settled in the 1800s to mine coal for the Northern Pacific Railroads, the population peaked in 1911 at 5,000 souls. When the "West Side Mine" closed in 1924, Red Lodge made some minor adjustments and built some "stills" in those abandoned mines and replaced black coal with bootlegged "syrup" which was shipped as far east as Chicago.

Today **Red Lodge** (www.redlodge.com, 888-281-0625) has a population of 2,000 and has all the trappings of an old mining town turned tourist mecca. As a result, the accommodations and eating facilities are plentiful, making this an ideal spot to have lunch. So take five, wander through town, do a little window shopping, and then grab a bite to eat. If you feel like splurging, drop by the **Bear Creek Saloon and Steakhouse** seven miles east of town on State Route 308 (406-446-3481). Well-known and well-publicized, the food here is great! Personally, I usually hit the **Red Lodge Pizza Company** in downtown Red Lodge for some hand-tossed pizza or visit **Natali's Front Bar** for some peanuts, a cold one, and a hamburger (406-446-3333). There are more eating establishments in Red Lodge per capita than any other town in Montana—I guarantee you won't go hungry.

One of the best things about this journey is that you get to ride the Beartooth Highway twice in one day. Heading south provides an entirely different perspective and since you have already stopped at the overlooks, you can test your driving skills and buzz right on by! An alternative route east on State Route 308 and then south on Route 72 can also be taken from Red Lodge. However, you will miss most of the Chief Joseph Scenic Byway and head straight into Cody. What's that old motorcycling adage? Something like, "if there is a longer way home, I'll take it." My advice, enjoy the Beartooth one more time and extend your motorcycling nirvana on the Chief Joseph Scenic Byway.

So, head back toward Cooke City and at the State Route 296 junction hang a sharp left toward Cody onto the Byway. Back in June 1877, Chief Joseph, Chief White Bird, Chief Ollokot, Chief Lean Elk, and Chief Looking Glass led 750 Nez Perce and a thousand horses over 1,100 miles from Oregon to Canada. Hoping to avoid pursuit by the U.S. Army, these Chiefs led the Nez Perce on a desperate journey away from the white man. Their odyssey lasted until October and about forty miles south of the Canadian Border. Route 296 memorializes that trek and is now part of the Nez Perce National Historic Trail.

Look down on Chief Joseph Highway with towering mountains in the distance.

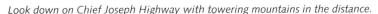

The Soda Butte Lodge is a good place to stop in Cooke City.

Cruising along the Chief Joseph Scenic Byway after the Beartooth Highway is like icing on the cake. To make it even better, the road is well-maintained with wide shoulders—a nice change after the narrow passes at Beartooth. The road hugs the Clark's Fork Yellowstone River, eventually thrusting you beside a 1,200-foot gorge commonly referred to as the box. You are soon spewed out and Sunlight Basin unfolds on the horizon. **Dead Indian Pass** at 8,098 feet provides wide open views as glorious switchbacks take you up and over this unforgettable expanse of black topped asphalt. This array of colors has taken you from gorges banded with browns and golds to the green and blue creeks of Sunlight Basin; and making this feast for the eyes even better—you may not see another motorist for miles!

Turn right at the State Route 120 junction and after fifteen miles you will arrive in **Cody, Wyoming**. Founded in 1896 by William Cody, better known as Buffalo Bill, Cody has grown considerably but still has an Old West-feel. There are numerous hotels and lodges, and many restaurants to help you unwind from your day's journey. If you want a piece of history, stay at the **Irma Hotel** (www.irmahotel.com, 800-745-4762) built by Buffalo Bill in 1902 and named after his daughter. His plan was to have tourists stay in a series of three properties owned by him on their way to the east entrance of Yellowstone: the Irma Hotel (railroad access), Wapiti Inn (one day's wagon ride) and Pahaska Teepee near the entrance. The Irma Hotel is showing its age, but is a fun place to stay and is now a National Historic Landmark. For more information on Cody visit their website at www.codychamber.org or call the chamber of commerce at 307-587-2777.

For dinner, you can certainly order some Prime Rib at Irma's, but my suggestion would be to unpack, take a refreshing shower and then head over to the **Cody Rodeo** held every night from June through August. Grab a hot dog and a drink and enjoy the cowboy atmosphere that is unique to hometown rodeos. The stadium is located just west of town on US Hwy 20.

DAY THREE

In the morning, after a quick breakfast at **Peter's Cafe Bakery** (1219 Sheridan Ave), point your mount westward on US Hwy 14-16-20 toward the east entrance of Yellowstone. You will soon pass the Buffalo Bill Reservoir on the south side of the road just outside of town. The landscape is arid with sagebrush and junipers dotting the terrain. The two-laner meanders across the North Fork Shoshone River where huge cottonwoods shade the riverbank. Gradually the road ascends into the Shoshone National Forest; the asphalt weaves methodically past funky colored rock spires and pinnacles created eons ago by volcanic eruptions.

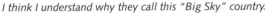

I think I understand why they call this "Big Sky" country.

The highway leads you gracefully upward as the turns become tighter and suddenly green forests surround you with colorful meadows pulling your eyes off the pavement. The road then becomes a series of switchbacks as you climb to **Sylvan Pass** (8,541 feet) and snow patches dot the granite slopes. As the road's twisting motion continues, Yellowstone Lake floods into view with all its glory. The road catches up to the lake and driving along its perimeter provides unimpeded scenes across this magnificent freshwater lake.

At the junction just past Fishing Bridge, turn left toward West Thumb. The Grand Loop continues to hug the former volcanic caldera-turned lake. Numerous turnoffs and picnic areas line the shoreline providing picture perfect stops to meditate on the tranquility of this great park. About eighteen miles north of West Thumb, turn left to Lake Village and visit the Lake Hotel. Originally built in 1891, it was completely renovated in the 1980s and has now been placed on the National Register of Historic Places.

Grab an ice cream at the local store at Lake Village and then continue onto the last leg of this journey to West Thumb and back to the Tetons on the John D. Rockefeller Memorial Parkway. Hookup onto the triple combo

The original Yellowstone Park tour buses replaced covered wagons and are still in use today.

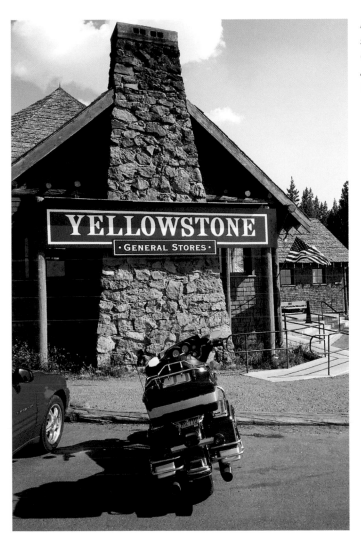

Drop by for a snack at the General Store just across from Yellowstone Lake.

26-89-191 for one last gasp at Mt. Moran and the jagged peaks of the Grand Tetons. The tourists and congestion are gradually increasing with each passing mile. Jackson's familiarity is welcome, but yearnings for the solitude of Beartooth and the Chief Joseph Scenic Byway linger. Although the road trip may be over, a saying from the Nez Perce echoes in the back of your mind, "this trail will live on in our hearts."

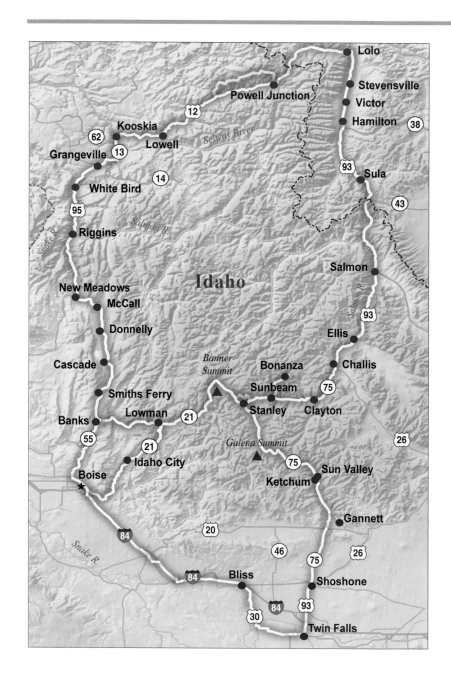

Boise

During the summer months many years ago (I'm not saying how many), my parents would take our family to visit grandma in Twin Falls, Idaho. Oftentimes in order to give grandma a break, we would load up one more time and see my Aunt Millie in Boise. At the time Boise was about one-quarter the size it is today. My aunt was a fanatic about keeping her home clean and had plastic covering all the living room furniture. I remember having to walk on plastic pathways through the house so the carpet wouldn't get dirty. Well, to say the least, my brother and I didn't spend much time inside. We would borrow some bicycles and go cruising through town (precursor to my eventual motorcycling days). Even at that young age, I can still visualize cycling down to the river and having a blast going up and down the neighborhood hills. Boise was a quaint, clean, all-American apple pie kinda town.

Blue sky stretches as far as the eye can see in the Boise Basin.

Boise still exudes that same charm. Although several times larger than in the 1960s, this city is still a relatively unknown little jewel. Like so many cities in the Rockies, the discovery of gold in 1862 became the major impetus for growth. Prospectors flooded into the Boise Basin creating more permanent settlements. The Oregon Trail ran right through the south side of town along the river bringing in even more pioneers to this part of the country. In the 1930s, Basques migrated here in vast numbers from the Spanish Pyrenees resulting in a very large concentration of this colorful culture. Today, the hi-tech boom with the likes of Micron and HP has further spawned significant growth, creating a mini-silicon valley.

The capital of Idaho since 1862, Boise merges western history and modern day growth into a great place to stay. Visit the State Capitol, take a walk down the Greenbelt or just hang out at Hyde Park and take a stroll down tree-lined Harrison Boulevard window shopping at some of the local boutiques. A host of restaurants are situated in this funky neighborhood. Try **Lucky 13**, **Parilla Grill**, or **Hyde Park Pub** to appease your appetite. All are conveniently located in this part of town. For more information visit the city's website at www.boise.org or call 800-635-5240.

Numerous lodging facilities are available in Boise. Although I usually stay at my Aunt's house, the **Doubletree Riverside** (www.doubletree .hilton.com, 800-222-TREE) and Idaho Heritage Inn Bed & Breakfast are high on my list as well. The Doubletree is conveniently located along a shaded stretch of the Boise River and is only a short distance from the Boise River Greenbelt for those interested in a morning walk or jog. Just remember there are two Doubletrees in Boise and this one is the **Doubletree Riverside**. It is also only a few blocks from **High Desert Harley-Davidson** (www.highdeserthd.com, 800-666-4644) if you are in town and want to rent a bike for the weekend. The people at High Desert are extremely friendly and helpful. They even gave me a free ride to the airport last time I was there. If you are interested in something a little more unique, try the **Idaho Heritage Inn Bed & Breakfast** (www.idheritageinn.com, 800-342-8445). This historic mansion is built on top of hot springs providing geothermal heat to your room and morning showers warmed "naturally." Occupied by a Governor and then Senator Church for many years, this B&B is now on the National Register of Historic Places and is home to two very cool cats—Mufasa and Simba (small cats).

If you decide to spend an extra day in town, be sure and visit the beautiful Mormon Temple on the cascading Snake River, take a leisurely ride on an inner tube down the Boise River, or just enjoy a scenic walk down the Greenbelt. You will not be disappointed.

Galena Pass crests at 8,701 feet before the road heads down to Sun Valley, a favorite playground for celebrities.

Trip 17 Sawtooth Sortie

Distance *414 miles (one to two days)*
Terrain *South Central Idaho is one of the most pristine and remote
wilderness areas in the United States. A diversity of terrain astounds the
visual senses from hot simmering thermal baths in Lowman to snow covered
mountain slopes near Sun Valley and from lava moonscapes to thundering
waterfalls at Shoshone Falls. Elevation change 3,800 to 8,800 feet.*
Highlights *Mostly mountain bends and twisties with gentle S-curves and
river crossings after Shoshone. If you stay in Stanley, take the "Nip and
Tuck" dirt backroad. Final leg is ninety miles of Interstate to Boise.*

When Count Felix Schaffgtosch was sent out west by Union Pacific Chairman Averill Harriman in 1936 to find the perfect mountain resort, he spent months trying to locate the right spot. On the verge of returning to Austria without any success, he made one last visit to an old mining town in Idaho called Ketchum. Upon his arrival to this small town nestled at the base of

The scenery is out of this world coming down from Galena Pass north of Ketchum.

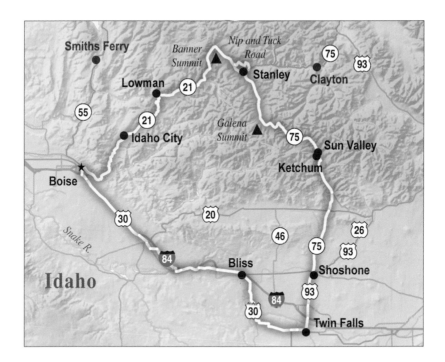

THE ROUTE FROM BOISE

0   Start in Boise. Take I-84 east to State Route 21

5   Turn north on Route 21 to Idaho City.

34 Arrive Idaho City. Continue on Route 21 to Lowman.

65 Arrive Lowman. Continue on Route 21 to Stanley.

124 Arrive Stanley. Continue on State Route 75 to Ketchum.

186 Arrive Ketchum. Continue on Route 75 to Shoshone.

241 Arrive Shoshone. Take US Hwy 93 south to Twin Falls.

267 Arrive Twin Falls. Turn left on Falls Avenue to Shoshone Falls Park.

272 Arrive Shoshone Falls, turn around.

277 Arrive Twin Falls, turn left on US Hwy 93.

278 Turn right on US Hwy 30 (Addison Ave).

324 Arrive Bliss, merge onto I-84 west to Boise.

414 Arrive Boise.

The road to Ketchum invites you to stop, breathe the clear air, and take it all in.

the Sawtooth Mountains, the Count wired Harriman saying he had discovered the "American Shangri-la" and within days Harriman had purchased 4,300 acres in what is now known as Sun Valley, Idaho.

After driving the San Juan Parkway or the Beartooth Highway or the Grand Canyon North Rim, you start to think it just can't get any better. And then you take a ride in the Sawtooths up to Stanley and down to Shoshone Falls and you realize that each trip and each road is unique. Each turn of the bend unveils mountain scenery unlike any other. The Sawtooths of Idaho are another sample of exquisite taste in this gourmet of Rocky Mountain Journeys. Twisting asphalt takes you by simmering hot springs, over alpine passes, past barren moonscape, and finally ends at the Niagara of the West, Shoshone Falls.

This trip is over 400 miles in length and can be done in one very long day. I would recommend an overnighter in Stanley along the banks of the Salmon River. Stanley is a small community situated beautifully in the jaws of the **Sawtooth Mountains**. Eat lunch in town and, if you have a dual sport bike, take the "Nip and Tuck" backroad through old Stanley Basin. Sun Valley is also an option if you want to enjoy first class accommodations. Remember this is not a contest for the Iron Butt Award, but rather a leisurely journey through some of the most majestic and diverse landscape in Southern Idaho.

Begin in Boise and head east on Interstate 84. Just outside of town, turn left (north) on State Route 21 to Idaho City 29 miles ahead. The road tugs at you immediately and after crossing the Boise River the bike is pulled toward surroundings rich with forests, streams, and lakes that make up the Boise Basin. The two-laner wanders gently upward eventually landing in the old mining town of **Idaho City** (www.idahocitychamber.com, 208-392-6000).

In 1862 while Civil War ravaged the eastern seaboard, gold was discovered in Idaho City. Within days of the discovery, this small town became the most populous area in the Northwest Territory, surpassing even Portland, Oregon. Fortunes were made and lost daily, with the loser often carted off to Pioneer Cemetery. Over just a few years $250,000,000 worth of gold was mined in the Boise Basin. Then just as suddenly as it started, the veins ran dry. Prospectors left in droves, searching for more profitable ventures, and the shell of an old mining town remained.

Though ravaged by fire several times over the years, Idaho City still exudes a natural "Old West" charm. The town has the look and feel of a rowdy mining town, maybe because it is a still a little run down and not very touristy. Several old brick and wooden structures line the streets. Rest your "rear end" for a moment and visit the old "merc" store where a pinch of gold use to buy a few items, peer into the old jailhouse and then peruse the paraphernalia at the **Boise Basin Historical Museum**. Try to imagine streets full of prospectors and saloons brimming with drunken brawls.

Fire has done its fair share of damage around Lowman, Idaho.

Time for a break in Idaho City at Harley's Pub & Spirits. Is it just for Harleys?

Continue north on Route 21 toward Lowman. Lowman is about thirty-one miles from Idaho City. The two-laner sweeps gently through the terrain, rocking you back and forth next to forested hills. Not far from Lowman, scarred black earth starts to dominate the countryside. In 1989, 46,000 acres were burned in a firestorm of unprecedented proportions along Route 21. Blazes from three separate lightning strikes merged into a fire ravaging the dry, drought-ridden forests. Interpretive signposts are placed adjacent to the road for more info on this once-blazing inferno.

At **Lowman**, continue on Route 21 and soon the smells of geothermal heaven will greet you. This area has one of the highest concentrations of hot springs in the United States. Several mineral-rich ponds are publicly accessible and located just off the road with their own National Forest Campground. **Kirkham Hot Springs** is one of the most well known and is located about four miles past Lowman. Although busy at times, during midweek this thermal delight (102 to 118 degrees) may be yours alone for a nice soak. Check it out, you might just get lucky!

After Kirkham Hot Springs, the road continues to hug the South Payette Fork River corridor and weaves gently through rolling hillsides toward Banner Pass. The Sawtooth Mountains inch upward across the horizon. Stop at the Sawtooth Overlook for your first glimpse of these teeth-like peaks. In early summer, the meadows are covered with wildflowers adding a floor of color beneath the distant, granite slopes.

After Sawtooth Overlook, the road soon starts to climb toward Banner Summit and crawls through a narrow-walled canyon. At **Banner Summit**

(7,056 feet), the blacktop doglegs through Cape Horn and begins its descent into Stanley. The asphalt beneath you flows like a black river through dense forests. Although your eyes remain fixed on the bend just ahead, glimpses of the Sawtooth beckon you forward.

Near milepost 126, turn right on Stanley Lake Road and continue for about three and a half miles to the Elk Mountain Overlook. The pullout is on the right and offers spectacular views of Stanley Lake and the surrounding area. This beautiful alpine lake is nestled between forest-cloaked foothills reminding you more of Switzerland then the Rockies.

Route 21 descends quickly into **Stanley** and the Sawtooths suddenly rear up in all their glory around this quaint mountain resort. Stanley caters primarily to outdoorsmen. Kayaking, fishing, hunting, hiking, and horseback riding are plentiful in and around this area. In the winter months, cross country skiers and snowmobiles swear this is the best place on earth. As a result Stanley is often referred to as the gateway to the **Sawtooth National Recreation Area** and the **Frank Church River of No Return Wilderness**. If you are interested in river running, fishing, or horseback riding, you may want to spend a day or two in this gorgeous spot.

Campsites are plentiful in the National Forest as well as lodging in either Upper or Lower Stanley. For information visit the United States Forest Service website at www.fs.fed.us/r4/sawtooth or call 877-444-6777. For information on Stanley check their website out at www.stanleycc.org or call 800-878-7950. The Stanley site includes numerous references for hotels, campsites, restaurants, and local activities.

If you want to stay clear of the uppity and exclusive allure of Sun Valley, then stay in Stanley. A convenient and clean place to overnight is the

I think I know why they call these mountains the "Sawtooths."

Forest and grasslands cover the landscape. What looks like mist is actually smoke from a forest fire in the northeast Sawtooth Range.

Salmon River Cabins (www.lowerstanley.com, 800-972-4627) owned and operated by Ben and Janet Forsgren in Lower Stanley. The location is beautiful as the Salmon River is just steps from the back door. At the very least, drop by **Bridge Street Burger and Brew** (208-774-2208) for a look at the antlered beaver on the wall, and enjoy a humongous burger and a piece of pie (hope there is one left!).

For you dual-sporters who decide to stay in town, a neat backroad detour is the "**Nip and Tuck Road.**" Used by freight wagons during the gold rush, this gravel and dirt road offers unparalleled views of the old Stanley Basin. About one mile north on State Route 75 toward Lower Stanley, turn left on Forest Road 633 (Nip and Tuck Road). After about three to four miles you will cross a cattle guard and views of the whole basin will be yours alone. Continue another four to five miles and then veer left on Forest Road 653 past the gravel pit to State Route 21. Follow Route 21 south back into Stanley. This is a great side trip. Don't miss it! If you can't find the turnoff, just ask any business in town, they will direct you right to it.

In the morning head south on Route 75 and after about four miles turn right toward **Redfish** and **Little Redfish Lake**. This five-mile-long, 300-feet-deep glacial lake epitomizes nature at its best. The blue lake reflects the jagged peaks off its surface with Mt. Heyburn at 10,229 feet as its centerpiece. Open skies, green lush forests, and cotton candy clouds attest to how Count Felix must have felt when he first saw this area. Drop by the historic **Redfish Lake Lodge** built in 1929 and nearby Little Redfish Lake before heading back to Route 75.

State Route 75 heads south toward Ketchum, but not before climbing another pass over the Sawtooth. The road continues its magical journey as it starts to ascend about five miles from **Galena Summit**. The movement enlivens your wrist as your boots scrape the pavement and the chilled air buffets your visor. About half a mile from the 8,701-foot summit, pull over at the Galena Summit Overlook for one last view of the Sawtooth Range. Groves of aspen and willows blanket the hills. Glacial valleys with ice-smoothed surfaces contrast with the pointed mountain peaks as the mighty Salmon flows 2,000 feet below you toward its final destination: more than 400 miles to the Pacific Ocean.

Continuing on our journey, drive south on Route 75 to **Sun Valley** about twenty-nine miles further along. The motorcycle churns quietly beneath you as the tires eat the miles all too quickly. Enveloped by the steep foothills of the Sawtooth, Sun Valley sparkles amidst meadows, streams, and forests. This playground of celebrities opened in 1936 and was frequented by the likes of Clark Gable, Errol Flynn, Lucille Ball, and Ernest Hemingway. This mountain "Shangri-la" is another great place to overnight and rest up before the ride home tomorrow. Lodging, restaurants, and bars run the gamut from haute cuisine to burger and fries. Sun Valley has numerous websites and free information available to tourists. Start with www.visitsunvalley.com or call the visitors' bureau directly at 866-305-0408.

In the morning, enjoy a leisurely breakfast at **Cristina's Restaurant** (208-726-4499) at 520 Second St. East, Ketchum, then go south on Route 75

The local gas station in Stanley, Idaho.

toward Bellevue and Shoshone. The road gradually descends into Magic Valley and the Camas Prairie toward Magic Reservoir. The reservoir provides water for Idaho's famous Russet Burbank Potatoes. In spring, the camas flower is in full bloom adding a rainbow of color to the rolling fields. Keep your eyes on the road as you may see some Basque Shepherds with their dogs driving sheep across the highway.

As the air warms, stop at the **Ice Caves** (208-886-2058) seventeen miles north of Shoshone for a cool respite. The temperature inside the caves drops to a cool thirty degrees so be sure and put the liner in your motorcycle jacket.

At Shoshone, State Route 75 becomes US Highway 93 to Twin Falls. This leg of the trip is about twenty-six miles and cuts straight through some of the most extraterrestrial landscape you will ever see. The lava formations rise like mummified aliens beside the road. You feel as if you're driving across moonscape and at any moment will see Neil Armstrong or Buzz

Try the natural hot springs east of Lowan on State Route 21.

Aldrin step out of their Apollo Spacecraft and hop in their moonmobile for a dry run.

Cross over Interstate 84 and just before Twin Falls, you will cross the deep **Snake River Canyon** on a 486 foot suspension bridge. The chasm is traumatic and the river rapids thrash along the canyon floor. I can see why **Evel Knievel** chose this abyss for his daredevil gravity-defying leap. The spectacularly stark scenery makes this a perfect place for this attempt at folly—and the public loved it.

Apparently, Evel's idea for this jump came while in a bar looking at a picture of the Grand Canyon. Since the park would not allow the stunt, Evel bought some land bordering the Snake River and built a rocket powered "Skycycle" to jump a quarter mile across the canyon. Well, he launched himself on that fateful day in 1974 and never made it to the other side. However, the parachute deployed and he landed with only minor injuries on the riverbank (and six million bucks richer). Not a resounding success, but definitely a lot of publicity and Evel Knievel became synonymous with "daredevil motorcyclist." Take a few minutes and try to visualize the immensity of what Evel attempted. Geez, I get jittery jumping two feet on my GS.

When you arrive in Twin Falls (I spent many summers here with Grandma), head east on Fall Avenue to **Shoshone Falls**. The Snake River plunges 210 feet down the canyon floor giving rise to its claim as the "Niagara Falls" of the west. During spring runoff the falls are quite impressive. However, due to drought conditions since 2001, the flow at times has been reduced to a trickle. Recently, southern Idaho has seen its fair share of rain and the drought has eased. Reservoirs are full and the river is flowing, making Shoshone Falls a sight not to be missed.

Cool yourself off from the mist covered overlook, and then turn around on Fall Avenue back to Twin Falls. Continue west on US Highway 30. The road winds gracefully through the high desert plateau surrounding the Snake Canyon. Except for possibly a tractor waddling on the side shoulder, the road is empty and the views endless. Accelerate through the curves and after about forty-six miles from Twin Falls merge onto I-84 at Bliss and crank another ninety miles home to Boise. The stark, barren landscape along the Interstate contrasts sharply with the memories of snowcapped, forest-cloaked slopes of the Sawtooth. Count Felix definitely got this one right. American "Shangri-la" is found in the unspoiled Salmon River country of central Idaho.

Trip 18 Lewis and Clark Country

Distance *756 miles (three days)*

Terrain *Follow the Payette River to US Highway 12 and on to untouched backcountry explored by Lewis and Clark in 1805. Continue to Salmon for some afternoon whitewater rafting, then head back through the Sawtooth Mountains to Boise but not before a side trip to a couple of ghost towns. Elevation change 1,500 to 8,000 feet.*

Highlights *Most of these roads hug the edges of the Payette, Lochsa, and Salmon Rivers resulting in ceaseless bends and sweepers. Unpaved dirt diversion available on the "Lolo Motorway" for those interested in following the actual trail used by Lewis and Clark. Another optional backway to some deserted mining towns on the "Backroad to Bonanza."*

The Payette River flows through forested terrain beside State Route 55 north of Boise.

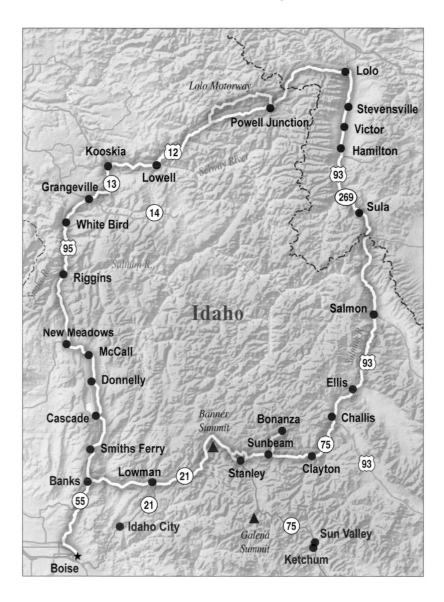

The **Selway-Bitterroot Wilderness** in north central Idaho and western Montana covers over 1,000,000 acres of a vast wild land. This area straddles the Bitterroot Range and Selway River. Dominated by granite peaks and coniferous forests, the heartland of Selway-Bitterroot is rugged and rarely visited by humans. As a result, little has changed since Lewis and Clark arrived in 1805 searching for a navigable waterway from the Missouri to the

THE ROUTE FROM BOISE

Day One

0   Start in Boise, take State Route 55 north

44   Arrive Banks, continue on Route 55

81   Arrive Cascade, continue on Route 55

97   Arrive Donnelly, turn right on Roseberry Road to Roseberry

99   Arrive Roseberry, turn around

101   Arrive Donnelly, turn right on Route 55 to McCall

114   Arrive McCall, continue on Route 55

126   Arrive New Meadows, turn right on US Highway 95

189   Arrive White Bird, see battle site

205   Arrive Grangeville, turn right on State Route 13

231   Arrive Kooskia, turn right on US Highway 12

254   Arrive Lowell, spend night if too tired to go on

326   Turn right to Powell and the Lochsa Lodge

327   Arrive Lochsa Lodge, get a good night's sleep

Day Two

327   Start at Lochsa Lodge, head north on Hwy 12 to Lolo or detour to Lolo Motorway

373   Arrive Lolo, Montana, turn left on US Highway 93

390   Turn left on State Route 269 (Eastside Highway) to Stevensville

413   Arrive Hamilton, re-enter Hwy 93 south to Salmon

506   Arrive Salmon, Idaho, go whitewater rafting

Day Three

506   Start in Salmon, continue on US Highway 93

566   Arrive Challis, veer right on State Route 75

611   Arrive Sunbeam and turn right on optional Backroad to Bonanza (side trip here to Bonanza/Custer on unpaved road).

621   Arrive Stanley, turn right on State Route 21

679   Arrive Lowman, turn right on Banks—Lowman Road to Banks

712   Arrive Banks, turn left on State Route 55 to Boise

756   Arrive Boise, Whew!

Columbia. Confronted with the Bitterroot Range, Lewis and Clark at first veered south to the Salmon River. Soon realizing that was not a viable option, they headed north and proceeded along an old Indian trail called the **Lolo Trail**. The Nez Perce had used this route for centuries to hunt bison in Montana. So with some help from their Shoshone guide, "old Toby" (I sorta like that name), Lewis and Clark continued west to the Pacific through the Clearwater National Forest.

Well, it just so happens that one of the world's most magnificent motorcycle rides parallels this journey of Lewis and Clark across the Bitterroot Range and through Clearwater National Forest on US Highway 12. Their ill-fated journey south to the Salmon River parallels US Highway 93. And for those on dual sport mounts, a detour on the unpaved "Lolo Motorway" follows the actual trail used by the expedition in 1805. All of these treks linked together with the Payette River Scenic Byway (State Route 55), the Ponderosa Scenic Byway (State Route 21) and the Wildlife Canyon Byway (Banks-Lowman Road) combine to create one grand circle of motorcycling ecstasy.

This journey is approximately 750 miles long and requires two to five days to fully appreciate the breadth of the history in this area. On the first day, head north on State Route 55 from Boise along the beautiful Payette

Sailboats in Idaho? Welcome to McCall.

Mile High Marina is one of the best spots in McCall to grab a burger, listen to music, and enjoy some breathtaking views.

River and then spend the night in the remote "Lochas Lodge" in Powell. Spend an extra day here if you want to enjoy the diversion on the dirt "Lolo Motorway." Then continue on the Lewis and Clark Highway (US Hwy 12) to Lolo, Montana. Head south on US Hwy 93 back into Idaho, overnight in Salmon (spend an afternoon or extra day if you want to go whitewater rafting) then hook up with the Ponderosa Scenic Byway (State Route 21) in Stanley heading west and at Lowman catch the Wildlife Canyon Scenic Byway back to Route 55 and home to Boise.

DAY ONE

All right, now that I have gotten you excited about this trip, let's get started. Boise is only about 2,200 feet above sea level and can be warm during the summertime. As a result, the landscape heading north of town on State Route 55 is not lush green forested mountains. Rather rolling hills are the norm, covered with green grass in the spring and dry brown splotches in late summer. The road winds lazily through the hillsides as it follows the Payette

River to Horseshoe Bend about twenty-three miles north of Boise. At this point the scenery starts to change and Ponderosa Pine begins to cover steep mountain slopes.

At Banks, about fourteen miles from Horseshoe Bend, the river splits and the forest becomes even lusher. The elevation is about 3,000 feet. At the confluence of the North and South Forks of the Payette River, rafters and kayakers are often seen rushing though the whitewater. Continuing north on Route 55, the road hugs the North Fork to Cascade, a well known recreational site about seventy-five miles from Boise. Turn left at the stoplight and about one mile from the intersection, Cascade Reservoir floods the horizon. A boat ramp and beach area is often crowded with sun worshipers enjoying the warm summer weather. There is a restaurant on the corner if you want to grab a drink.

Back on Route 55, continue north toward McCall. The road sweeps gently beside the river and soon you will arrive in the small town of Donnelly, population 138. Don't blink or you will miss the turnoff to **Roseberry**.

In the 1890s the first Finnish homesteaders arrived and established several communities in Long Valley, Idaho. The primary town was Roseberry located about one mile east of Donnelly. Between 1890 and 1912,

The Salmon River Valley

Roseberry was a hub of activity boasting a twenty-three-room hotel, various businesses, schools and even a bowling alley. Then the railroad came to town—but not this town—and by 1959 the last class was held in the local school and the town, in essence, shut down. Starting in 1973, the Long Valley Preservation Society took up the Roseberry Banner and now fifteen restored structures line Farm-to-Market and East Roseberry Roads. If you have the time, drop by this quaint, restored town for a glimpse into our "Finnish" past.

Heading north again on Route 55 past Donnelly, you will enter the resort town of **McCall**. This city is everything you could ask in a resort community. A beautiful lake, nearby ski resort, western style storefront veneers, and forest clad mountain slopes surrounding the whole town. To enjoy this scenic interlude a little longer, veer right at the main intersection and head toward the lake. A beautiful park with picnic tables lies adjacent to the lake providing a picture perfect spot to unpack your tuna sandwiches. Or right next to the boat ramp park your bike at the "Mile High Marina" and order a Buffalo Burger on the outside patio. A local guitarist was strumming some old Jim Croce tunes last time I was there. I could have stayed quite a bit longer!

The Salmon River has been cutting this canyon for some fifteen million years.

The Old Outpost at the Lochsa Historical Ranger Station is well worth a visit.

Continuing through McCall, the road doglegs left and after only a few miles at New Meadow, turn right on US Highway 95 to **Riggins**. You are now following the Little Salmon River and the road descends relatively quickly through meadows and dry basalt canyons to this small community. Located at the confluence of the Little Salmon and Salmon Rivers, Riggins is often referred to as the whitewater capital of Idaho and numerous outfitters are located here. As you drive alongside the river, don't be surprised to see rafters paddling madly through the rapids set between steep canyon walls.

The elevation continues to drop and at White Bird you are only 1,500 feet above sea level. Just after the turnoff to town, the road ascends over a small pass with well marked passing lanes providing a wrist cracking spurt of speed up the road. Don't go too fast or you will blow right past a turnout for the historic **White Bird Battlefield.** On June 17, 1877, Yellow Wolf of the Nez Perce was fired upon while attempting to make peace with the U.S. Cavalry. This was the opening salvo for the Nez Perce War and the demise of this great Native American tribe. Time permitting, head down the narrow single-laner through the battlefield itself. Interpretive signs are posted with more detailed information along the road. The asphalt runs like a coiled snake through the valley and up the side of the low lying hills. Fun and rarely traveled . . . what more could you ask! For best access, head back to White Bird and turn into town. The road is about fifteen miles long and eventually wiggles itself up past the turnout and reconnects with Hwy 95 just south of the Salmon River outlook.

At Grangeville, turn right on State Route 13 to Kooskia. Running through the Camas Prairie, this little winder cuts back and forth through the lowlands and rolling hills before connecting with US Highway 12. Last time I drove it, two crotch rockets blew past me going—I don't know how fast. I can still see their smiles etched permanently in their rear view mirrors.

Soon even more fun beckons you ahead. Be sure your gas tank is full as the next eighty miles will keep you focused on this wild and scenic ride beside the Lochsa River to **Lolo Pass** on US Highway 12. No gas stations are available until Powell and the next fuel stop is about fifty miles miles after that. US Hwy 12 is often referred to as the **Lewis and Clark Highway** or the Northwest Passage Scenic Byway. Various interpretive signs mark the way making this not only an incomparable motorcycle ride, but a trip back in time to one of the most significant events in our nation's history. As you drive this route, little has changed over the past two centuries. The area is still remote, the river still clear, the panoramas still pristine and the trail still windy. I can see why this stretch of pavement has been voted by many motorcycling magazines as one of the top ten rides in the United States.

You can also opt to spend the night in Lowell, about twenty-three miles up Hwy 12, if you're feeling tuckered out. Lowell has a nice resort set right on the Lochsa River called the **Three Rivers Resort** (www.three riversresort.com, 208-926-4430). I know 327 miles is a long day to Powell, but the setting at Lochsa Lodge, in my opinion, is also well worth it. Another bonus is that you are right next to a convenient loop excursion on the "Lolo Motorway" in Powell. Just remember the sun doesn't set until 9:00 in

The Lolo Trail Crossing was made famous by Lewis and Clark.

Camping just outside of Powell, I'm getting a good night's rest before heading south toward Salmon.

the summer, so you should have more then enough time. A shorter trip to Salmon in the morning may also provide extra time for an afternoon white-water rafting trip down the "River of No Return!" So if you can, keep on truckin'!

Now, if you can force your right wrist to decelerate (I know this will be hard), there are a couple of places worth stopping at along the way. The first is the **Lochsa Historical Ranger Station** built in the 1920s and used by the early forest service to watch for forest fires. Not accessible by road until 1952, this site is a living memorial to the rustic and difficult life rangers lead prior to tourists flocking to our National Parks. Park in the lower lot and walk up the steps to the visitors' center. An older couple usually acts as hosts and is more than willing to give you some background into the Ranger's daily routine. The old living quarters and work barn are also open as part of the self guided tour. My appreciation for the Forest Service and the sacrifice made by these dedicated Rangers increased ten fold after walking through this living museum. Don't miss it.

The other stop is **Powell**—definitely worth your time as this is where you will be spending the night! Tucked neatly in a pine covered glen, Powell is about fourteen miles from the Montana border. Turn right on exit 162

Enjoy a remote stop in the pines as you follow Lewis and Clark's historic route.

into the wooded grove off Hwy 12 and you will find a remote rest stop with a small gas station, food, and lodging. In 1805, Lewis and Clark stopped here totally exhausted and had to kill one of their colts for food. You may feel the same way, but don't do anything drastic—the restaurant serves up plentiful portions to satisfy your gnawing appetite. The blackberry cobbler is particularly scrumptious. The **Lochsa Lodge** was recently renovated in 2002 and offers both motel rooms and cabins. A restaurant, mini-mart, and campground are also on the premises. This is an ideal spot to relax and spend a quiet evening. You couldn't ask for a better setting. Visit their website at www.lochsalodge.com or call ahead for reservations at 208-942-3405.

DAY TWO

If you do spend the night here and are on a GS or dual sport, consider spending another night. The historic **Lolo Motorway** is just a hop and a skip from Powell. This motorway was built in the 1930s by the CCC to replace the historic trail that once bore the footprints of the Nez Perce. This is the actual trail Lewis and Clark hiked on their trek to the Columbia River. The motorway is definitely *not* a motorway, but rather a narrow and rocky dirt single-laner along a mountainous ridgeline. Although the motorway extends quite some distance down to Lowell, I would suggest taking a fifteen- to twenty-mile portion of it. If you are interested, take Parachute Hill Road 569 on the north side of Hwy 12 just before the turnoff to the Powell Ranger Station. Follow this road to Forest Road 500—this is the "**Lolo Motorway**." Turn left and get a real taste of Lewis and Clark country from the seat of a motorcycle. Follow the motorway until you arrive at Saddle Camp Road 107 and turn left back to Hwy 12. You are now about twenty-two miles west of Powell. Total loop is around sixty miles. Plan on four to six hours to do the entire trip. Pack a lunch and stop along the way for a hike to really appreciate the excitement of this fascinating episode in our American history. For more information contact the Powell Ranger Station District, Lolo, Montana, 59847 or call 208-942-3113.

From Powell, continue north on Hwy 12 over Lolo Pass. Stop at the newly rebuilt visitors' center for more information of the Lewis and Clark Expedition and the 1877 flight of the Nez Perce. The road then descends into Montana and sweeps past the Lolo Hot Springs Resort (stop for some hot chocolate www.lolohotsprings.com, 800-273-2290) and after forty-six miles from Powell enters the town of Lolo, Montana. At Lolo, turn right on US Hwy 93 and just outside of town stop at the Travelers Rest Historic Site. Lewis and Clark camped here in 1805 while traveling toward the Pacific as well as on their return journey in 1806. Continue south toward Florence and then turn left on State Route 203 (East Side Highway). Follow this through Stevensville onto Route 269 and then back to Hwy 93. State Routes 203 and 269 run parallel to and just east of US Hwy 93. I prefer this side road as it is less traveled and, in my opinion, a more enjoyable ride. Before leaving Florence, though, **Glen's Mountain View Cafe** just west of the Highway bakes some awfully good double crusted berry pies. You may want to try one before turning onto the East Side Highway!

Just before Stevensville, the Lee Metcalf National Wildlife Refuge appears on the west side of the road. The highway then cuts through Stevensville toward Hamilton. Just north of Hamilton, cottonwoods dot the landscape as you approach the **Daly Mansion**. This Victorian mansion was built in 1890 by Marcus Daly, a copper mining magnate. The 22,000 acre farm surrounding his former home was used to raise some of the greatest racehorses in the country. Called Bitterroot Stock Farm, this area is now a National Historic Site owned by Montana and open from 11 to 4 (www.dalymansion.org, 406-363-6004). Upon his death, these horses were sold for what was considered a fortune in his day.

Continue south past Hamilton, veer back onto Hwy 93 toward Daly and Lost Trail Pass. The Bitterroot Range looms to the west with Trapper Peak at over 10,000 feet as its centerpiece. In the springtime the bitterroot lily blooms with a pinkish hue adding a streak of outlandish color to this rugged wilderness area. The road runs relatively straight as it hugs the East Fork Bitterroot River and then starts to climb toward Lost Trail Pass. This is a steep, four-lane sweeper with historical markers along the way noting the ill-fated detour of Lewis and Clark to the Salmon River. Certainly a pleasant journey today, back in 1805, Lewis and Clark were momentarily lost on this

Rafters make their way down the Salmon River.

US Highway 12 is also known as the Lewis and Clark Highway or the NorthWest Passage Scenic Byway.

part of the expedition. Their journal records this trek as being one of "the worst" episodes of their entire journey as they struggled over the steep ridges. As your motorcycle zigzags along the mountain crests, try to visualize hiking through this remote wilderness with no map and only a vague notion of what lies ahead.

At North Fork, the Salmon River churns wildly along a rock strewn riverbed and hugs the highway pretty much all the way to Stanley. Squeezed by narrow cliffs, the Salmon gushes forward like a hemmed in hose. The Shoshone Indians realizing the savage nature of the river centuries ago named it the "River of No Return." Today, experts have mastered its unruliness and rafting trips are numerous and readily accessible along its shoreline.

The town of Salmon (www.salmonidaho.com) nestled within the mountain valley is a convenient spot to overnight before completing this journey back to Boise. Several hotels are located in the small downtown area. Or if you prefer, several historic B&Bs are located just outside of town. Roger and Sharon Solass provide fresh, bountiful breakfasts at an old stagecoach stop in the town of Baker. **Solaas Bed and Breakfast** (www.salmonidaho.com/solaas) is located on 3 S. Baker 208-756-3903, nine miles west of Salmon. Another B&B is the **Greyhouse Inn Bed & Breakfast** built in 1894 and run by Sharon and David Osgood. The Greyhouse is located twelve miles south of Salmon on US Hwy 93 just across from the 293 marker (www. greyhouseinn.com, 800-348-8097). Rooms and cabins are available. Some local eateries are **Bertram's Brewery** located on Main and Andrew (208- 756-3391). For more upscale dining (relatively speaking) try the **Shady Nook** right on Hwy 93 (208-756-4182). If you really want a taste of this community, stay an extra day and indulge in some whitewater rafting down the Salmon. Or, since today's trip was relatively short and you got here by noon (assuming you took my advice and got to Powell last night), take a half-day trip down the river! Just ask anybody in town who the best outfitter is. You'll get an earful.

DAY THREE

In the morning, continue south on US Hwy 93 toward Ellis. The road me- anders alongside the Salmon River, scrapes its way through Cronks Can- yon, and then slides through low lying hills into Challis. Challis is a small town of 1,200 people and was originally founded in 1876 as a supply depot for miners in the surrounding area. Hwy 93 and State Route 75 intersect here. Continue east on Route 75 toward Stanley. About forty-five miles from Challis, you will arrive in the small town of Sunbeam. If you are inter- ested in visiting two old mining communities turned ghost towns, hang a right on the dirt road to Bonanza and Custer (**Backroad to Bonanza**). The mother lode was discovered in 1876 and these towns hosted upward of 1,500 inhabitants at one time. Several structures still remain and are now under the management of the U.S. Forestry Service. Some of the buildings are being reconstructed and a self guiding tour is available. A very worth- while side trip to a couple of well preserved ghost towns. It is best seen on a GS or dual sport type bike.

Fourteen miles further east of Sunbeam on Route 75, the outdoorsmen's mecca of Stanley greets you. You are now well into the Sawtooth and some of the most beautiful countryside in Idaho. At Stanley, turn right on State Route 21 and follow the Ponderosa Scenic Byway toward Lowman. This journey is covered in my chapter titled "Sawtooth Sortie," but in the oppo- site direction. I've discovered in my motorcycling travels that re-riding a route in the opposite direction provides quite a different vantage point and is almost like a new journey. Anyway, brush up on the other chapter for more details on this great run from Stanley to Lowman.

Now, when you arrive in Lowman, instead of heading south on Route 21 to Boise, turn right on the Banks-Lowman Road to Banks and State Route 55. This thirty-three-mile run is called the **Wildlife Canyon Scenic Byway**

At historic White Bird Battlefield, Yellow Bird of the Nez Perce was fired upon while attempting to make peace with the U.S. Cavalry.

and provides some sweet sweepers along the South Fork of the Payette River. The road is a two-laner with no passing lanes, but there are several turnouts for viewing.

As your wrist re-engages for one final lap before returning to Boise, keep a lookout for gravity-defying kayakers leaping through Class IV rapids on the river next to you. Don't be surprised if some of them beat you to the finish line! Keep your other eye focused on the horizon for elk or deer grazing lazily in the meadows (that is until a motorcycle flies by!). Bald eagles flying overhead may also distract you, so do be careful! This short span of byway through another remote and unspoiled part of Idaho is not only a great way to end your three-day adventure through this great state, but is another testimony to the rugged beauty of this entire wilderness area once visited by Lewis and Clark in 1805 and still enjoyed by us today.

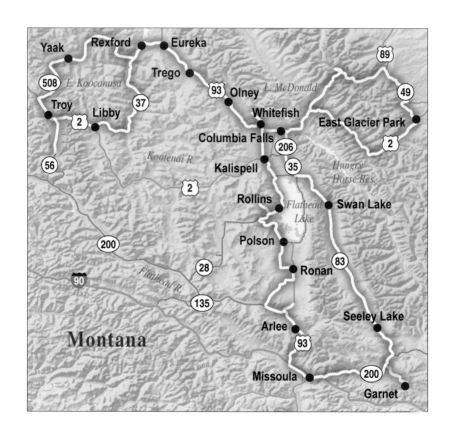

Whitefish

Like I have always said on these journeys, it's amazing the little tidbits of trivia and undiscovered gems you come across while motorcycling. **Whitefish, Montana**, is one of those gems. Did you know that this small community hosts two high caliber theater companies, the musical Alpine Theatre Project and the Whitefish Theatre Company? Or did you know that on the corner of 4th and Central you will find a building designed by none other then Frank Lloyd Wright? Or that golf courses and a world-class ski resort are just a few minutes from town and to top it all off, Black Star Beer originates from and is made locally at the Great Northern Microbrewery? No wonder Whitefish is not only an avid recreational playground, but also an up and coming retirement community as well. Now all that's needed is an annual motorcycle rally!

The alpine village of Whitefish offers gondola rides, hiking, chuckwagon dinners, fine village and summit dining, and music festivals in the outdoor amphitheater. Try some of the local microbrews such as Black Star Lager, Big Fog, Black Lager, and Huckleberry Wheat Lager at Great Northern Brewing Company.

Situated in the Flathead Valley on the shores of the Whitefish Lake, this little town combines its natural setting and community spirit into a heck of a great place to stay. Originally founded as a fur trading post in the 1800s, the Great Northern Railroad really got the town started in 1903 as a division point and switchyard to transport logs due to the booming timber industry. Toward the 1930s as the timber business dwindled, Whitefish evolved into a recreational haven boasting golf courses and a ski resort at **Hellroaring Mountain.** And most importantly, Whitefish got a real tourist boost by being only twenty-five miles west of Glacier National Park. Due to its prime location, Whitefish is used as a base for three Rocky Mountain motorcycle journeys—the Going-to-the-Sun Road, Flathead Lake Loop, and The Lake Koocanusa Loop.

Coming home to Whitefish is a welcome sight as numerous lodging facilities, restaurants, and activities are located here. Taking a stroll along the sandy shores of Whitefish Lake, visiting the historic Whitefish Railway Depot, attending a local theater company performance, or just wandering around the weekly Farmer's Market are like icing on the cake after a scrumptious 200-mile motorcycle ride.

For information on places to stay or dine, visit their website at www.whitefishchamber.com or call 877-862-3548. I usually stay in town at the **Best Western Rocky Mountain Lodge** (www.rockymtnlodge.com, 800-862-2569). I like being close to town and the hotel has a fireplace downstairs to warm me up. Another highly recommended B&B is the Good Medicine Lodge run by Betsy and Woody and located just north of town (www.goodmedicinelodge.com, 800-860-5488). Their hospitality is

The historic Great Northern Railroad Depot and Stumpton Museum was restored by the Whitefish Historical Society in 1990 to its original chalet-like appearance.

In the 1930s when the timber business dwindled, Whitefish evolved into a recreational haven boasting golf courses and a ski resort at Hellroaring Mountain. (Photo by Michael Jaffe)

legendary and food is fantastic. If you want to mix it up, try **McGarry's Roadhouse** just across the street from the lodge (510 Wisconsin Ave 406-862-6223). Or if you are downtown, try the **Buffalo Cafe's** (516 E. 3rd Street) huevos rancheros for breakfast and then in the evening drop by **The Palace**, Whitefish's oldest bar, for a nightcap. A host of other restaurants from fast food to pizza and fine dining are also located around the downtown area.

After a long day of riding, sipping a cup of hot chocolate as you rest on the lake's shoreline watching the sun slip behind the horizon is a near perfect end to another day of riding through the Rockies in the "Big Sky" country of northwestern Montana.

Trip 19   The Going-to-the-Sun Road

Distance *201 miles (full day)*
Terrain *Drive the famous "Going-to-the-Sun Road" through Glacier National Park then loop back around via the south end of the park along the old Great Northern Railroad route. Elevation change 3,300 feet to 6,600 feet.*
Highlights *Narrow two-laners carved into granite cliffs on the "Going-to-the-Sun Road," sweeping bends on US Hwy 2.*

Glacier National Park is referred to by its founder as the "Crown" of the continent. Ice fields lingering from times past have cut across granite slopes creating a wonderland of alpine valleys and hundreds of deep azure lakes. One solitary road weaves through the park beside creviced slopes so high above the valley floors that it has been named none other than the "Going-to-the-Sun Road." Winter storms often bring eighty-plus feet of snow along

Motorcyclists seem pretty small next to these towering slabs of granite.

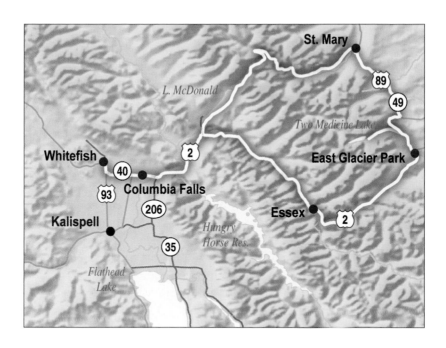

THE ROUTE FROM WHITEFISH

0	Start in Whitefish, head south on US Hwy 93
2	Turn left on State Route 40
6	Route 40 turns and becomes US Hwy 2
25	Turn left on the "Going-to-the-Sun Road"
75	Arrive St. Mary, turn right on US Hwy 89
94	Turn right onto State Route 49
101	Turn right on Two Medicine Road
109	Arrive Medicine Lake, turn around
117	Turn right on State Route 49
121	Arrive East Glacier Park, turn right on US Hwy2
150	Arrive Essex, continue on US Hwy 2
195	US Hwy 2 turns into State Route 40
199	Turn right on US Hwy 93
201	Arrive Whitefish

this corridor, keeping it closed until late spring. The traveler's patience is well rewarded driving alongside snow banks ten-feet-high with views of green valleys and spiraling waterfalls. The pavement itself is often wet from the spray of water cascading down the vertical cliffs towering above the road.

A journey through the Rocky Mountains would not be complete without visiting **Glacier National Park**. This motorcycle trip takes you east from Whitefish to West Glacier and then over the continental divide on the Going-to-the-Sun Road to St. Mary at the east end of the park. After a detour to Two Medicine Lake, you complete the loop following US Highway 2 beside the old Great Northern Railway line that skirts the southern boundary of Glacier Park. The route is just over 200 miles long and through some of the best scenery the Rocky Mountains has to offer. Don't forget your raingear, liner, and some sunscreen. The weather can be unpredictable and at these altitudes, the ultraviolet rays are unforgiving.

Begin this trek by heading south on US Highway 93 from Whitefish for about two miles and then turn left on State Route 40. After four miles Route 40 becomes US Highway 2 and then after nineteen miles becomes

Roads like this twist and turn all the way from Arizona to Montana. Time to get going!

Hey, slow down! Remember I'm the one taking the pictures!

the **Going-to-the-Sun Road** at West Glacier. Glacier National Park (www.nps.gov/glac, 406-888-7800) is a huge wilderness area bisected by only the one road. As a result, this park remains a pristine natural habitat for bear, moose, elk, and other wildlife. Designated a National Park in 1912 by President Taft, Glacier National Park also has the distinction of being an International Peace Park, Biosphere Reserve, and World Heritage Site. Touted as the "American Alps," the Great Northern Railroad under the direction of its Chairman Louis Hill promoted this area as a destination unto itself. Before 1932, there was no road access so the railroad company constructed two enormous hotels and several backcountry chalets. This series of accommodations were linked by horseback, boat trips, and day hikes into a truly remarkable trek across the innards of this mountain wilderness. Several of the original chalet style lodges are still being used today and are National Historic Landmarks.

Due to the heavy influx of tourists, constructihttp://o.forums.go.com/abc/oceanic/thread?threadID=1139206on of a road through the park's interior began in 1921. The final portion of the road at Logan Pass was completed eleven years later. What took days to traverse now takes hours and the Going-to-the Sun Road became a National Historic Landmark. If you can, time your visit in September when most tourists are gone, the colors are changing, and wildlife is abundant.

Today's 200-plus mile journey is relatively long, so leave early from Whitefish. You might even get lucky and see some moose grazing at Moose Turnout at the east end of Lake McDonald. Drop by the Agpar Visitor Center to become more familiar with the park. Maps and recommended hikes are available from the Rangers.

For around ten miles before the Moose Turnout, the asphalt runs adjacent to the lake through wooded glens and forests. **Lake McDonald** is the largest in the park and was carved out by a huge glacier. The lake is 472 feet deep and is surrounded by the Lewis Range. The mountains act not only as a scenic backdrop but cause significant rainfall in the valley, creating a shoreline that is dense with undergrowth, western red cedar, and hemlock trees. Reminds me of the Pacific Northwest.

The pavement tunnels through the vegetation and begins to climb beside McDonald Creek. At the end of McDonald Lake, a waterfall comes cascading downward and a marshland unfolds revealing limitless shades of green. Thanks to the beaver population, a moist wetland invites moose to search for one of their favorite foods, aquatic plants. Stop at the Moose Turnout and if you get here early enough, you may just see a few of these 1,000-pound mammals.

The asphalt continues to hug McDonald Creek and after about four miles you will see a turnoff on the right for the "Trail of the Cedars" and

The road is still wet from an afternoon shower but there are clear skies ahead.

Many roads in the Rockies run parallel to the old train routes used by miners.

"Avalanche Lake." Pull into the parking area and put on your walking shoes. The **Trail of the Cedars** is a short half-mile elevated walk through moss draped hemlocks and cedars. If you have the time, I would highly recommend the two-mile hike to **Avalanche Lake**. It is relatively easy and a myriad of waterfalls plummeting into the lake will greet you. During late spring and early summer, avalanches from the surrounding mountains tumble frequently onto its surface.

After putting your kevlar padded motorcycle boots back on, the Going-to-the-Sun Road continues to climb and eventually the dense vegetation turns to fir and spruce. Then abruptly the ridgeline of **Garden Wall** rises on the horizon and you begin to understand why this is, indeed, called the Going-to-the-Sun Road. The two-laner then quickly hairpins from northeast to southeast at a point called The Loop.

The Loop doubles back with several pullouts available in both directions providing great panoramas of the surrounding mountain range. The six percent grade up Logan Pass now follows the Garden Wall and about two miles after the Loop, **Birdwoman Falls** drops majestically into view. As you continue to ascend toward Logan Pass, the sky may be clear but the road may be slick with a film of water. **Weeping Wall** on your left definitely weeps! Snowmelt splashes down the cliffs and water seeps through cracks and crevices on its way down to the valley floor. Drive carefully and if it is a warm day, make a hasty switch into your swimsuit and have a refreshing outdoor shower!

After Weeping Wall, the road will wind around Haystack Bend and a parking lot. Wildlife is abundant here and if you want to take a chance pull over and hike around a bit; mountain goats and bighorn sheep are known to roam these parts. Also, about half a mile from the summit **Alpine Meadow** comes into view. During the early summer, this meadow is covered with yellow glacier lilies.

At Logan Pass, the highest elevation in the park at 6,640 feet, pull into the large parking area and spend some time at the visitors' center. On my last trip, a crowd of tourists had congregated just off the parking lot to befriend one of the local inhabitants—a shaggy mountain goat. Two trailheads are also located at Logan Pass. One is the easy one-and-a-half-mile hike to Hidden Lake Overlook and another is the "not for the faint of heart" seven-and-a-half-mile hike on the Highline Trail. The **Hidden Lake** hike eventually ends up at a platform overlooking this scenic alpine lake. **Highline Trail** is one of the most popular hikes in Glacier as it climbs around sheer cliffs on a toothpick-sized trail gouged into the rock. The hike ends at the Granite Park Chalet overlooking Bear Valley.

Now that you're out of breath, take a break by hopping back on your bike to begin the descent down the eastside of Logan Pass. About one mile from the summit, keep a lookout for Creek Falls just north of the road. Take your sunglasses off driving through the tunnel and then pop open your umbrella for yet another refreshing waterfall on the opposite side. At Siyeh Curve the road twists tightly and drops quickly into the more heavily forested area just west of St. Mary's Lake.

A single-laner weaves its way to a high mountain lake.

A tranquil alpine lake nestles high in the Rockies.

Another stop worth noting before the lake is the **Jackson Glacier Overlook**. A bluish white glacier, now just a remnant of the huge ice bands that once covered the landscape, can be seen tucked between the mountain slopes.

Now, if you waited until September to make this journey, you will be rewarded when descending into yellow and gold foliage falling off forests of aspen and alder. The blacktop frolics through the trees swaying back and forth like a pendulum. Stop at the turnout for views of **Virginia Falls** across the valley. Various other pullouts are located strategically along the north shoreline of **St. Mary's Lake**. Sun Point, Goose Island View, and The Narrows are all worth mentioning and provide picture postcard panoramas of the idyllic location. In the background Triple Divide Peak rises like a shadow along the continental divide. Rain showers over this peak will either end up in the Pacific, Atlantic, or the Arctic Oceans. Your guess is as good as mine!

The park's boundary edges right up to the east end of St. Mary Lake and after just a few miles the Going-to-the-Sun Road officially ends in the town of St. Mary. If you haven't eaten yet try **Johnson's Cafe** located just off US Highway 89 in St. Mary. The hot soup and fresh, homemade bread will definitely hit the spot and warm your chilled bones. Take a moment and chat with Lester or Ruth and have them share their experiences starting this restaurant. Apparently a tent behind the cafe was their home for a number of years when they first opened up and water had to be hauled up from the river in barrels. What a life! Their daughter Kristin now runs the place.

The next part of this journey takes you south on US Hwy 89 to State Route 49 for a short detour to Two Medicine Lake and then down to East

This train was used for years to haul silver from the Rockies.

Glacier where you join up with US Hwy 2 back to Whitefish. So continue on Hwy 89 south and enjoy the next twenty miles as the road weaves through the foothills of Glacier's Rocky Mountains. This is Blackfeet Indian Reservation territory and as you approach the junction of Hwy 89 and Route 49, the foothills fan out and eventually merge with the endless yellow grasslands of the Great Plain. Originally, the Blackfeet Indian Reservation included Glacier National Park but due to miners' greed the Blackfeet were forced further east of the park.

Turn right on State Route 49 toward East Glacier and then if you have time for another venture into Glacier Park, turn right to Two Medicine Lake. This lake is less touristy then the Going-to-the-Sun Road and is only nine miles from the junction. The road ultimately ends on the eastern shore of clear blue water surrounded by snowcapped mountains. A boat service is available at the dock and various trailheads exploring the interior of the park begin here.

After a quick look, head back to Route 49 and turn right to East Glacier about four miles further on. If you want to spend more time hiking or boating in the park, East Glacier is a good midpoint. Lodging, camping, and restaurants are all available in town (www.eastglacierpark.org, 800-338-5072). At the very least drop by the **Glacier Park Lodge** built in 1913 (www.bigtreehotel.com, 406-892-2525). The lobby's timbered posts reach majestically toward the ceiling making this an awesome sight (the restrooms aren't bad either).

In East Glacier, Route 49 joins US Highway 2 skirting the south end of the park and pretty much following the old Great Northern Railroad Line over **Marias Pass** to Essex, and then West Glacier to Whitefish. Railroad buffs should love this historic run along Hwy 2. The linking of the Central Pacific and Union Pacific Railroads at Promontory Utah in 1869 was only the beginning of a huge rush to the markets just opening on the West Coast. The Southern Pacific had taken the "lowland" route through New Mexico and it was now time for the Great Northern Railroad to find another crossing through Montana's Rocky Mountains to the Puget Sound. Construction over the Rockies took over a year following a path along the southern boundary of Glacier National park and was completed in 1893. In addition to crossing the continental divide at Marias Pass, two mammoth trestles were built over Cut Bank and Medicine Creek. Now operated by the Burlington Northern and Santa Fe Railroads, this stretch of railway history can for the most part be seen from the seat of your motorcycle along US Hwy 2.

There is nothing more enticing then a bend in the road with scenery like this.

East Glacier to Marias Pass Summit is ten miles and then another twenty miles to Essex. As most tourists cross the divide via the Going-to-the-Sun Road, Hwy 2 is less traveled and in its own way more fun to ride. No major stops along the way, just an open windy piece of blacktop enticing you along. Enjoy the solitude of this ride as you skirt the edge of Glacier up and over Marias. Ride alongside modern day locomotives as they crawl up the grade and over the summit.

At Essex, visit the famous **Izaak Walton Inn** (www.izaakwaltoninn.com, 406-888-5700), a converted rail bunkhouse used by the Great Northern Railroad and built in 1939. Named after the 16th century sportsman Sir Izaak Walton, this hotel is tucked in the backcountry and truly gives a whole new meaning to "getting away from it all." Train service is still very active on this line, making this inn a great layover for rail fans.

Continue north on Hwy 2 toward West Glacier. The road will cross the rail line several times along the way. Impressive bridges span Medicine Creek and Cut Bank. Enjoy the lack of motorists. Open up your throttle. The serpentine asphalt flows in a small valley between Glacier National Park and the Flathead Mountains in the Great Bear Wilderness. Nestled

These motorcyclists have it figured out! Bring along some collapsible chairs and have a picnic lunch.

The sun sets on a lake high in Montana; the end of another perfect day.

between two mountain ranges racing beside a Burlington Northern locomotive is a picture I will never forget. Hopefully, you'll have a similar
experience.

At West Glacier, follow Hwy 2 east to the small towns of Coram, Martin
City, and Hungry Horse. Hook back into State Route 40 for a short jaunt to
US Highway 93 north back home to Whitefish.

The quiet solitude of the last eighty miles on Hwy 2 has given you time
to reflect on the grandeur of Glacier National Park and its surrounding wilderness refuge. Motorcycling through the Rockies is not only about racing
toward the next bend, but also gaining a deeper appreciation of the great
natural wonders this country has to offer. Being encompassed by snow-clad
peaks on a toothpick size two-laner beside a mile-long train makes you feel
puny indeed! But, then again, I don't care how puny I am; life sure is great
cruising along on a two-wheeler. What journey is planned for tomorrow?

Trip 20 Flathead Lake Loop

Distance *332 miles (one to two days)*

Terrain *Cruise by Montana's largest body of water, Flathead Lake, and then drive to the National Bison Range where herds of Buffalo still roam. End the journey driving by numerous lakes in the Seeley Swan Valley. An optional backroad is available on this tour: The twelve-mile Garnet Back Country Byway to one of the Rockies best ghost towns. Spend the night in Seeley Lake if you want to take it a little slower and do some side trips. Elevation change 3,000 to 6,000 feet.*

Highlights *Curvaceous lake shore runs and gentle bends through rolling hills and lake filled valleys. Some roads to lakes are on well groomed gravel.*

Montana is not only big sky country, but big lake country as well. Located just south of Whitefish is the largest freshwater natural lake west of the Mississippi encompassing 188 square miles. Flathead Lake lies just north of the Mission Mountains with its southern half intruding halfway into the Indian Reservation. This huge lake nudges into the Rockies and is surrounded with pine and grasslands. Smaller lakes dot the countryside between the Swan and Mission Mountain Ranges in what is known locally as the "chain-of-lakes." The Seeley Swan Valley is the watershed for the Clearwater and

The Rocky Mountains ring the perimeter of this alpine lake.

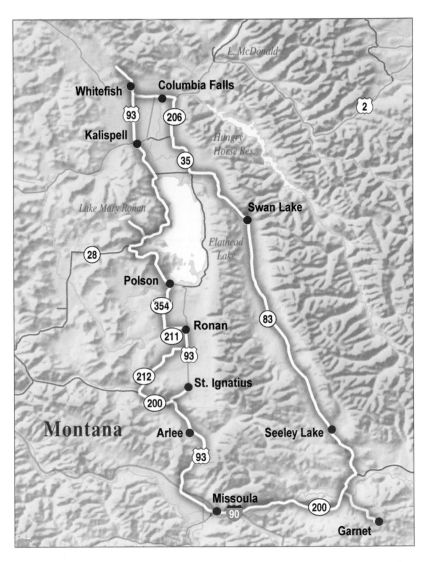

Swan rivers resulting in a myriad of lakes lining this mountainous corridor. Take your pick with the likes of Seeley Lake, Salmon Lake, Placid Lake, Holland Lake, Lake Inez, Rainey Lake . . . and the list goes on. For those on dual sport bikes, head up that dirt track to some less frequented alpine lakes and enjoy the setting in absolute solitude. Camp at one of several state, local, or national sites located right on the shoreline or stay at a B&B with balcony views overlooking many of these lakes. Hope you remembered your fishing gear!

THE ROUTE FROM WHITEFISH

0   Start in Whitefish, go south on US Hwy 93

15   Arrive Kalispell, continue south on Hwy 93

44   Arrive Dayton, turn right to Lake Mary Ronan

48   Arrive Lake Mary Ronan, turn around

52   Turn right on Hwy 93 in Dayton

62   Arrive Big Arm (optional boat ride to Wildhorse Island available here)

74   Arrive Polson, drive south on State Route 354 to Kerr Dam

82   Arrive Kerr Dam, continue south

92   Turn right on State Route 211 to Ronan

99   Arrive Ronan, turn right on US Hwy 93

104 Turn right on State Route 212 toward Ninepipe National Refuge and Bison Range

117 Arrive Moiese and entrance to the National Bison Range. [Continue south on Route 212 toward Dixon.]

121 Turn left on State Route 200 to Ravalli

127 Arrive Ravalli, head north on US Hwy 93 to St. Ignatius

132 Arrive St. Ignatius, turn around, continue south on Hwy 93 to I-90

164 Merge into I-90 east

178 Take exit 109 to Bonner on State Route 200

203 Optional turnoff to Garnet on twelve-mile Garnet Back Country Byway (dual sport only)

211 Turn left on State Route 83 to Seeley Lake. Route 83 lined with numerous side trips to mountain lakes. See narrative for choices and more specific directions.

226 Arrive Seeley Lake. Spend the night or continue north on Route 83

302 Turn right on State Route 35

313 Connect with State Route 206 north to Columbia Falls

323 Turn left on US Hwy 2, State Route 40

325 Arrive Columbia Falls

330 Turn right on US Hwy 93 to Whitefish

332 Arrive Whitefish

This trip is over 300 miles and requires a full day (or two) of riding. Starting in Whitefish, this trek follows US Hwy 93 south along the shores of Flathead Lake and down to the National Bison Range on State Route 212. It then moves in a counterclockwise motion to Missoula and back north through the Seeley Swan Valley and eventually home to Whitefish. If you want to break this trip into a two-day jaunt and spend some extra time exploring, then stay in Seeley Lake (www.seeleychamber.com, 406-677-2880) on State Route 83. The pleasant, peaceful surroundings will sooth your aching joints in a truly tranquil Rocky Mountain setting. Another good website with short descriptions of each lodging facility is www.montanascenicloop.com/selleylake.htm. Some of the lodges such as the **Emily A. Bed & Breakfast** are set right on the Lake's edge (www.theemilya.com, 406-677-FISH). Camping facilities are available at most lakes as well, although some are more primitive then others. If it's bathrooms you're concerned about, I know both Salmon and Placid Lakes have flush toilets!

Begin bright and early on US Hwy 93 south to Kalispell. This town's name is an Indian word for "prairie above the lake." With a population of 14,000 it is one of the larger towns in northwestern Montana. If you're hungry, drop by **Norm's News** at 34 Main Street for breakfast. Then the real fun begins as you approach Somers on the northwestern end of **Flathead Lake**. The road narrows and follows the shoreline to Lakeside and Rollins. The lake appears huge as the road hugs the rocky perimeter. The expansive views stretch far onto the horizon with glimpses of the Mission Range to the southeast.

At Dayton, thirty miles south of Kalispell, turn right to Lake Mary Ronan for your first of several detours on this chain-of-lakes journey. Head

Montana is not only big sky country, but big lake country as well.

northwest on a paved/gravel road and after about three miles you will arrive at the lake's edge. Surrounded by ponderosa pine and rolling foothills, this small lake is a delightful introduction to what lays ahead. Visit the **Lake Mary Ronan Lodge Restaurant** (www.lakemaryronan.com, 406-849-5459) if your stomach is still grumbling or just take a short walk to stretch your legs.

Hop back on your bike and continue south toward Big Arm. There is a marina in town and if you decide to take two days to complete this trip then enjoy a short boat ride to **Wildhorse Island**. The island was originally used by the Indians to hide their horses from enemies and is now a state park. In the early 1900s the island was bought by Colonel Almon A. White for real estate development. The anticipated buyers never materialized and ultimately the government repossessed the island and turned it into a park. Private property is still found around the perimeter, but the interior is home to wild mustangs and a variety of plant and wildlife. The island is only accessible by water and boats can be chartered in Big Arm.

From Big Arm, Hwy 93 veers southwest from the lake heading over grassy hills to Polson. The rocky shoreline soon re-emerges and wind-filled sails are seen moving along the lake's shimmering surface. Tiny coves and summer homes dot the perimeter. The beauty of this lake is reaffirmed the closer you drive toward its glistening mass.

After around twenty-eight miles, you will arrive in **Polson**. Set on Flathead Lake's southern end and former glacial moraine, Polson is situated in Reservation Land and is a homey community with a mixed population of Flathead Salish, Kootenai, and retired Caucasians. Grocery stores, gas stations, lodging, and camping (one of the best KOA campgrounds from what I've heard) are all found in this quaint town. Known for its cherry orchards, Polson also has a nice waterfront area worth a visit. The Cove Deli or **Lake House Grill** provide needed nourishment—a little ice cream can do the trick as you stroll along the Lake and admire the views.

Head south on Seventh Avenue to Kerr Dam Road and follow the signs to the dam. You will drive by Pablo National Wildlife Refuge and then after eight miles arrive at **Kerr Dam**. This dam stands 204 vertical feet above the Flathead River and was completed in 1938. Walk to the lookout point just above the dam for some magnificent panoramas of the Flathead Valley. The dam itself is a sight to behold. After getting your fill, continue south on what is State Route 354 for just a few miles and then turn left on State Route 211 to Ronan.

Turn right at Ronan to rejoin Hwy 93 and about four miles south watch for signs to the **Ninepipe National Wildlife Refuge** (www.fws.gov/bisonrange/ninepipe, 406-644-2211). Turn right on State Route 212. This road will hug the western boundary of the refuge. Ninepipe is a wildlife and waterfowl management area. The wetland has a 1,700 acre reservoir and hundreds of different bird species. If you're interested, dust off your binoculars and stop at any of the signed parking areas along the way.

Continue through Charlo and then on to Route 212 through rolling prairie lands. Soon you will arrive in Moise, which marks the entrance to the **National Bison Range** (www.fws.gov/bisonrange/nbr, 406-644-2211). This 18,500-acre preserve is located east of Route 212 and west of Hwy 93. Created in 1908 to protect the once endangered buffalo, the park is now home to bison, mountain goats, and pronghorns. Drop by the visitors' center for a brief introduction. Some of the pictures will astound you—a picture is definitely worth a thousand words! If you want to continue through the park, take the four-mile half-hour Buffalo Prairie Drive. Driving this

Be sure to take your fishing gear. You might get lucky and have fresh trout for dinner.

short spur road transports you back to the days when bison roamed freely on our Great Plains—just remember they're bigger then your motorcycle.

When you reconnect with Route 212, continue south toward Dixon about five miles from Moise and turn left on State Route 200 to Ravalli. Grab a real live (you know what I mean) Buffalo Burger and a huckleberry milkshake at the **Bison Inn** in Ravalli to recharge yourself, and then head north on Hwy 93 to St. Ignatius for a short detour (about five miles). Although the town itself is not all that charming, the Mission Church is worth a short visit. Open from ten am to four pm, the church's interior is adorned with over fifty frescoes. The paintings are more reminiscent of an Italian chapel than a mission found in northwest Montana. What is most impressive is that the frescoes were painted by the mission cook, Friar Joseph Carignana, in his spare time!

Turn around in St. Ignatius back to Ravilli and veer left at the intersection to Arlee on Hwy 93. The road meanders through the Jocko Valley to Arlee (home of the northwest's largest Powwow held every July) and then climbs to Evaro amidst ponderosa and fir. The ascent to Evaro reveals the Mission Mountains in all their glory. Rising abruptly from the earth's crust these mountains provided a natural barrier and enclave to the Native Americans who once lived here. Seven miles after Evaro, Route 93 connects with I-90. Merge onto the freeway heading east toward Missoula. Drive right

Mountain roads lush with fir, pine, and more shades of green than you can count.

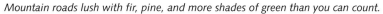

Can you see it? Keep an eye out for wandering wildlife.

through town and after fourteen miles take State Route 200 north toward Clearwater and Seeley Lake.

State Route 200 winds by the southern boundary of the Rattlesnake Wilderness (don't stop to change a flat tire here!) and runs through the "don't blink or you'll miss" towns of Milltown and Potomac. After about twenty-five miles between mile markers twenty-two and twenty-three there is a turnoff to the old mining town of **Garnet**. Founded in the late 1800s, this town struck gold in the 1890s and swelled to over 1,000 people by 1898. Unlike other mining towns, big mining companies laid claim to the gold and as a result a mellower community resided here (relatively speaking). By 1905 the gold was gone and the population dwindled to 150. A fire in 1912 all but closed the door on this mining town turned bust, but what remains are some very well-preserved turn-of-the century buildings and one of the best ghost towns in the Rocky Mountains.

The **Garnet Back Country Byway,** a dirt road about twelve miles in length, takes you to this once thriving mining town. More suited for a dual sport bike or GS, the road ascends 2,000 feet through forested pines into the Garnet Range. In addition to visiting the town itself, the journey along this backroad offers up great panoramas of the Swan Range and the Blackfoot River Valley. This diversion is best suited if you plan on spending the night in Seeley Lake. You can either do this run in the afternoon or in the morning before heading back to Whitefish. One of the best off-road treks I've done in the Rockies!

After seven miles, Route 200 connects with State Route 83. Turn left. You are about to embark on one of the most beautiful spans of asphalt in the Rocky Mountains. Route 83 cuts through the Swan Range/Bob Marshall Wilderness Area on the east and the Mission Range/Wilderness Area on the west. The road follows the Clearwater and Swan Rivers through countryside dotted with a myriad of lakes, some of them easily accessible, while others require some more serious effort. This ninety-mile "chain-of-lakes" scenic drive is one to be enjoyed and savored.

One of the first lakes you see just off the road is **Salmon Lake**. The lake reflects Montana's big blue sky and green ponderosa from the shoreline. Private homes and retreats are seen surrounding the lake as the road swings gently around its perimeter. Camping and picnic facilities are conveniently located along the way.

The road continues to wind through lower Clearwater Valley and at the twelve-mile marker you will arrive at the Placid Lake turnoff. If you feel up to it, drive three miles west on a gravel road to **Lake Placid**. More private homes dot the shoreline. A camping facility is also available here. Water skiers and sailboats are often seen here as well.

Continuing north on Route 83, the road soon juts up to the south end of **Seeley Lake**. The forest-lined shore invites you to stop and enjoy the peacefulness of the scenic area. If you are planning on spending the night, this is the area to settle in. Lodging facilities and restaurants are located here. Several lakes have accommodations and/or campsites situated nearby. The population nearly doubles in the summer months due to the influx of tourists. Hiking, fishing, horseback riding, boating, and mountain biking provide most everyone visiting with something to do. Another popular activity is paddling down the **Clearwater Canoe Trail** (www.fs.fed.us/rl/lolo, 406-677-233). This one- to two-hour canoe trip through a willow marsh

This road beckons you to great motorcycling in the mountains ahead.

provides rare glimpses into the wildlife and waterfowl along an isolated and picturesque portion of the Clearwater River.

Now comes the hard part. A myriad of lakes line this corridor on Route 83 going north. I will quickly mention a few and you can choose which one (or ones) to see. If you have time all are gorgeous and worth a visit! Starting about six miles from Seeley Lake look for a small forest service road to Lake Inez. A parking area, boat launch, picnic area, and campsites are all available at the end of Lake Inez Road. Another two miles north of Lake Inez is a larger sign for the turnoff to Lake Alva. Again similar facilities are available here. One mile north of Lake Alva at the top of the hill is the turnoff to Rainey Lake. Turn left and go one quarter of a mile to the parking area. If you want to see a lake off the beaten path, travel east on Clearwater Loop Road just north of Rainey Lake. This forest service road is about five miles long and goes to Clearwater Lake.

If you have time to see just one lake, then head north of Rainey Lake about eleven miles and turn right on Holland Lake Road. After about three miles you will arrive at the lake. Mosey down Summer Home Road on your right or just stop at one of the pullouts to enjoy the setting. **Holland Lake** butts up against the remote **Bob Marshall Wilderness Area** giving this lake a sense of natural isolation. Several trailheads into the Wilderness Area begin here. Reward yourself for getting this far by having a cup of hot chocolate at the **Holland Lake Lodge**.

After Holland Lake, take a "lake break" and roll the throttle down a bit. The road's gentle sweeping bends lull you into the zone. Traffic is light, sprinting the final lap along Route 83 toward Columbia Falls and back to Whitefish. Swan Lake and the Swan River National Wildlife Refuge appear on your left. It just keeps getting better! Pull over for a quick look, or slow down a tad and enjoy this one last lake from the seat of your motorcycle. Continue on Route 83 as it veers west and connects with State Route 35. Turn right to Columbia Falls and then continue straight on State Route 206 into town. You are now in familiar territory. Turn left on State Route 40 and then right on US Hwy 93. Whitefish is just a few miles ahead. Be patient, you are almost home!

I know it has been a long day and without a doubt you will feel it. But it will, hopefully, be a "good" feeling with pleasant memories of crystal lakes and abandoned ghost towns. Northwestern Montana is undoubtedly one of the most scenic areas in the Rocky Mountains. The state's big sky and towering mountains combined with flowing rivers and glass-surfaced lakes have transported you to an era of unrivaled natural beauty once known only to herds of roaming buffalo.

Trip 21   Three Rivers Scenic Run

Distance   *322 miles (full day)*

Terrain   *This trip takes you through an isolated and sparsely populated corner of northwest Montana. Lake Koocanusa and the surrounding Kootenai National Forest are fed by multiple rivers and streams. A huge forest blankets this area of rolling hills and cascading waterfalls. Elevation change 1,800 to 6,000 feet.*

Highlights   *Sweeping bends and S-curves are abundant on this run. They seem to carve a path right through the area. Very narrow road to Ross Creek Cedars.*

This final journey takes you through one of the most isolated areas of the Rocky Mountains. The Kootenai National Forest encompasses 2.2 million acres of northwest Montana. In the farthest corner is a land blanketed with fresh scented pine and roaring waterfalls. The Whitefish and Cabinet Mountains rise to heights exceeding 8,000 feet and then tumble to less than 2,000 feet at the lowest point in Montana. The Kootenai, Yaak, and Tobacco rivers flow down the mountain slopes to valleys covered with lush green vegetation and trout-filled lakes. The locals have tried to keep this place a secret and refer to the roads that carve the landscape as the Lake

Few things can compare to riding together with friends on mountain roads.

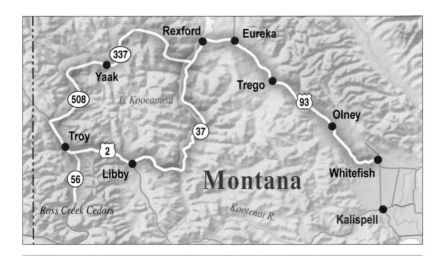

THE ROUTE FROM WHITEFISH

0	Start in Whitefish, Montana, on US Hwy 93 heading north
51	Arrive Eureka, continue on Hwy 93 north
53	Turn left on State Route 37
66	Turn right on Koocanusa Bridge and cross to other side
67	Turn right on State Route 337 to Yaak (continue straight on spur road to Amish Settlement)
108	Arrive Yaak, continue on State Route 508
137	Turn left on US Hwy 2 to Troy
147	Arrive Troy, continue on US Hwy 2 east
149	(optional detour to Ross Creek Cedars) Turn right on State Route 56 (Bull Lake Road)
164	Turn right to Ross Creek Cedars
168	Arrive Ross Creek Cedars, turn around
172	Turn left on State Route 56
187	Turn right on US Hwy 2
191	Arrive Kootenai Falls turnout
203	Arrive Libby, continue on State Route 37
270	Turn right on US Hwy 93 to Eureka
272	Arrive Eureka, continue on US Hwy 93 to Whitefish
322	Arrive Whitefish

Koocanusa, Kootenai River, and Yaak Loop Scenic Byways. I refer to this journey as the Three Rivers Scenic Run and, by the way, the secret is out! The trip starts in Whitefish, heads north on US Hwy 93 and follows the Tobacco River to Eureka. Just past Eureka, you cross Lake Koocanusa where you follow another river, the Yaak, to Troy located on US Hwy 2. The road then meanders beside a third river, the Kootenai, through the Cabinet Mountains to Libby. The return leg hugs the gorgeous manmade reservoir, Lake Koocanusa, on State Route 37 back to Eureka and then home on US 93 to Whitefish. There are only a handful of small communities on this route, so be prepared for wide open roads and be sure your tank is full. If your right wrist has a tendency to twist a bit, I'd keep a lookout in your rear view mirror as well!

This journey covers about 280 miles and if you take the detour to Ross Creek Cedars it is just over 320 miles. So get up nice and early, put your liner in and head north on US Hwy 93 from Whitefish to Eureka. This fifty-one-mile morning run skirts the Flathead National Forest and Stillwater State Forest as it wanders through the small towns of Olney and Stryker. Even at these lower altitudes, the forests are ripe and the scenery divine. The road carves giant S-curves through the landscape. What a great way to start the day!

At Trego, the asphalt links up with the Tobacco River and after sixteen miles enters the small town of **Eureka**. On the south side of town the Tobacco River flows lazily next to the **Tobacco Valley Historical Village**. Several historical buildings have been relocated here and are now open to the public. Some of the structures were moved from Rexford when the original town was covered by Lake Koocanusa. Take a minute and walk around or, if you haven't had breakfast, grab a bite to eat at one of several restaurants located in Eureka. An alphabet soup of eateries line Hwy 93 starting with the Three C's Restaurant to the Big E's. Take your pick!

Keep a watchful eye on the side of the road. You don't want to be surprised.

I love the solitude!

After some fresh huckleberry pancakes, head north out of town, then turn left on State Route 37. The road swings south and runs adjacent to the lake. Drive over the Koocanusa Bridge and connect with State Route 228. Turn right on State Route 337 toward Yaak. If you want to see an old order Amish Settlement, continue north at the intersection on a spur road. The road will end at a small Amish community just a few miles up the road. Please respect their wishes and ask before taking any photographs.

Back on Route 337 to Yaak, the asphalt takes on a life of its own as it twists like a snake. Boulder Mountain rises 7,000 feet to your left. The scenery is green and the forest abundant as you follow a ribbonesque route through the northern edges of the Kootenai National Forest. Thirty miles from the bridge, you will arrive in Yaak where the road becomes State Route 508. It continues to follow the Yaak River and after about twenty miles there is a turnoff to **Yaak Falls**. This waterfall runs down a narrow valley and is a perfect spot to stretch. There is a pullout just off the Route 508. In this sparsely populated area of Montana, the sound reverberating from the cascading water will probably be the only noise you will hear!

From Yaak Falls, continue on to US Highway 2 and turn left to Troy. You are now following the **Kootenai River**. The green valleys and curvaceous asphalt soothe your spirits as you lift your visor to smell the fresh pine. If you are making good time, turn right on State Route 56 for a quick detour to Bull Lake and Ross Creek Cedars. This is about a thirty-eight-mile round-tripper that ends at a grove of spectacular old growth cedars. To get there go about fifteen miles south on Route 56 and take the Bull Lake Road exit to Ross Creek Cedars. Watch for cyclists on this narrow road as it climbs the Cabinet Mountains. After two miles there is a scenic turnoff for views of Bull River Valley and the surrounding mountains. Another two miles later you will arrive at the parking lot for **Ross Creek Cedars**. This area is home to a grove of 400-year-old Red Cedars that are eight feet in diameter. Walking along the nine-tenths of a mile self-guided trail amidst 175-foot cedars makes you feel very puny and very young (don't mind the young part!).

After a quick tour, head north on Route 56 back to US Hwy 2 and turn right to Libby. About twelve miles from town look for signs to **Kootenai Falls**. There is a parking area next to the highway and a trail that leads to the falls. For those of you who remember the movie "River Wild" with Meryl Streep, this particular falls provided the climatic setting when the boats went over the roaring rapids called "The Gauntlet." Take a look for yourself by following the trail to the "Swinging Bridge" and some great views. There is also a picnic area right by the parking lot if you brought some munchies.

Continue east to Libby on US Hwy 2. Many of you may have heard of **Libby** and the controversy surrounding the mining of vermiculite. Around 200 miners and residents (out of a total population of 2,600) have died due to causes linked to asbestos. Lawsuits have been filed, books written, and documentaries filmed about this small community. Libby now caters primarily to tourists and makes a convenient place to stop and eat. Numerous restaurants line US Hwy 2: Beck's Montana Cafe, Four B's, Red Dog Saloon, Pioneer Junction Restaurant, to name just a few. Or if you want a fresh trout dinner on the lake, try the **Koocanusa Resort & Marina** about twenty-three miles north of Libby on State Route 37. Either way you can't go wrong!

Sorry, can't wait for ya, Toby. That bend ahead looks too tempting.

And this is Memorial Day weekend! Where are all the tourists?

After a quick recharge, continue east on State Route 37 to Libby Dam. There is a visitors' center just off State Route 37 on State Route 228. Drop by and see the exhibits on this 422-foot dam built in 1972, or just keep on cruising along Route 37 past the south end of Lake Koocanusa. This lake has a ninety-mile shoreline that extends all the way into Canada. When the dam was built a contest was held to name the lake. The winning contestant combined the first three letters from Kootenai, Canada, and then added USA. Not bad!

The lake itself sets between the Purcell and Salish Mountains in a heavily forested valley. Inadvertently, the Corps of Engineers has created one of the most picturesque settings for a motorcycle ride in the entire state. The gentle sweeping bends combined with forest-cloaked hills and sweeping lake view vistas make this an unforgettable ride. The sixty-eight miles to Eureka will fly by as you ratchet up the speed and enjoy the absolute solitude of this run.

When you hit Eureka and turn right on US Hwy 93 to Whitefish, the sun will probably be setting behind you. Close to 300 miles today and maybe a little more if you took the detour to Ross Creek Cedars. You may be tired but the solitude of this run has also rejuvenated you. The picturesque rivers and wonder of Kootenai Falls, the languid beauty of Lake Koocanusa and timbered shores leave an indelible impression on your mind. Far from civilization in this remote little corner, you are reluctant to return. As you approach the lights of Whitefish, this small town seems like a huge city and visions of that old Amish settlement flash back into your mind. Hmmm . . . living without electricity doesn't seem so far fetched anymore. If only they had motorized buggies!

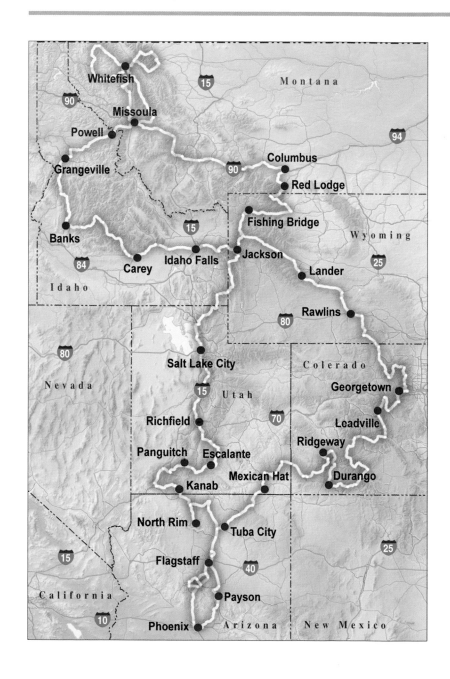

Rocky Mountain Grand Loop

Distance *4,500 to 5,000 miles (three to five weeks)*
Terrain *Most of the trips in this book are linked together into one grand adventure through the Rocky Mountain States. A once in a lifetime journey! Elevation change 1,100 to 12,000 feet.*
Highlights *I will leave this to your imagination!*

Taking a summer journey through the Rocky Mountains will be one of the most rewarding experiences in your life. These mountains are a statement in diversity and resplendent natural beauty. Combine that with a little old west history, a few abandoned ghost towns, some of the world's grandest national parks and, of course, the ultimate in black tarred twisties and you have the formula for a trip you cannot afford to miss. I hope you have saved up a little extra vacation time!

First, a little housekeeping before we begin this adventure. The best way to enjoy this trek is on your own two-wheeler. If you can, drive your own bike and connect at any point along the route. That is really the way to go. The other option is to fly into one of several cities along the way. Naturally,

THE ROUTE FROM PHOENIX

Week One

0   Start in Phoenix, Arizona, and go north on State Route 87 to Payson

90   Arrive Payson, continue on Route 87 to Pine

128   Turn left on State Route 487 to Flagstaff

188   Arrive Flagstaff, continue north on US Hwy 89

298   Veer left at Junction 89A to Marble Canyon and Jacob Lake

353   Arrive Jacob Lake, turn left on State Route 67 to the Grand Canyon

395   Arrive North Rim Grand Canyon. (Point Sublime Backroad). Turn around.

437   Arrive Jacob Lake, take US 89A to Kanab, Utah

474   Arrive Kanab, continue on US Hwy 89 to Mt. Carmel Junction

492   Turn left at Mt. Carmel Junction to Zion National Park on State Route 9. Drive through park. Smithsonian Butte Backway optional at Rockville.

537   Arrive La Verkin, take State Route 17 to I-15

542   Merge onto I-15 to Cedar City

572   Arrive Cedar City, turn right on State Route 14

592   Turn left on State Route 148 to Cedar Breaks National Monument

600   Turn right on State Route 143 to Panguitch

632   Arrive Panguitch, go south on US 89

639   Turn left on State Route 12 to Bryce National Park

652   Turn right on State Route 63 to the Park

655   Arrive Bryce National Park, turn around

658   Reconnect with State Route 12, turn right

704   Arrive Escalante. Hell's Backbone Road turnoff here.

758   Turn right on State Route 24 to Capital Reef National Park.

768   Turn right on optional 11-mile scenic drive at visitors' center, otherwise turna round and take State Route 24 to Fish Lake

809   Turn right on State Route 25 to Fish Lake

818   Arrive Fish Lake, turn around

827   Reconnect with State Route 24. Turn right.

847   Turn left on State Route 119 to Richfield

857 Arrive Richfield, go east on I-70

873 Take US Hwy 89 exit 54 and then veer left on US Hwy 50 to I-15

903 Merge onto I-15 to Salt Lake City. Continue to Brigham City.

1076 Take exit 364 to Brigham City, direction US Hwy91/89 to Logan

1102 Arrive Logan, continue on US 89 to Bear Lake and Jackson, Wyoming

1289 Arrive Jackson, Wyoming

Week Two

1289 Start in Jackson, Wyoming, head west at State Route 22 to Wilson and Victor

1313 Arrive Victor, Idaho, turn left on State Route 31 to Swan Valley

1234 Arrive Swan Valley, turn right on US Hwy 26 to Idaho Falls

1380 Arrive Idaho Falls. Take US Hwy 20 to Arco

1448 Arrive Arco. Take US 20/26/93 to Carey

1492 Arrive Carey. Take US 20 west to State Route 75.

1510 Turn right on State Route 75 to Ketchum.

1536 Arrive Ketchum. Continue to Stanley.

1598 Arrive Stanley. Turn left on State Route 21 to Lowman.

1657 Arrive Lowman. Turn right to Banks.

1690 Arrive Banks. Turn right on State Route 55.

1772 Turn right on US Hwy 95 to Grangeville

1851 Arrive Grangeville. Turn right on State Route 13 to Kooskia

1877 Arrive Kooskia. Turn right on State Route 12 to Missoula, Montana

1972 Arrive Powell and Lochsa Lodge. Turn off for Lolo Motorway across from Powell

2021 Arrive Missoula. Head west on I-90

2029 Take US Hwy 93 exit to Kalispell and Flathead Lake

2156 Arrive Whitefish. Take 93 south, head east on State Route 40 and US Hwy 2 to the Going-to-the-Sun Road and St. Mary

2231 Arrive St. Mary. Take US Hwy 89 south to State Route 49 and US Hwy 2. Loop around south end of park.

2348 Turn left on State Route 206, stay straight on State Route 35 then left on State route 83 to Seeley Lake

2445 Arrive Seeley Lake.

Week Three

2435 Start in Seeley Lake, go south on State Route 83

2460 Turn right on State Route 200 to Missoula

2468 Turn off for Garnet Back Country Byway

2493 Arrive Missoula. Take I-90 east to Columbus.

2794 Turn right on State Route 78 (exit 408) to Columbus

2841 Arrive Red Lodge. Take US Hwy 212 south (Beartooth Highway)

2892 Turn left on Chief Joseph Scenic Byway, State Route 296

2938 Turn right on State Route 120 to Cody, Wyoming

2955 Arrive Cody, turn right to Yellowstone on US Hwy 16/20/14

3032 Arrive Fishing Bridge, go south on Grand Loop Road US Hwy 20

3052 Connect with US Hwy 287/191/89 south
     to south entrance of Yellowstone

3100 At Moran Junction take loop through Grand Tetons and then return here to head east on US Hwy 26/287 to Lander, Wyoming

3230 Arrive Lander. Take State Route 789/US 287 to Rawlins

3355 Turn left (east) on I-80

3374 Turn right (south) on State Route 130 to Saratoga
     (exit 235 on I-80)

3402 Take State Route 230 to Riverside

3439 Take State Route 125 to Walden and Granby, Colorado

3514 Turn left on US Hwy 34 to Rocky Mountain National Park

3576 Arrive Estes. Take State Route 7, 72, 119 (turn off for Oh My God Road) and US Hwy 6 south to I-70

3643 Merge onto I-70 west to Georgetown

3659 Arrive Georgetown

Week Four

3659 Start in Georgetown. Go south on State Route 381
     (Guanella Pass) to Grant

3681 Arrive Grant. Take US Hwy 285 to Fairplay

3709 Arrive Fairplay. Turn right on State Route 9 to Frisco

3740 Arrive Frisco. Head west on I-70.

3745 Take State Route 91 exit to Leadville

3769 Arrive Leadville. Continue south on US 24

3806 Stay straight on US Hwy 285

3827 Turn right on US Hwy 50 to Gunnison

3896 Turn left on State Route 149 to Lake City

3940 Arrive Lake City and take Alpine Loop to Ouray or continue on Route 149 and US Hwy 160 to Pagosa Springs

4054 Arrive Pagosa Springs. Take US 160 west to Durango

4114 Arrive Durango. Head north on US Hwy 550 to Ouray

4188 Arrive Ouray. Continue north on State Route 62 to Ridgeway

4200 Arrive Ridgeway. Take 62 and then State Route 145 to Delores

4299 Arrive Delores. Take State Route 184 west

4307 Turn right on US Hwy 491 to Dove Creek and Monticello

4358 Arrive Monticello. Turn left on US 191 to Blanding

4383 Turn right on State Route 95 toward National Bridges Monument

4411 Turn left on State Route 261 to the Moki Dugway and Mexican Hat

4437 End of Moki Dugway and turnoff to Valley of Gods backroad

4444 Turn right on US Hwy 163 to Monument Valley and Kayenta

4467 Arrive Monument Valley, continue on 163

4491 Arrive Kayenta. Turn right on US Hwy 160 to Tuba City

4573 Turn left on US Hwy 89 to Flagstaff

4640 Arrive Flagstaff. Take US 89A south to Sedona

4668 Arrive Sedona. Turn left at stoplight on State Route 179 (Schnebly Hill Road turnoff about one quarter of a mile on your left). Follow 179 to I-17

4683 Turn right on I-17 to Phoenix

4783 Arrive Phoenix (Congratulations!)

Phoenix, Denver, and Salt Lake City are the largest and offer the most amenities. Lodging and motorcycle rentals are plentiful and just a keystroke away from a "Google" search. Even smaller cities like Boise and Flagstaff now offer motorcycle rentals if you want to stay away from the larger metropolitan areas and all the traffic. For purposes of this chapter, I will start in Phoenix, as this is my home, and head north from here. Remember, this is a three to five week journey over about 5000 miles. I would suggest four weeks, which is about 175 miles per day. I know that doesn't sound like much, but if you are like me, there may be a side road that beckons you on a detour to parts unknown. Or you may want to hang out in Ouray and do some dirt tracking to some old abandoned mining camps, or perhaps in

Stanley that whitewater rafting trip looks appealing, or fishing in Seeley Lake or more time at Yellowstone or . . . the list can go on and on. By the way, the route I'm suggesting is just that: a suggestion. I've summarized it into four week-long phases that primarily discuss the roads linking the journeys you've just read. Use the chapters as more detailed references. Use this route as a template to discover the Rockies. This is your trip, you decide which side roads you want to take and in the process create your own version of "Motorcycle Journeys Through the Rocky Mountains."

All right, let's begin.

WEEK ONE

I know Phoenix has a reputation for being hot in the summer, but just one and a half hours out of town, you are at 5,000 feet of elevation enjoying the cool pines of the southern Rockies. Start this trip by taking the "beeline" (State Route 87) to Payson and then continue north to Pine. Hang a left at Clint's Well on US Route 487 past Mormon Lake to Flagstaff. See the chapter on "Sedona and Mormon Lake Loop" for more details. Once in Flagstaff, cruise north on US Hwy 89 and follow the journey as described in "The Grand Canyon North Rim." This will take you to Cameron, over to Lee's Ferry, past the Vermilion Cliffs, up to Jacob Lake and then down State Route 67 to the north rim. If you know your exact timing, try to book a cabin on the rim, otherwise camp out or stay in Jacob Lake.

If you like, spend a day or two in Rim Country or try the backroad to Point Sublime. Then turn around on State Route 67 and at Jacob Lake turn left on US Hwy 89A to Kanab. In Kanab continue north on State Route 89 to the Mt. Carmel Junction and turn left on State Route 9 to Zion National Park. Refer to the chapter on the "Kolob Loop" and follow the directions (reverse order) through the park, up to Cedar City and Cedar Breaks and then over to Panguitch. Don't forget to take the **Smithsonian Butte Backway** at Rockville. From Panguitch go south on US 89 to the State Route 12 turnoff. You are now entering the chapter on "Up the Staircase." This trek takes you to Bryce, Escalante Staircase, and Fish Lake. A couple of nice diversions are **Hell's Backbone Road** off State Route 12 at Escalante and, since you have all summer, do a quick trip into Capital Reef by turning right on State Route 24. Try the eleven-mile scenic drive at the visitors' center just inside the park. Turn around and now head north on State Route 24 to Fish Lake and then continue on to Richfield. Take I-70, US Hwy 50 and then 1-15 to Salt Lake City. Keep going to Brigham City and take the US 91/89 exit to Logan. Follow US 89 past Bear Lake (beautiful ride!) and then up to Jackson, Wyoming. Week one is officially over after about 1,300 miles!

WEEK TWO

From Jackson, Wyoming, use my "Teton Rendezvous" chapter for a loop up to the Grand Tetons and then swing over to Victor and Swan Valley, Idaho on State Route 22 and 31. In Swan Valley take US 26 to Idaho Falls, US 20 to Arco and onto State Route 75. Do the "Sawtooth Sortie" in reverse and at Lowman head over to Banks on the Wildlife Canyon Byway. You are now on State Route 55 which will eventually lead to US 12 and Missoula, Montana. The chapter on "Lewis and Clark Country" covers this stretch of road in detail. The "Lolo Motorway" is definitely worth it at Powell if you happen to be on your dual-sport!

At Missoula, catch I-90 west and after a few miles take US 93 to Kalispell and Flathead Lake. You are now in "Flathead Lake Loop" territory. Head north to Whitefish, veer right on US 2 to the "Going-to-the-Sun Road," swing through Glacier National Park to St Mary. Take US 89, State Route 49 and US 2 around the south end of the park and then turn left on State Route 206 to State Route 35 and State Route 83. Follow the "chain-of-lakes" to Seeley Lake. Spend a relaxing evening or two here. Paddle down the Clearwater Canoe Trail for a leisurely change from that motorcycle seat or just go fishing! Week two is now over.

WEEK THREE

From Seeley Lake, head south to State Route 200. If you can, take the **Garnet Back Country Byway** then continue to Missoula and I-90 east. This will be your longest stretch of Interstate. It is 300 miles to Columbus and State Route 78. Go south on State Route 78 to Red Lodge and another majestic run begins on the **Beartooth Highway.** See the chapter on "Yellowstone and the Beartooth Highway." Connect with the Chief Joseph Scenic Byway on State Route 296, head to Cody, Wyoming, back west to Yellowstone then south to the Grand Tetons.

If you are ahead of schedule or have a few extra days, spend some time exploring Yellowstone National Park and the Grand Tetons. Otherwise, just downshift at Moran Junction and take US 26/287 to Lander, Wyoming. At Lander take State Route 789/US287 to Rawlins, connect with I-80 east and turn off on State Route 130 (exit 235) to Saratoga. Connect with State Route 230 and then take State Route 125 to Walden and Granby, Colorado. Then head east on US 34 through Rocky Mountain National Park to Estes. Refer to "Rocky Mountain High" for further directions on State Route 7, 72, 119, US 6 and I-70 to Georgetown (reverse order). **Oh My God Road** to Idaho Springs is also on the way. You are now in Georgetown, one of my favorite places to stay and 3,700 miles into the trip.

WEEK FOUR

This final week links four truly amazing journeys together into one heck of a good ride home. The "Top of the Rockies," "Silver Thread," "San Juan Parkway," and "Grand Circle Loop" all come together into one grand finale. If at all possible, start by taking State Route 381 (**Guanella Pass**) to Grant and then zig zag on State Route 9, I-70, State Route 91, and State Route 24 to Leadville. Continue south on US 24, 285 and 50 to Gunnison. Take State Route 149 south to Lake City (Chapter on Silver Thread). At this point either take the **Alpine Loop Backway** to Ouray as a short cut or follow State Route 149 and the US 160 to Pagosa Springs. Continue into Durango and take the San Juan Parkway up to Ouray and Ridgeway. Head west on State Route 62 and south on State Route 142 to Delores. Just outside of Delores take State Route 184 west, US 491 to Monticello, Utah, and then US 191 to Blanding. Head west on State Route 95 the "trail of the ancients" before going south on State Route 261 and the Moki Dugway. See the chapter on "The Grand Loop" for more details. At the bottom of the Moki Dugway either take the side trip to **Valley of the Gods** or continue on to Monument Valley. At Monument Valley, stay on US 163 to Kayenta and then turn right on US 160 to Tuba City. At US 89 turn left and after sixty-seven miles you are back in Flagstaff.

If you are totally beat, just boogey on down to Phoenix and you'll get there in time for a round of golf. Or take 89A to Sedona for an even cooler round of golf. Who knows, the vortex may make that ball go just a little bit farther. Read the chapter on "Sedona and Mormon Lake Loop" if you're interested in heading back through Jerome or just take State Route 179 to I-17. **Schnebly Hill Road** is just off State Route 179 for one more dirt track. At the end of State Route 179 connect with I-17 and after about 100 miles you are back in Phoenix.

As this is summer, Phoenix will definitely be hot. So take it easy, drink lots of liquids, and try to think of those cool pines you just left in Flagstaff. When you arrive at your hotel crank down the A/C and sleep like a baby. Congratulations! You just completed a 5,000-mile trek through six western states. Memories of glacier filled valleys, cobalt blue lakes, fresh scented pine and abandoned ghost towns are now yours and yours alone. Hopefully, you took some notes and can begin writing your own version of *Motorcycle Journeys Through the Rocky Mountains*. If not, just send me a postcard (care of the publisher) so I can enjoy it one more time, but this time through your eyes.

Favorites

Whenever I read a travel book, I am always interested to know if the author had any "favorites." Often, that is the first section I will read! So I decided to compile my own list of favorites for *Motorcycle Journeys Through the Rocky Mountains*. My list includes not only rides, but places to stay, campgrounds, backroads, and so on. All right, here goes . . . my top ten "favorites" are (drum roll please):

- Favorite Place to Stay: Georgetown, Colorado. Never ravaged by fire, this old mining town has a quaint feel about it. The restored Victorian homes and buildings nestled between towering peaks make this an ideal base to explore the Rockies in central Colorado.

- Favorite Campground: Goulding's Campground at Monument Valley. Maybe I'm just lucky, but the campsite I usually get is perched on a small bluff with views straight between sheer cliffs. I can open my tent flap in the morning and "voila," Monument Valley is framed like a postcard. The facilities and showers are great at this campground as well.

- Most Unique Road: Maybe this sounds weird, but I didn't know a road like New Mexico's State Route 503 (Jemez Mountain Trail Chapter) existed. This relatively short single-laner truly does feel like you have been transported to another country.

- Most Historical Ride: Without a doubt the Northwest Passage Scenic Byway on Idaho's US Hwy 12 (Chapter on Lewis and Clark Country) combined with the Lolo Motorway backroad win the prize. Following Lewis and Clark's 1805 journey through this remote territory really brought their experiences to life.

- Favorite Overnighter: If I could do just one three-dayer, it would be the "Yellowstone, Beartooth Highway, Chief Joseph Byway and

Grand Teton Loop" through Wyoming and Montana. A never-ending journey across the ultimate in scenery, wildlife and twisties.

■ Best Road for "Excessive Acceleration:" I didn't want to say speeding, but State Route 95 in Utah from the east end of Lake Powell to Hanksville is unbelievable (chapter on the Grand Circle Loop). Not only is the road in good shape, but nobody is out here. Plus the sweeping turns are wide open for excellent views (if you know what I mean!).

■ Best Paved Road: Maybe my timing was just right, but State Route 67 to the Grand Canyon's North Rim has asphalt as smooth as silk. It's like driving on an unrippled, glass-covered lake.

■ Favorite Lake Drive: Lake San Cristobal just south of Lake City, Colorado sits beneath forested slopes and towering peaks (chapter on the Silver Thread). The ride around this lake is not only breathtaking, but far from fellow tourists.

■ Favorite Backroad: The Alpine Loop in the San Juans from Lake City to Ouray is well known and one of the best backroad adventures in the Rockies (The Silver Thread).

■ Number One Favorite Ride: This may strike some readers as a little unusual, but due to a combination of remoteness, beauty, and continuous sweepers and twisties, my favorite ride is in northern New Mexico on US Hwy 64 to Chama and State Route 17 through the San Juans in southeastern Colorado (Chapter on High Road to Chama). I admit, the road from Chama to Antonito was a little rough, but the Rocky Mountain scenery was unparalleled. Plus, nobody really travels to this remote corner of the Rockies; it's just too far out of the way!

Index

About the Author

Toby Ballentine has lived in the Rocky Mountain area (Utah and Arizona) for over 20 years.

His parents were raised in Idaho, and his original heritage is from pioneer stock. They crossed the Great Plains back in the mid-1800s. His great-grandfather was one of the original founders of Pine, Arizona (he's even got his picture in the local museum!).

His mother comes from a family with ten siblings so he has uncles, aunts, and cousins in just about every state in the Rockies, whom he spent many summers visiting as a kid. He grew to appreciate the mountains at a very young age.

Ballentine has been riding motorcycles since he was twelve. His first bike was a Honda PF50 with pedals and an engine mounted on the rear wheel. Eventually, he got a Honda 100SL and has never stopped since. He spent tens of thousands of miles riding and camping through the Rockies on his GS and a Yamaha FJR (his wife says the FJR is hers). He has motorcycled all over the world, but his favorite rides are right here at home—in the Rocky Mountains.